AF279490

DEDICATION

In memory of Harold Milford Watson (April 14, 1940, to October 3, 2010) a best friend and best partner. Writing this book has brought back a lot of wonderful memories of the good times we had building and racing the roadster together.

I would like to dedicate the book to my wife, Barb. My background was definitely not in electronics or literature. There were times that I was ready to throw the computer out the window. However, Barb's support and encouraging influence enabled me to see this book through to completion. The computer has since been replaced, but Barb is here to stay.

ACKNOWLEDGMENTS

I must confess to all of you gearheads out there reading this book that I am not an engineer, machinist, or mechanic. I'm just a retired coke oven worker, who as a kid became infatuated with Buick Nailheads, and 60 or so years later, I still don't know any better. I used these engines in various applications from the early 1960s to date. Early on, I learned about motors from those *older* guys in our local car club. Then, there is Carmen Faso, who is not only a great go-to guy for Buick parts but he is also the most knowledgeable Nailhead person that I know. Mike at TA Performance, Russ at Centerville Auto Repair, and Tom Telesco are Nailhead dealers, who not only have good experience and reputations with these motors but also are your go-to guys for parts.

Harold Watson was not only my cousin but also a best friend, and through our mutual interests with Nailheads and land speed racing, we became partners in a Buick-powered 1928 Ford roadster. Building that roadster and racing it on the Bonneville Salt Flats was a hoot and the best years of our friendship. I have to acknowledge that we could not have had nearly as much fun and success without the invaluable mentoring from Jack "The Motor Man" Greenhalgh. Jack built our first race motor and then nursed me through the transition from building street motors to racing Nailheads. He would always rein me in when my mind wandered too far outside of the box.

In today's world of disposable engines and relatively cheap crate motors, automotive machine shops are a dying breed. Then you factor in trying to find one with Nailhead experience and you are left with a very small market. I have been fortunate to find a local automotive machine shop (Forrest & Forrest Racing) where you can have confidence in getting quality work. When you come across a good, reliable automotive machine shop in your area, give it your business (whether it is through the shop's machine services or complete rebuilds) and support it by sending your friends there. These shops are only able to sustain profitability with a steady supply of work coming from racers, street rodders, and restoration projects.

For those of you who do not have the facilities or time to do your own motor work and do not have the luxury of a good local automotive machine shop, your first option is through the those mentioned above. I am sure there are specialty engine shops that are experienced with these engines throughout the country, but they are becoming fewer and fewer every day. There were many, including Al Anderson, Hans Boks, Peter Foulds, Ernie Nagamatsu, Garry Thomson, and several more who helped with photos and moral support to make this book possible.

There are a lot of peculiar things about these engines that I have learned from my own experiences and from others who have generously shared their knowledge. I would like to share with you what I have learned from using these motors in both street and race applications over the past 50 years.

Buick Nailhead 1953–1966

HOW TO REBUILD & MODIFY

Gary Weldon

CarTech ®

CarTech ®

CarTech®, Inc.
838 Lake Street South
Forest Lake, MN 55025
Phone: 651-277-1200 or 800-551-4754
Fax: 651-277-1203
www.cartechbooks.com

Edit by Bob Wilson
Layout by Connie DeFlorin

ISBN 978-1-61325-558-2
Item No. SA493

Library of Congress Cataloging-in-Publication Data

Written, edited, and designed in the U.S.A.
Printed in China
10 9 8 7 6 5 4 3 2 1

DISTRIBUTION BY:

Europe
PGUK
63 Hatton Garden
London EC1N 8LE, England
Phone: 020 7061 1980 • Fax: 020 7242 3725
www.pguk.co.uk

Australia
Renniks Publications Ltd.
3/37-39 Green Street
Banksmeadow, NSW 2109, Australia
Phone: 2 9695 7055 • Fax: 2 9695 7355
www.renniks.com

Canada
Login Canada
300 Saulteaux Crescent
Winnipeg, MB, R3J 3T2 Canada
Phone: 800 665 1148 • Fax: 800 665 0103
www.lb.ca

FOREWORD

Gary Weldon has been our Nailhead guru for many years. My first contact with Gary was at the steel company where we both worked. I heard many accounts of his trips to the Bonneville Salt Flats, first as a spectator and then as a crew member of one of the prominent race teams. He made the trip out in his Model A Ford chopped coach with a turbocharged Nailhead, a '57 Chevy 3-speed overdrive transmission, and an Oldsmobile rear end.

That prompted him to consider building a car to compete. He wanted a highboy roadster with a Nailhead engine. His cousin and very good friend, Harold Watson, who shared that same enthusiasm for the Salt Flats, pooled their resources and built a Nailhead-powered roadster to compete at Bonneville.

The team consisted of Harold with his 1940 Ford truck, Gary with his 1948 Ford pickup with a Nailhead engine, and as many friends as they could convince to make the trip to Bonneville. Gary had an influence on a number of people. One of them was Larry Lamb from Des Moines, Iowa. He came by the pits with a beautiful 1940 Ford chopped convertible in gray primer with a Chevy V-8. Larry saw the Nailhead engines and went home and converted his car to a 425 dual-quad Nailhead. He became a valuable member of the team for many years after that. Two more team members, Mike Moreau and Bill Melville, were from Michigan. They showed up with a Model A roadster with a Nailhead. For years, they convoyed out to Bonneville with us.

My first involvement with Bonneville was 2001, when I drove my Dodge van towing a car trailer with the team. Later, I drove my 1950 Willys panel van out to the salt.

We had many mechanical problems with the race car and tow vehicles over the years. One memorable problem involved the 4-speed transmission. The second-gear bearing seized to the shaft, and Gary spun the car at 180 mph on the track. We disassembled the transmission and tried heating and pounding but could not remove the bearing. We went through the pits looking for a solution. Fortunately, there was a Nissan Factory Race Team that was running the new 350Z car. It had a complete machine shop in a trailer. The team allowed us to use its hydraulic press to remove the seized bearing. We then went about making a spacer and assembled the transmission as a 2-speed, using only the third and fourth gears. It worked very well.

When we returned home, we built a new transmission with only third and fourth for the next year. We didn't need the lower gears because we used Gary's pickup as a push vehicle to get up to about 40 mph, and then he took off in third gear.

Gary made many modifications and improvements to the engine and car every year. He never lost the desire to make the car go faster. I have to thank him for all the enjoyment that he gave me and all those who worked with him over the years.

— Wayne Hamilton

NAILHEAD HISTORY

The first Buick car was built in 1899 by a company owned by David Dunbar Buick, but the Buick Motor Company was not formed until 1903. William Durant became involved in 1904 as a financier and ultimately became controller of the Buick Motor Company. David Buick left his namesake company in 1906 to pursue other interests. Durant then developed Buick into one of the largest-selling US automobile manufacturers by 1908 and established General Motors Corporation with Buick as one of the premier marques. Buick was the first overall in General Motors sales for 1908.

The status of Buick was firmly established for its innovation prior to the formation of General Motors, when it introduced the overhead-valve (OHV) motor in 1904. As part of General Motors, Buick Engineering (and later the Buick Experimental Division) were entrusted with significant portions of General Motors development programs. Among the numerous achievements that were pioneered through this division were the first straight-8 OHV engine and synchromesh transmissions in the early 1930s, and it was the first manufacturer to provide turn signals as standard equipment in 1939, which was well before any of its competitors. This is a very brief overview of a significant era in automotive history, but for the purpose of this book, we need to see how the Nailhead evolved from all of this.

I feel that the most important information is my observations and comments from a paper presented at an SAE conference in 1953 by Buick Chief Engineer Verner P. Mathews and Joe D. Turlay, staff engineer of special projects. These gentlemen were credited with designing the Nailhead. This will provide some insight into the logic of their design, although you would have to read to entire paper to reap the full benefit of their project.

New Era and New Engines

When World War II was coming to a close, vehicle man-

This roadster was originally built in Brantford, Ontario, during the 1950s with a flathead motor and soon after was upgraded to Nailhead power. Chris Matthon found and restored his new hot rod with a fresh 401. (Photo Courtesy Peter Foulds)

ufacturers looked ahead to the predictions from stylists of a new era of automobiles. The trend to lower, sleeker cars mandated physically shorter and more-compact powerplants to fit within the confines of these new cars. Cadillac broke the ice in postwar styling that introduced rear fender fins and, along with Oldsmobile, developed V-8 engines.

Beginning in the early 1950s, engine development was as exciting as the new car models. Car enthusiasts anxiously awaited the annual (in some cases midyear) introduction of each manufacturer's latest innovations. Cadillac and Oldsmobile previewed their all-new OHV V-8s in 1949.

Very quickly, all the marques of the Big Three (General Motors, Ford, and Chrysler), Studebaker, and AMC jumped in and the race began. We had moved into the OHV V-8 horsepower race. Competition developed among all manufacturers to see who had the bragging rights for the largest displacement and the most horsepower. This competitiveness was not only among General Motors, Ford, and Chrysler. It even ran deeply through the divisions within each of the Big Three.

A similar competitive spirit evolved with car enthusiasts, whether it was through drag racing, road racing, or non-competitive segments of the automotive market, such as hot rodders or car clubs dedicated to a specific brand. There were some very devoted groups that pitted themselves against each other, whether it was Pontiac versus Chevrolet, Chevrolet versus Mercury, Mercury versus Dodge, etc.

That fan enthusiasm continues in various forms today with the most obvious being NASCAR, where a whole new industry evolved by selling souvenirs and attire of all the favorite drivers and corporate race entrants. Car enthusiasts became and continue to be a very partisan group, with the Ford camp pitted against the Chevy camp versus the Mopar camp versus the Studebaker camp, etc. The fact that we still embrace these rivalries today has allowed the Nailhead group (among others) to evolve. We may not have the numbers of those other guys, but we are a dedicated bunch.

Intense Competition

During those developing years of the 1950s and 1960s, you could stand back and watch the comedy act within the Big Three, as their marques competed with each other to produce the largest and most powerful engines. The corporations kept a rein on the development of each marque and tried to ensure that it did not step beyond its status within the company.

For example, look at General Motors. Oldsmobile initiated the race in 1949 with the all-new Rocket 303-ci OHV V-8. However, because it was not the premier marque, Cadillac immediately elbowed its way back to the top of the heap with the new 331-ci OHV engine. Buick entered in 1953 with the new Fireball V-8 at 322 ci. This upset the ranks within General Motors, so Oldsmobile responded with a 324-ci Rocket. By 1956, all GM marques introduced their OHV V-8 with cubic inches in an ascending order with respect to their status within the corporation: Chevrolet had the 265, Pontiac the 316, Buick the 322, Olds the 324 Rocket, and the king of the fleet was Cadillac with its 365. This little charade carried on with each model year as each marque wrestled to not only keep ahead of each other but also to maintain an edge on the status quo over at Ford or Chrysler.

Each of GM's divisions had a pet name for its new OHV motor. The Oldsmobile Rocket was the most recognizable, and the Buick Fireball was probably one of the more obscure monikers. Buick's Nailhead nickname was quickly adopted by automotive enthusiasts, who perhaps mocked its peculiarly small exhaust valves, comparing them to carpenter nails. Buick Motor Division (and more specifically Chief Engineer Vice President Verner Mathews and Staff Engineer Joe D. Turlay) was entrusted with a mandate to design a more lightweight and compact motor as a replacement for the straight 8.

One of the primary concerns was that the new engine had to be shorter than the current straight 8 to fit within the confines of what was predicted to be the new extremely low styling, which led them to pursue the V-8 configuration. For this new engine to be competitive in the expected upcoming power race, it had to have improved combustion chambers that could withstand higher pressures with more durability and efficiency than previous motors. This also pushed the engineers toward the V-8 design to achieve significantly lighter castings with more strength than the inline engines.

The Nailhead Design

In spite of the competitive horsepower atmosphere, Mathews's team purposefully opted for the small valves and corresponding restrictive intake and exhaust ports to maintain high flow efficiency at lower RPM and provide a smoother-running engine. I am sure it was by design that the cross-sectional square-inch area of both the intake and exhaust port paths were consistent all the way through to and from the valves to help maintain constant flow velocities.

Buick competed in the luxury car market, where a quieter and smoother-running engine gave it an edge over competitors. Keeping the valves in a vertical position allowed a narrower profile but mandated a different style of combustion chamber in an inverted V form, better known as a pentasphere.

A major benefit was that the spark plug was more centrally located than in most other American engines of that era. The piston crown was raised and shaped to conform closely to the shape of the head, which resulted in a very compact combustion chamber and minimum flame travel from the spark plug. All the combustion chamber research at Buick from as early as 1937 showed the great importance of shorter flame travel and high turbulence to reduce octane requirements and result in greater efficiency. The close clearances around the outer part of the piston crown caused high turbu-

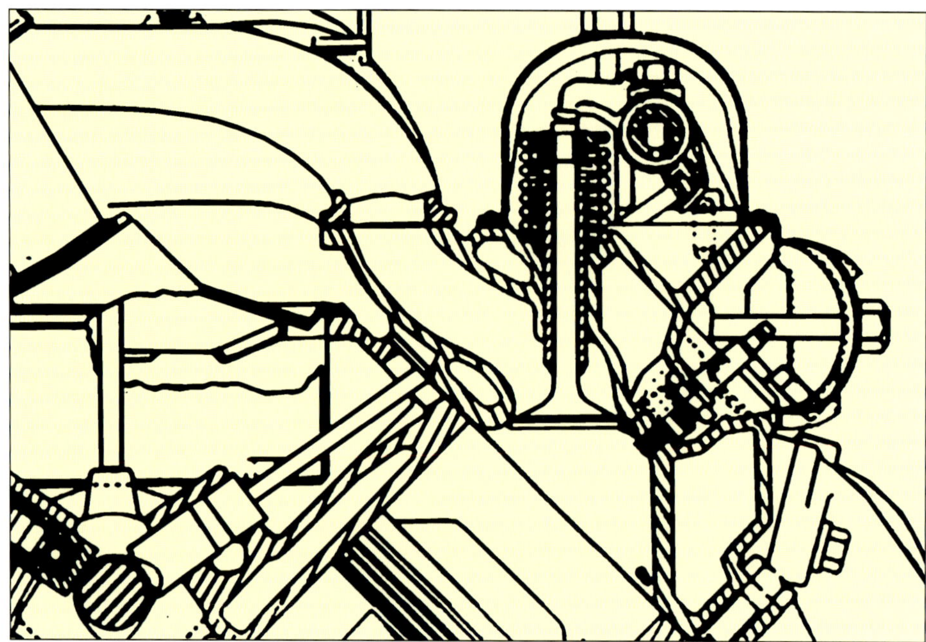

Looking at the side profile of the low-roof design of the intake port and that the exhaust valve is also upright and inline behind the intake valve, you can now imagine how restrictive the exhaust port routing becomes. This makes it easier to understand how this design promotes accelerated velocities at a low RPM but also is a limiting factor for the flow rates at a higher RPM. Consequently, this is not a high-RPM motor. (Photo Courtesy Bill McGuire/Mac's Motor City Garage)

lence in that area to force the bulk of the cylinder charge closer to the spark plug and result in shorter flame travel and more complete combustion. Buick was one of the pioneers to take advantage of this quench area.

The efficiency of this design also allowed higher compression ratios without knocking, resulting in more power. Today, we routinely manipulate this squish or quench area when building high-performance or race engines to optimize the power output.

Buick's V-type engine was designed to be lighter and more rigid structurally than the previous inline version so that it could withstand the higher cylinder pressures. Given its mandate, I believe that Buick hit the nail right on the head, and that is

what I prefer to believe is the true origin of the Nailhead moniker. At least that's my version, and I'm sticking to it. You can ask seven other Nailhead enthusiasts about the origin of the Nailhead nickname, and I expect you might get eight different expert versions. So, take your pick.

I had a recent discussion with a current engineer from GM Performance and Racing Division about the Nailheads in general but more specifically about the design of the head that evolved from Mathews's engineering team. To understand from where his thoughts emerged, look at a schematic of the motor from a frontal view. Concentrate on the relationship of the combustion chamber, exhaust port, and pushrod angle to each other. Suppose that the exhaust valve had been mounted horizontally. The head of the valve would approach the outboard side of the piston dome as it opened, much like the intake functions on the inboard side. The geometry of the pushrod location could easily support a long-reach rocker arm to operate the exhaust similar to the Chrysler hemi. This format would allow for a much more streamlined port alignment and possibly elevate this motor into a front-runner as a competition engine.

I understand the mechanics of this theory, but I also understand why it would have been sidetracked, given the commitment to using the restrictive ports for high-velocity flows at low RPM. It is an interesting thought. Bear in mind that Buick's engineering team in Flint flirted with a hemispherical combustion chamber in an overhead-cam (OHC) motor less than 25 years later. It could have been that Mathews's first choice design was abandoned to comply with the original mandate of a narrow powerplant, or maybe it was shelved due to the urgency of getting the Nailhead into production. Imagineering is a wonderful freedom that can lead to many exciting thoughts. It was the driving force for our forefathers throughout the industrial revolution and carries on to today.

Well, let's get back to reality for our rebuild. We will try to optimize and take advantage of the engineering that Mathews, Turley, and many others involved with their team at Buick Motor Division put into the development of our favorite Nailhead more than 65 years ago.

Early Nailhead Pioneers

You cannot delve into the performance background and subsequent racing success of the Nailhead Buick without a tribute to Max Balchowsky and his wife, Ina. Ernie Nagamatsu was a friend, customer, and co-racer with Max and is the caretaker of the Balchowsky's historical archives and memorabilia related to the *Old Yeller* racing days. I don't believe there is anyone more suitable than Ernie to graciously present this tribute. As shared by Ernie Nagamatsu:

"Max and Ina opened a garage in 1950 that was called Hollywood Motors. The garage never had a sign for all the years it was open.

"It was the meeting place for the sleek cars and fastest hot rods in Southern California. It was only a matter of time until Ina and Max challenged every factory team car sent from Europe in 1953 to the International Sports Car Racing races at Pebble Beach with a channeled 1932 Ford roadster called *Whistling Willie* (later changed to the *BuFord Special*). It was powered by a mighty, earthshaking, fire-breathing Buick Nailhead that made children run and hide and birds take flight. It struck fear into the eyes of fellow racers.

"Soon, Max and Ina (with welding torch in hand) built a yellow race car named *Old Yeller II* from used junkyard parts, and the rest is history. With crew chief and head mechanic Ina by Max's side, it was a little team with big dreams . . . and sometimes dreams do come true in Hollywood."

You cannot discuss Nailhead performance without some focus on the innovative thinking of Max Balchowsky. His successful campaigns with Buick's first V-8 are well documented and more than familiar to Nailhead enthusiasts. What is not so common knowledge is his involvement with Hollywood as a stunt man and that he prepared the suspension for the vehicles in the movie Bullitt. *(Photo Courtesy Ernie Nagamatsu)*

For those who may not be familiar with the Balchowsky achievements that Ernie Nagamatsu alludes to, the *Old Yeller II* was built by Balchowsky and was a formidable competitor on road-race circuits. Many of the high-dollar factory sports car race teams that came from Europe considered the Balchowsky entry as just an old jalopy. At least that is what they thought until Max drove circles around them and embarrassed them back to the pits.

There have been many (most notably Tony Nancy and Tommy Ivo) who had a lot of success squeezing more power from Nailheads thanks to the role that Max played in mentoring them with their motors.

Max Balchowsky was the most formidable pioneer in developing Nailhead performance. Max mentored Tommy Ivo and Tony Nancy through their introduction to engine building and Nailheads in particular. Both of these gentlemen had respectable careers in drag racing that was over and above careers as an actor and upholsterer. (Photo Courtesy Ernie Nagamatsu)

Balchowsky, as a result of his previous successes, seems to have had a foot in the door with General Motors. He was brought on as the chief mechanic to a project headed up by Sam Hanks to develop the 322 Nailhead into a competitive road race motor. The project was sponsored by the Bill Murphy Buick dealership in Culver City, California, and was pretty adventuresome for that era. The motor was taken out to 354 ci, fitted with Hilborn fuel injection, and put out more than 410 hp on alcohol. These motors were installed into Kurtis Kraft 500S roadsters and successfully campaigned across the US by Bill Murphy himself, who shared the driver's seat with Bill Stroppe and

A succession of road race cars that the Balchowskys built were initially based on a 1932 ford roadster. It started with Whistling Willie, *which became the* BuFord Special. *These were raced by Max and his wife, Ina, in the late 1950s. I think it would have been hilarious to watch as they competed in International Sports Car Racing in California. They frequently embarrassed the factory race teams from Europe and Great Britain. (Photo Courtesy Ernie Nagamatsu)*

Max and Ina followed their initial efforts by building their most notorious and successful race car: Old Yeller II. *The car was raced by Max and several other notable drivers, including Carroll Shelby, Dan Gurney, Bob Bondurant, Billy Krause, Bobby Drake, and Paul O'Shea. After it was restored, it has been invited to many prestigious vintage events, including the Goodwood Festival of Speed in the UK and Pebble Beach Concours de Elegance, where my partner Harold finally caught up to it. (Photo Courtesy Ernie Nagamatsu)*

Tommy Ivo and his famous T were two of the most recognizable individuals and vehicles from the early Nailhead years. It is hard to tell if this picture is of his original famous T because there are so many clones around. However, if this is the real thing, was Ivo the first to use stepped headers? I took this photo at the 2020 Detroit Autorama, where it was displayed with Norm Grabowski's T.

Was it coincidental that upholsterer Tony Nancy and actor Tommy Ivo both emerged from such different backgrounds and each built roadsters that became icons of 1950s hot rodding? Both cars were Nailhead powered and impeccably detailed, and both gentlemen became Top Fuel dragster owners and drivers. Both of their paths went through Hollywood Motors. (Photo Courtesy 3 Dog Garage)

Sam Hanks. This was not an official General Motors endeavor, but I suspect there was financial support somewhere in the background.

In 1959, Balchowsky marketed a 364-ci Nailhead-powered British sports car called the Doretti. However, it was not successful. It may have faltered due to a poor marketing strategy, or perhaps the public was not ready for a vehicle so lightweight with 300-plus hp. It certainly could have set the bar at a significantly higher level for Ford when it introduced its new Cobra a few short years later.

In my area of southern Ontario, Canada, Harvey Lennox was inducted into the Canadian Motor Sports Hall of Fame in recognition of his successes in Canada and the US campaigning a Nailhead-powered Super Modified known as *Tammy 10*. Lennox terrorized tracks with his alcohol-injected Buicks from Ontario through Michigan, Ohio, New York, and Pennsylvania from the mid-1950s to 1969 before he

Jack Greenhalgh began racing in the early 1950s and quickly earned a reputation as a car builder. His reputation as an engine builder began with flathead Fords and then Chevrolet and Studebakers and continued with Black Jack engines. During the early 1960s, Jack had an affiliation with Andy Granatelli and STP and raced Studebaker R-3 and R-4 engines. (Photo Courtesy Jack Greenhalgh)

gave in to the big-block Chevrolets.

The current popularity of Nailheads and the succession of aftermarket accessories that are available today are in no small part thanks to the creativity of the Balchowskys, Ivos, and many other pioneers like them who spawned Nailhead followers. If this is your first experience with a Nailhead, you are about to learn that it is an individual with its own character and personality in the world of the North American V-8s.

WHY BUILD A NAILHEAD?

There are many reasons to justify building a Nailhead versus any other brand of engine. However, there are also some significant reasons to look elsewhere. If you are concerned about the cost, consider these factors. Rebuilding two vintage small-block Chevrolets is less expensive than a quality rebuild on a Nailhead. You can purchase modern crate engines that produce more horsepower for a lower cost than rebuilding a Nailhead. Parts availability has improved immensely in the past few years, but the demand is still low enough that it does not warrant your local parts store to stock Nailhead parts.

Sourcing Parts

In today's world, your local supplier might be able to source the items you need and have them delivered in the next day or two, but they may not have that intimate familiarity with the origin or the quality of those parts. The automotive parts market in general has been flooded with offshore parts, and some of those are even labeled with recognized brand names. However, some of them may also be substandard. The people who you can trust to decipher whether parts meet the standards that we have come to expect from Buick are dealers who specialize exclusively in Nailheads.

The market for Nailheads is very narrow compared to that of the more popular vintage engines. Consequently, there are a limited number of dedicated dealers whom I have referenced in this book. OEM Buick parts for Nailhead-powered cars of the 1950s and 1960s were priced for the affluent when they were new. I remember the shock when I rebuilt my first Nailhead.

Believe it or not, it has been claimed that this torque monster has 708 ft-lbs of torque and was on the doorstep of going into production. The plug was pulled when the decision was made to discontinue Nailhead production. There are rumors that the drivetrain division breathed a sigh of relief when the news was announced. (Photo Courtesy Bill McGuire/Mac's Motor City Garage)

I purchased Buick lifters at $4.65 apiece from my local GM dealer's parts department (compared to $1.92 each for 283 Chevrolet lifters a few weeks earlier from the same dealer).

Parts Interchangeability

Be aware that parts for the first-generation 264- and 322-ci Nailheads are less available than the more-popular 364, 401, or 425 engines. These earlier 1953–1956 motors share very few parts with their later big brother. The 364 version may appear identical to its big brothers, but there are a few significant differences: the deck height and main bearings. Intake manifolds for the 264 and 322 are common to each other, the 364 intake is a standalone unit, and the 401 and 425 manifolds are wider. The only reason these are not interchangeable is because the different deck heights resulted in a wider spread between the head flanges, so the intake ports do not line up with each other. There are adapters available, and I have seen examples where people filed the bolt holes oblong to facilitate switching these manifolds, but the problem is that you still end up with misaligned intake ports. There are very few automotive machine shops left with Nailhead experience, and I will go into this further with machining and preparation.

Transmission Options

The availability of transmissions to fit restored Buicks powered with a Nailhead engine is very limited and they are certainly not at Chevrolet prices. Buick introduced the Dynaflow transmission with the first Nailheads in 1953. It earned the horrible reputation of being known as the 30-mile or 30-minute transmission. Improvements were made during the 8-year run of that transmission, but the damage was done and the reputation remained.

Buick finally phased out the torque tubes in 1961 in favor of the open-drive format used by the rest of the General Motor marques. The closed-drive system used a solid steel rod as a driveshaft inside of a steel tube that was hinged from the rear of the transmission via a large ball socket and flanged to the differential. This was like having Model T Ford suspension technology in a 1950s luxury vehicle. Buick engine swaps with the torque tube–era Nailheads could only be done by using adapters to alternate transmissions. During this same time frame, Buick discontinued the Dynaflow transmission, but it was unable to admit defeat in the automatic transmission field, so it followed up with a couple of other not-so-successful automatics through 1963.

Finally, by 1964 Buick succumbed to being a failure with its own automatic transmissions and adopted General Motors' new corporate standard, but it was not going down without a fight and changed the name from Turbo Hydra-matic 400 to the Super Turbine 400. I can't help but wonder if that decision was aided by the rumored introduction of the turbocharged Nailhead from the experimental division.

Transmission options are pretty limited for those restoring a pre-1964 Buick. Cores for rebuilding the Turbo Hydra-matic with the Nailhead bellhousing flange are becoming difficult to find. The situation is similar for those who prefer a manual transmission. At the beginning of the Nailhead era, most Buicks had an automatic transmission, and by 1966, virtually all Buicks came with an automatic. Factory stan-

This start cart is another testament to Buick power. As you can see from this photo, the start cart was powered with a pair of 401-ci Nailheads that put out 445 ft-lbs of torque each stock, plus headers had been added. This is the only photo I have seen of the AG 330 with red motors. A curious observation that I have not seen before is the provision for threaded plugs at the top of each exhaust port. A best guess of the head casting number is 1376912.

dard transmission bellhousings are difficult to find and not just because of the low production numbers. Hot rodders through the 1950s and early 1960s took a Buick standard bellhousing and modified it to accept Chevrolet standard transmissions. There was a standard bellhousing available for the 1965 and 1966 Buick Skylark Gran Sport option that mated a 401 Nailhead to a Muncie 4-speed with a Chevrolet bolt pattern. These are highly sought after for restorations, and the prices have escalated accordingly. This all sounds pretty grim, but there is encouraging transmission information later in this chapter.

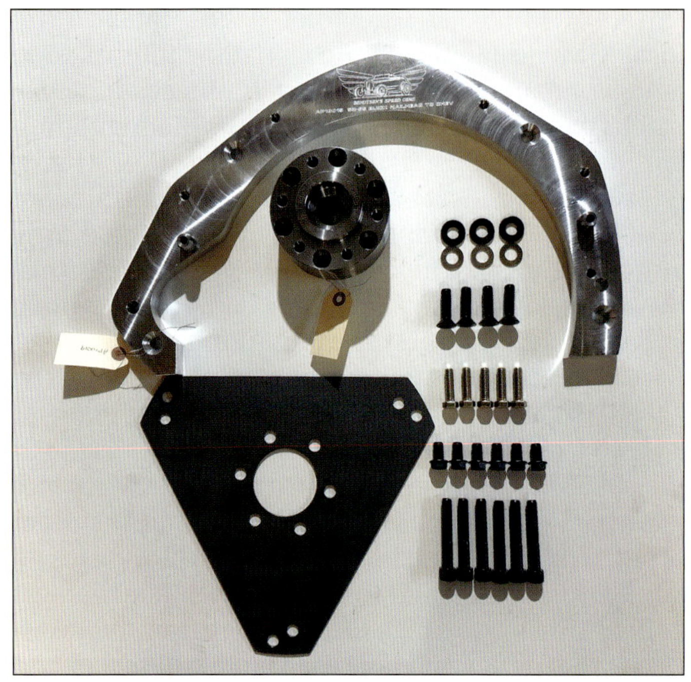

Bendtsen's Speed Gems manufacturers automatic transmission adapters to fit the first generation of Nailhead from 1953–1956. Their parts are available online or through a network of dealers. (Photo Courtesy Bendtsen's Speed Gems)

Nailhead Upsides

Now let's look at the positive aspects of running a Nailhead. If you don't want a belly-button motor like 95 percent of those other people, then you are on the right track and about to delve into one of your best options. When properly rebuilt and maintained, these motors are very reliable, and it doesn't seem that you can wear one out.

I have a few friends who think Nailheads should be used in dump trucks or school buses, and they are quite vocal about it. Well, these guys and anyone else who thinks like them should read the rest of this paragraph and refer to the next chapter, where even General Motors acknowledged that Chevrolet wasn't up to the torque task from 1956 to 1959.

The most significant testimony to the reliability and recognition of the brute torque from

Stock flexplates from the 1964–1966 engines are becoming more difficult to find as more people are adapting the Super Turbine 400 transmission to the earlier motors. Be aware that Nailheads are externally balanced and require rebalancing when changing a flywheel or flexplate. TA Performance carries flexplates to fit various years of Nailheads. (Photo Courtesy TA Performance)

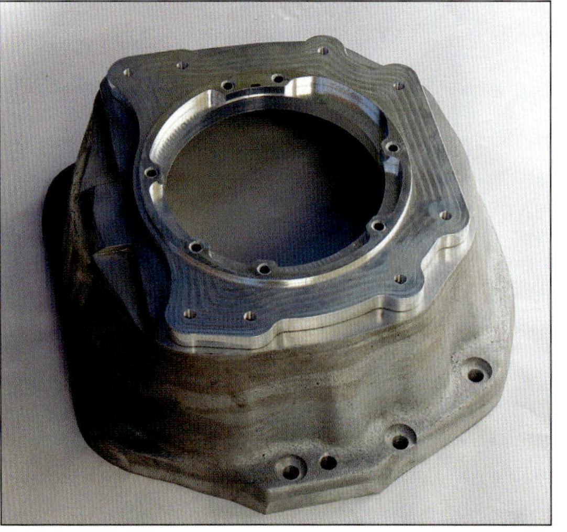

This adapter will mate a Nailhead to GM's 4L60 and is available through Centerville Auto Repair. This swap is going to become more popular as the 400 transmission cases get used up. (Photo Courtesy Centerville Auto Repair)

a Nailhead that I have been able to unearth is the AG-330 start cart. For those not familiar with the AG-330, it was a starter motor package driven by a pair of 401 Nailheads that was designed to fire up the Lockheed SR-71 Blackbird aircraft.

There's no doubt in my mind that the US military diligently researched motors, looking for the most reliable engine with the highest torque output before commissioning the AG-330. For those who may be concerned about the reliability of the Nailhead, perhaps that information will help ease your mind.

My first Nailhead experience was a turbocharged 364 that I put into a Model A Ford. That was over 50 years and 200,000 trouble-free miles ago. All Nailhead connecting rods and crankshafts are forged. They are strong and seldom fail unless there are mitigating factors.

The supply of the good old stuff like Clevite 77 or Johnson main bearings may have since dwindled to almost nothing, but thankfully there are new Rebuilders Special offshore main bearings now available. The name almost implies that these are bargain basement items, and you may be a little hesitant about using them without any knowledge of the quality or source. I have used these in rebuilds, including the engine in the race car. They appear to be a quality bearing and have performed well without any problems.

Cam bearings and rod bearings are still readily available. Shop around before purchasing parts. Local distributors may add an extra fee for shipping, an extra markup for the less-common parts, or claim to be the only source in town.

Although they may not be in your immediate locale, your best parts sources are Nailhead-specific dealers, such as Carmen Faso, Centerville Auto Repair, or TA Performance. These businesses are reputable, will have virtually everything that you need, and (most importantly) are knowledgeable about what they are selling. The most reassuring aspect of sourcing parts from these dealers is the quality. I am not aware of anyone who has received substandard parts from them. There may be other dependable dealers that sell Nailhead parts. I am not purposely ignoring them.

Light at the End of the Transmission Tunnel

I want to reiterate my previous comments. The selection of Buick transmissions up to 1964 was poor at best for anything other than a stock application, especially when you factor in the obstacle of the earlier closed-driveshaft

Carmen Faso makes this pilot bushing adapter. There are different-sized receiver holes in the end of the crankshaft, so be sure to get a good measurement before you order so that you order the right size. You will need to use a locking compound to secure it. (Photo Courtesy Carmen Faso)

design. My dad bought four new Buicks from 1953–1956 and got rid of them as fast as the Dynaflows failed.

The introduction of the Turbo Hydra-matic 400 (Super Turbine 400) in 1964 quickly became the automatic transmission of choice for Nailheads in any open-driveshaft applications, especially behind a motor built for performance. It was an excellent, strong unit that used all GM Turbo 400 parts and can be mated to all 1957-and-newer Nailheads but only in a non-torque-tube application.

Parts are readily available because this unit shares parts with the other GM marques. More good news is that this transmission can be built to accept any level of horsepower output

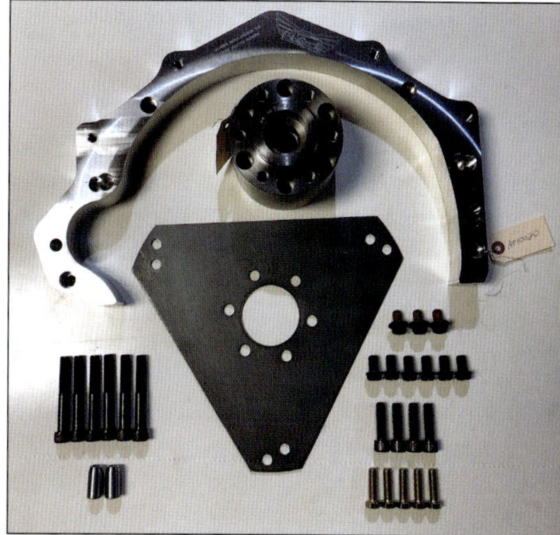

Another product from Bendtsen's Speed Gems is this adapter that will mate a Chevrolet automatic transmission to 1957–1966 Nailheads. The company also makes standard bellhousings to fit all of the Nailheads up to 1966, and it even produces the Nailhead predecessor straight 8s. (Photo Courtesy Bendtsen's Speed Gems)

Bendtsen's Speed Gems sells its bellhousing as a complete standard shift conversion kit that includes all the necessary hardware or separate components. One-stop shopping can save you an immense amount of time searching out all the little pieces needed to complete your conversion. (Photo Courtesy Bendtsen's Speed Gems)

Billet steel flywheels are also available from TA Performance and are another welcome addition from the aftermarket. The supply of aluminum flywheels from the 1960s is drying up. The early Buick cast flywheels are not acceptable for performance applications because they were cast. (Photo Courtesy TA Performance)

you could build into your Nailhead. Good cores for rebuilding are still available, but they are not as plentiful as they once were and are becoming more expensive.

The aftermarket industry has stepped up to the plate and now offers adapter kits to mount either automatic or standard transmissions to all years of the Nailhead. Bendtsen's Speed Gems and Centerville Auto Repair offer a complete line for both automatic and standard on their websites.

Standard transmissions account for a very small portion of Buick's production. The 3-speed standard transmission was a

Vintage bellhousings, such as this adapter, were made by companies such as Ansen and Offenhauser through the 1950s and 1960s in different configurations. This particular one mated 1957–1966 Nailheads to Chevrolet 3- or 4-speed transmissions. Other adapters fit the 1953 to 1956 engines.

Many of these adapters that mated either the early or the late Nailheads to pre-1948 Ford transmissions used to be available at swap meets. I am not sure why they are so hard to find now. Maybe it's because some people are using them as picture frames.

Aluminum accessory pulleys, such as these, are dress-up items that were never available in the 1950s or 1960s. The pulleys and valve covers were sent out to be chrome plated. Along came the 1980s with billet aluminum, and you can now get pulley sets to fit your Nailhead with either V-belts or a serpentine belt. (Photo Courtesy Centerville Auto Repair)

It is good to see the billet aluminum crankshaft pulley come on the market. In areas where the roads are salted in the winter, the original steel pulleys are prone to corrosion from salt and road dirt that accumulates inside the pulley. (Photo Courtesy Centerville Auto Repair)

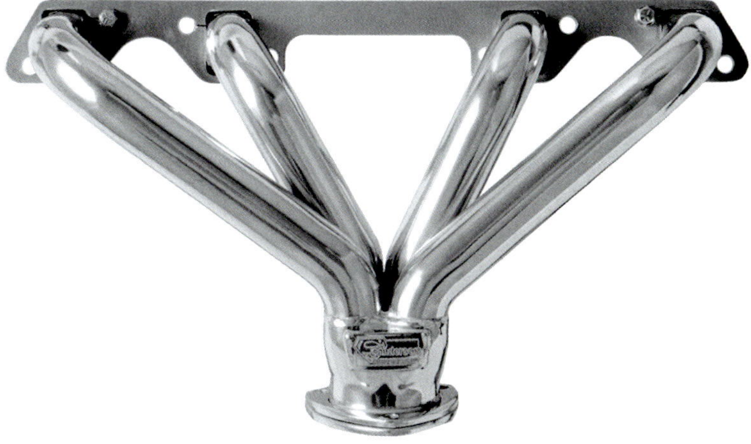

These block-hugger headers from Sanderson have one of the best-quality ceramic coatings that I have seen. They make these in two different shorty versions that will fit full-size Buicks and Skylarks that came with Nailheads. (Photo Courtesy Sanderson Headers)

good, strong unit, but most could only be used with a closed driveshaft and parts availability can be an issue. I would not recommend them unless you are committed to originality. There is not a General Motors part number that I am aware of to fit a pilot bushing into a Nailhead crankshaft, but it is available through all of the Nailhead dealers. You will need to specify the year of the crankshaft.

Vintage standard transmission adapters were available from Ansen, Offenhauser, and others through the 1960s. However, they have become very expensive due to dealers and collectors hoarding them. The vintage adapters did not have the advantage of CNC machining like today's pieces and may have developed damaged threads or oversized dowel holes from many years of use. A close inspection is warranted for any used speed equipment.

Engine Dress Up

The Nailhead is a very attractive engine when it is dressed up with optional Buick goodies like the finned aluminum valve covers

---

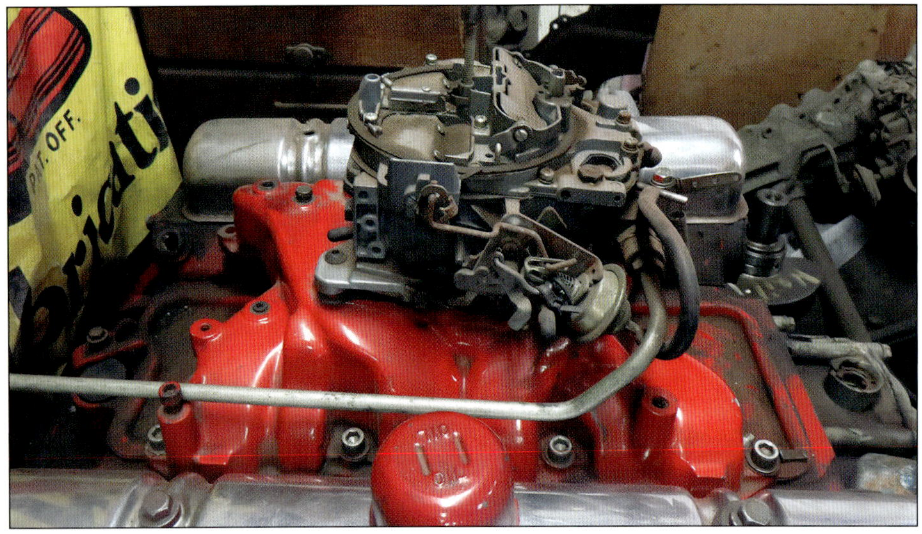

The 1966 Buick was the only year there was an intake manifold available to fit anything other than a Carter AFB. The one-year-only Quadrajet carburetor and manifold are very popular and a good fit for the Nailhead; the small primaries were for cruising until the large secondaries were opened up.

that are being reproduced today. Buick offered a very impressive 2x4 manifold option with a pair of Carter AFB carburetors and a huge chrome air cleaner in the mid-1960s. It later produced a Quadrajet carburetor and manifold that was only available in 1966. Both of these induction setups are highly sought after today. Other than the products developed in the Experimental Division in Flint, Michigan, Buick did not pursue any further performance options because its first obligation was to the luxury car market status.

The automotive aftermarket industry has picked up the slack to fill the void left by Buick for accessories and performance-enhancing products. Actually, I believe there are more dress-up items available today than there ever were in the 1960s.

PML YourCovers.com produces a wide array of cast-aluminum valve covers, valley covers, and oil pans in various finishes that range from powder coating to show-polished aluminum. It has numerous distributors throughout North America, and you can order directly from the website if

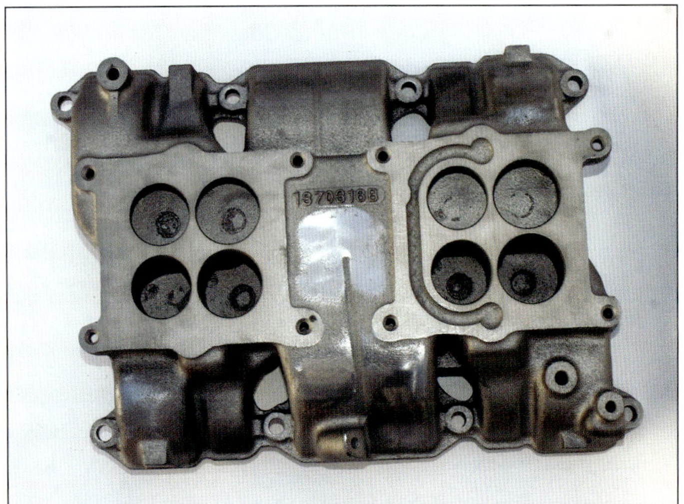

Buick had an optional 2x4 manifold available for 1964 to 1966 on the 425 engine. This unit was factory installed in the 1964 models, but the complete manifold and carburetors setup was delivered in the trunk and became a dealer-installed option for the next two years. This has become a highly sought-after and consequently high-dollar option for restorations. (Photo Courtesy Centerville Auto Repair)

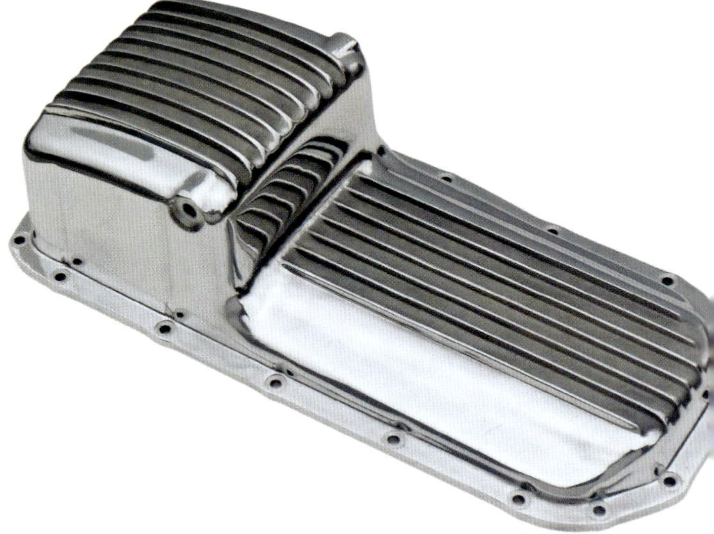

PML YourCovers.com is a relatively new player and it looks like it has its act together by putting out some quality parts. Original rear sump pans are becoming pretty scarce, so hopefully this company will fill the void. Rear sump oil pump pickups are available from Carmen Faso. (Photo Courtesy PML Yourcovers.com)

This aluminum valley pan is another product from PML and comes with or without a breather tube. It also comes in various finishes from cast to powder coated to show polish. This particular pan has a provision for a positive crankcase ventilation (PCV) valve. (Photo Courtesy PML Yourcovers.com)

The spark plug wire covers come in a variety of finishes. All of PML's products can be purchased through its dealers or online from yourcovers.com. (Photo Courtesy PML Yourcovers.com)

These valve covers are available in different styles (with or without the fins or script) and the same variety of finishes as the rest of its products. The valve covers are also a GM-licensed product. (Photo Courtesy PML Yourcovers.com)

This is an interesting adapter from TA Performance for those of you running an early motor with the old canister oil filter. The filter elements for those are almost non-existent. This adapter uses the later 401-425 spin-on filter and saves the mess of working with the canister. (Photo Courtesy TA Performance)

I call this Buick Mr. Subtle. If you look closely, the headers tuck around behind the inner-fender panels to feed an 800-plus hp twin-turbo setup. Air intake flow is fed back through the firewall, into a pressure chamber made to resemble the original air cleaner, and blows through a TBI unit. Cool! (Photo Courtesy Rad Rides by Troy)

Forged pistons are usually a custom order because of the low volume and variety of different dome volumes and bore sizes. Due to the low volume, Nailhead pistons cost a bit more, and you will seldom see them on the shelf. The advantage to that is that you are not limited to what is available. Everything from compression height or valve pocket depth to the ring package can be determined through discussions with the piston supplier. (Photo Courtesy TA Performance)

there is not an outlet in your area.

Other manufacturers make different finned aluminum parts, such as air cleaners, coil covers, and belt drives that you can use for the wow factor with your motor. Otherwise, you can do the over-the-top subtle detailing route like the Rad Rides–prepared 1956 Buick. These options are yours to pursue to achieve your

Nothing makes more of a statement on top of a Nailhead than a set of injectors standing straight up. Hilborn now makes an electronic version that is very streetable and has the look. It still makes its original mechanical fuel injection. (Photo Courtesy Hilborn Fuel Injection)

Roller cams used to be a race-only item. They have been resurrected by the auto manufacturers and aftermarket in either hydraulic- or solid-lifter format with grinds that range from mild street applications to all-out racing. Remember, the cam supplier is the expert and will work with you to tailor a cam for your specific needs. (Photo Courtesy TA Performance)

ultimate goal. There have been significant improvements in the quality of the manufacturing and finish of new products compared to the items that were available years ago. That progress in quality doesn't end there with the dress-up parts.

Performance Parts

This book is also about high performance, and like the cosmetic accessories already mentioned, performance-enhancing products have also benefitted from the progress in manufacturing quality. The engineering and production controls of today's performance and race engine parts far exceed any of the offerings from the 1960s heyday of Nailheads.

We still must be aware of the bottom-feeders that provide offshore fasteners and other substandard parts. Buyer beware because they are not going to go away. The legitimate manufacturers have superior machinery and elevated standards to work with, and we all benefit. Companies such as Diamond Pistons and RaceTec Pistons can make custom pistons to order, or they can scan a piston and make exactly what you need.

For street and racing applications, there are numerous options for coatings, forging versus billet, ring packages, etc. Piston ring technology has progressed immensely in the past few decades, and the piston manufacturer will supply the rings and machine the ring grooves to the appropriate package for your needs.

Schneider Racing Cams makes

Racing Nailheads were mostly injected with the occasional supercharged version turning up. The few blown Nailheads that I recall from the past were homemade setups. There is now a commercially available manifold for the 4-71 supercharger. (Photo Courtesy Centerville Auto Repair)

A log manifold is a challenge to tune. The best use I got out of my 6x2 manifold was to put it on the coffee table and plant a cactus in it. There seems to have been enough resurgence of interest in these from the nostalgia contingent that Centerville Auto Repair has started to reproduce them. You can now get electronic fuel injection that looks like the old 97 carburetors to fit these manifolds. (Photo Courtesy Centerville Auto Repair)

This is a vintage Offenhauser manifold with Offy adapters to mount the Holley carbs. It is a lot of carburetor but sure looks impressive. In case you are curious, this casting is significantly different from the base of the no-name tunnel ram pictured in chapter 9.

several hydraulic grinds for Nailheads and can custom-grind hydraulic or solid rollers or flat-tappet cams on request. When you are looking to buy a camshaft, discuss any planned modifications to the engine and the intended use of the vehicle with the supplier. The key to this dialogue is to speak with a person who has intimate knowledge about camshafts and not a salesperson who is just going to point and pick out of a catalog. Camshaft selection is one of the most important purchase decisions you will make building your performance motor; seeking advice is a prudent approach. You only want to make one purchase.

Discuss all aspects of planning this project with your camshaft grinder, including the intended use of the vehicle, whether it will be a dedicated race car, cruise night special, or any combination in between. The camshaft grinder also needs to know the weight of the vehicle (whether it is a 6,000-pound Wildcat or a 3,000-pound street rod), induction and exhaust system modifications, automatic or standard transmission (converter stall speed if using an automatic), gear ratio, tire size, and any other engine modifications you intend to do. All of these factors are an important part of the equation to ensure that you get the best results. Nailheads respond well to the addition of electronic fuel injection, but the camshaft grind can make or break how well it works. Your cam grinder is the expert, so listen carefully to the advice.

Here is a great bad example. During the early 1960s, speed shops in Canada were emerging, and the cool thing to do was to drive across the border to Gratiot Auto Supply in Detroit, buy some speed parts, install them on a side street, and try to return across the border unnoticed. An acquaintance of mine drove across the border in his new 1963 Pontiac, and he purchased and swapped in a 2x4 intake and carburetors for the 2-barrel manifold on his 283 (Canadian Pontiacs in this era were actually on Chevrolet chassis). We were not quite sure how he made the 200-mile drive home—I mean, this thing smoked so bad you could have dusted crops with it.

The moral of that story, (aside from the fact that the parts could have been confiscated, including the vehicle itself) is that using the biggest cam or largest carburetor are not necessarily the best decision, depending on the purpose of the vehicle and the level of performance that you desire. Each change made to the operating parameters of the engine must complement other modifications to work as a package. If one function of the motor overwhelms or underperforms the rest of the package, you will likely be disappointed and probably wasted a lot of money.

There has been tremendous growth with electronics, such as generic TBI electronic fuel injection kits with computer controls, that are reasonably affordable. The most impressive unit is available from Hilborn with its original-style mechanical fuel injection now available in electronic form. Other manufacturers are marketing turbocharger packages that can go from mild street applications to a more exotic level of 800-plus hp that would have

I haven't seen this motor, nor have I forgotten about it, since I first saw it on the cover of Hot Rod *magazine in May 1970. This motor is another product from the Flint Experimental Division, and the original turbocharged engine is still alive and well in storage at General Motors. (Photo Courtesy Bill McGuire/ Mac's Motor City Garage)*

These are probably the two most recognizable T buckets and for good reason. Norm Grabowski is credited as being the initiator of this styling trend, and Tommy Ivo followed a few months later. Rumor has it that young Tommy Ivo would sneak over to Grabowski's after dark to get measurements for his new hot rod. (Photo Courtesy Todd Ryden)

been unheard of not many years ago. The choice of ignition plays a huge role in the level of power you want to make, ranging from solid-state modules that fit inside the stock distributor to electronic control boxes to Vertex electronic or magneto distributors.

Parts Selection and Consideration

There is much to consider before purchasing parts. Regardless of which avenue is followed, upgrading the rod bolts is a no-brainer. All Nailhead connecting rods and crankshafts are forged and will stand up well to a reasonable increase in horsepower, but these engines are 55 to 65 years old, and you can't expect anyone to know what one has been through in the past.

Get your parts Magnafluxed as part of the reconditioning, and upgrade to ARP rod bolts. A mild performance street Nailhead is still a formidable powerplant. Buick advertised a stock 401-ci Nailhead with more than 440 ft-lbs of torque. Do you want a relatively original-appearing

engine, a nostalgia look, or an exotic-appearing torque monster? From a cost standpoint, the original look using a carburetor, mild cam, and stock 10.25 compression is the least expensive approach

and will provide respectable performance. Upgrading the ignition even with a stock motor from the old points and condenser to a solid-state module is a good start.

The nostalgia appearance can

What can I say about this iconic dragster? Through the 1950s and early 1960s, there were a lot of adventuresome efforts from racers as they strived to break through various speed barriers. That was an exciting era to live through as drag racing evolved into what we see today. The Showboat became a profitable venture, making exhibition runs across the country.

This well-dressed Nailhead has a set of vintage valve covers, an Edelbrock drive adapter, and Edelbrock water-cooled exhaust manifolds. Note that the engine is mounted in reverse and the transmission feeds back under the motor. This is normal for a marine application. (Photo Courtesy Garry Thomson Metalworks)

This is another nautical Nailhead that is relatively current, as it is dressed up with PML aluminum valve covers and spark plug wire covers. It also has pretty significant water-cooled exhaust manifolds and uses a magneto. (Photo Courtesy Garry Thomson Metalworks)

When is the last time you saw a cast-iron oil pan for a Nailhead? This one came with its own dedicated pump pickup and windage tray. This is an example of the different accessories that were made exclusively for the marine enthusiast. (Photo Courtesy Carmen Faso)

depend how drivable you want it to be and will cost as much as you want to spend. I know it looks really neat, but don't try to run mechanical fuel injection on the street unless you can tolerate poor drivability. These were designed for racing. Period. You can tune the high-RPM range and maybe some of the midrange, but it will not capture low speed without some serious sacrifices. If this is the look you want, buy the electronic version. The multiple carburetors look neat and can be tuned to work well on the street, although the six-carb log manifolds are a little more of a challenge.

Further upgrades to the ignition are the most important modification as you continue to increase the power output of your motor. Either the new electronic or the original magneto Vertex will get the right look and are very streetable. Keep your compression ratio stock or at no more than 10.25:1 unless you want to use premium fuel or race gas exclusively. Headers are a necessary part of the nostalgia look. Both Sanderson Headers and TA Performance have Nailhead headers in either inside-the-frame or outside-the-frame formats. The cost of this motor will escalate depending on how far you want to go with the performance accessories and the amount of additional dress-up items.

Building a Nailhead to produce a serious amount of power or to be raced is an entirely different project. The entire motor will need to be built to accommodate the expected power output. (I will go into this further in chapter 9.)

An interesting side note about turbocharging: Buick built a turbocharged 425-ci test motor in 1964, although, photos I have seen show it with a generator. I suspect that the project took place prior to the introduction of alternators in 1964. This engine was reported to make 708 ft-lbs of torque and was purportedly scheduled to go into production. Nonbelievers need to read that again: a Nailhead produced more than 700 ft-lbs of torque 50 years before Hellcats were even imagined.

However, Buick was near the end of Nailhead production, and the project was aborted. Judging from the pictures that I have seen of that motor, I think this project was in its infancy because it does not appear that they even installed a wastegate. With the potential for this amount of output, not having any control could be a disaster. It is interest-ing to see how they dealt with the traditional throttle lag with a suck-through system by using side-draft carburetors at the inlet to the compressor housing and the housing mounted on top of the intake manifold. I am willing to bet that the engineers at the Flint plant stayed in school a little longer than I did. This motor was testament not only to the durability of Buick's forged connecting rods and crankshafts but also the strength of the skirted block design.

When thinking about performance Nailheads, we automatically focus our thoughts on the Ivos and Balchowskys and their achievements. However, from some of the photos that I have seen, there is also a significant interest in these engines with the marine enthusiasts. They also put together some really cool-looking motors. There is a whole new world of parts that were manufactured specifically for marine use that are seldom found in the automotive market, such as marine front drives and water-cooled exhaust manifolds.

The options for a Nailhead build are infinite depending on your resources and what is desired as an end product. Remember that a Nailhead is not a cheap motor to rebuild, but the good news is that you do not need to deviate too far from stock or spend a fortune to wake up this sleeping dog. Are you going to build your own motor? It can be a very rewarding experience to assemble your own motor and even more if you actively participate in determining the level of performance you want. The limiting factor to how far you can go is your wallet.

Mild Performance Building

If you are going to rebuild your Nailhead for a mild performance level, the best bang for your buck is to first spend your money on the heads and get a good street-performance porting job, which will include new valves, springs, milling the head surfaces, and cc-ing the combustion chambers.

The second most important area is getting a true 10.25:1 compression ratio. This may seem excessively high, but the penta-spherical combustion chamber is very efficient and will work well when you take advantage of the quench area. Many engines will not tolerate this much compression without using race gas or octane booster. This does not mean you can just call your local parts source and order a 10.25 set of pistons. Remember the quench area.

Work with your automotive machinist and use a formula to calculate your desired compression ratio. Then, calculate how much material to mill from the deck with a stock-sized piston dome to get as close as you can to 0.045- to 0.050-inch squish area. Don't jump in and cut a whole lot of material from the piston dome; you need to measure the dome thickness to verify how much you can safely remove. Do not take the dome to less than 0.200 inch. The other areas that you can control to achieve this are the amount that you remove from the block deck and head surfaces and the compression height of

Buick had an optional manifold with two Carter AFB carburetors that looked pretty sedate compared to this more exotic setup that Vern Buehler put on top of his D heads. He had success street racing this coupe in the 1970s, although I thought we had grown out of that by then.

your pistons if you place a custom order. There are good fiber or steel shim gaskets of different thicknesses that can be used to tune in the compression as well. If you order copper head gaskets, they are available in different thicknesses. A good automotive machinist will work with you to hit your target.

The third item is a good ignition system. There are a few options that range from complete aftermarket distributors to a simple module that fits inside your stock distributor. They are all only as good as the rest of the ignition system, which means that quality wires and plugs must be used. No matter which type of ignition you use, it is a good practice to use a dab of silicon grease inside the plug wire boots and at the cap to keep moisture out.

When it comes to ignition timing, don't listen to your Chevy buddies. Nailheads have a pretty efficient combustion chamber with a centrally located spark plug, and they do not like a lot of advance. You will get maximum power with as little as 28 degrees total advance but seldom more than 32 degrees.

In summary, do these three things: optimize airflow (intake and exhaust), optimize combustion efficiency, and make sure it fires completely. Then, you will have a mild-mannered and strong-running Nailhead.

Additional Performance Upgrades

There is a grocery list of other modifications that could be done to build on what you have already completed. Buick has a reasonably good camshaft, and some of you may be perfectly content with that selection. If you want to step up to something more aggressive, I suggest a dual-pattern cam— the extra emphasis being on the exhaust with the duration around 215 to 220 and a wide lobe center in the 112- to 114-degree range.

Any camshaft duration numbers referred to here are taken at 0.050 lift, which has been adopted as a standard by most of the aftermarket racing cam companies, such as Schneider Racing Cams. Unfortunately, Buick used 0.002 as its standard for referencing camshaft duration. This means that the measurement began when the lifter was just barely off the base circle of the cam and continued until the lifter had gone all the way over

The turbocharger has been on this motor for close to 50 years without the protection of a wastegate. The turbo was adapted from an 800-ci diesel engine and is obviously not properly sized to the motor. However, the Nailhead and turbo have survived more than 200,000 miles with as much as 32 mpg.

the lobe peak and back to only 0.002 from the base circle. The net effect of the 0.002 measurement is an exaggerated duration number, and you cannot compare its specifications with those used by the aftermarket camshaft grinders. The 0.050 measurement is much more accurate.

A 750-cfm carburetor is an optimum size for a build like this. As your level of your modifications increase, the motor becomes thirstier. The ultimate test is where your horsepower peaks on the dynamometer. If it starts to fall off early, you need more carburetor and vice versa. This is where a chassis dyno is more effective as you are testing the motor in full street trim. Headers and less-restrictive exhaust are always going to help optimize the flow, which equals additional horsepower.

The vehicle that your new motor is going into and whether it has an automatic or standard transmission will dictate how the engine will respond. If it is an Electra 225 sedan, you probably want it to be mild mannered with lots of bottom-end torque. Keep the wider lobe center so the motor will have a longer torque band to pull around a heavy, old vehicle.

On the other hand, if it goes into a gasser-style '55 Chevy with an M22 Muncie 4-speed, you probably want it to sound ferocious like there is big cam in there. Don't go with more than 230 to 235 degrees of duration for the sake of drivability. However, you can get some of that *plump, plump* sound by going to a tighter lobe center like 108 to 109 degrees. That will make some noise (but not likely any more power), and it will probably be a little less driver friendly.

Whichever direction you want to pursue with your rebuild, keep in mind that you want to build it as a package. I will stress this again that each modification must be made to complement any other performance enhancements planned for that particular engine. Some of these upgrades may also create side effects for which you will have to compensate.

Something as simple as a less-restrictive exhaust system or headers may require larger jets in the carburetor. A combination of head milling and decking the block or thinner head gaskets may necessitate shorter pushrods. Use an adjustable pushrod adjusted to zero lash with a solid test lifter on the base circle of the cam. Be certain that the height of this test solid lifter is the same as your hydraulic lifters from the face of the lifter to the pushrod cup. This provides a base length. Then, add 0.030 to 0.050 inch to the length of the pushrod to provide preload to the lifters. Changes to the deck height may cause intake port misalignment and will also have to be checked. A high-lift camshaft will reduce the piston-to-valve clearance and may require cutting the valve reliefs deeper in the pistons. Newton's third law states, "for every action there is an equal and opposite reaction." Keep that in mind with each change you make.

Identification and Parts Interchange

The Buick family of vehicles through the 1950s are easily recognized by their portholes. The Buick family of V-8 engines from the 1950s to the mid-1960s had one motor that could be easily recognized and identified by the upright valve covers: our infamous Nailhead.

There were a few similar motors produced by Buick that made a meager effort to copy the Nailhead's identifying trait. The primary factors that distinguished the 215- and 300-ci V-8s from the Nailhead were their front-mounted distributors and the valve covers that appeared straight up but were slightly canted.

Both of these engines were less successful and had a much shorter life span. In spite of those similarities, these engines were distinct among themselves and did not share any interior or exterior motor parts with the original Nailhead family. For that reason, I excluded the aluminum 215 V-8 and the later 300-series iron engines from this book.

Interestingly, the 215 was only in production for three years by Buick before the aluminum block and head casting format was abandoned in 1963 and replaced by a 300-ci iron version. After the 215 was discontinued by General Motors, the rights were purchased in 1967 by the Rover Company, which later became part of British Leyland Corporation, where it lived on as a Rover powerplant well into 2004.

For those of you Nailhead enthusiasts who thought you may have seen a Nailhead trans-

Do you recognize the motor in this show car? Below the eight carburetors, the carburetor plenum box, and the supercharger and the adapter from the blower to the 2x4 manifold is one of the infamous Nailheads. The owner has gone way over the top (no pun intended) relative to the performance modifications we are going to cover in this book. This incredibly well-detailed hot rod was photographed at the Grand National Roadster Show. (Photo Courtesy Al Anderson)

Perhaps you can identify the engine in this street rod. This is a more traditional approach by Chris Matthon's restoration of a vintage hot rod roadster that was built in Brantford, Ontario, in the 1950s. (Photo Courtesy Hans Boks)

planted into an MG, Morgan, Triumph, or TVR, you weren't seeing things. British Leyland loaned out the aluminum 215 V-8 to several of its lower-production makes that wanted to produce a V-8 option for their vehicles.

This one should be simple. Just count the pipes. Believe it or not, there are four all-out Nailhead race motors hidden here. Imagine the innovation and just how far outside the box that Tommy Ivo and Kent Fuller were thinking when they created this work of art. This was built in the early 1960s, and virtually every part of the dragster was handmade. It sure had the NHRA technicians scratching their heads, and it ran as well as it looked. (Photo Courtesy Jeff Koch/Hemmings Motor News)

The First Nailheads

When the first-generation Nailhead came into production, it was Buick's first V-8 engine. It displaced 322 ci and replaced the 320-ci straight-8 powerplant in the more-expensive 1953 models. It continued on through 1956 in Buick cars. A smaller 264-ci version of the 322 V-8 was introduced in 1954 to replace the 263-ci straight-8 powerplant in the baseline Specials. This was the standard engine for the entry-level Special but only for 1954 and 1955 when it was phased out of production. The 322 V-8 was the only motor used in Buick cars in 1956, but it lived until 1959 as a truck engine.

General Motors decided that Chevrolet needed a gasoline motor with more torque for its commercial vehicles, so it rebranded the 322-ci Fireball as the Torque Master and started putting Nailheads into 3-ton-and-over-capacity Chevrolet truck chassis. That only lasted until 1959. A company in Toronto, Ontario, Canada, picked up the ball and continued to transplant the new, larger Nailheads into big GM trucks and bus chassis until 1965.

The 264 and 322 motors were easily distinguished from the second generation because they had only three motor-mount bosses on the side of the block versus four on their big brother, the new 364 engine. The oil-bath air cleaners were discontinued beginning with the 1957 model year and replaced with the new paper filter elements. All the block and head casting numbers for the 264 and 322 motors were from the

116-series. The exhaust ports were round as opposed to the rectangular ports of the next generations of 364- to 425-ci motors. These early motors had a cast front pulley, whereas the 1957-and-later engines had a cast harmonic balancer and stamped-steel pulleys. Only a few parts interchanged with the next generation of the Nailhead.

A 364-ci V-8 was introduced in 1957 as the second-generation Nailhead and was the only motor available for the next two model years. The third-generation 401-ci Nailhead entered the picture in 1959. The 364 was then relegated as a powerplant for the base models for the next three years until it was phased out at the end of the 1962 model year. The differences from the 364 V-8 engine to the 1959 to 1966 401 V-8 and later the 425 V-8 were very subtle, but most of the parts were interchangeable.

Casting Numbers

You can identify your engine's era from this list of casting numbers. Keep in mind that the casting numbers were not specific to a model year because they only represented a particular production run and may have been used for many years. The numbers from one production run frequently overlapped other casting numbers.

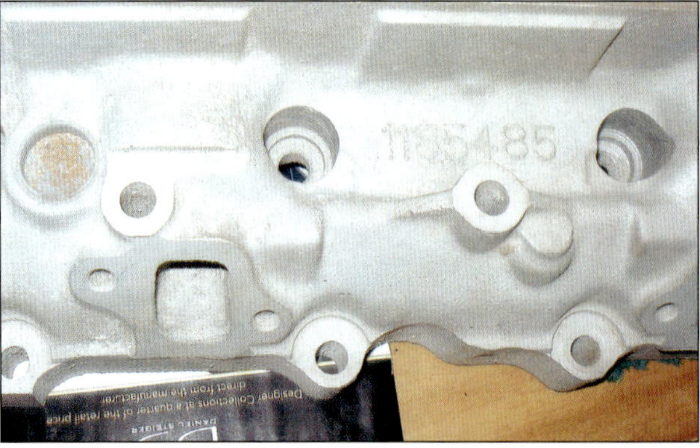

The aluminum head casting number was shared with a regular production head casting number that was produced from 1961 to 1966. Rumors are floating around about how many aluminum heads were made at the Buick Experimental Division in Flint. Rumor 1: three sets were produced. Rumor 2: a night-shift employee made an additional three sets for his dragster and that two did not have water jackets.

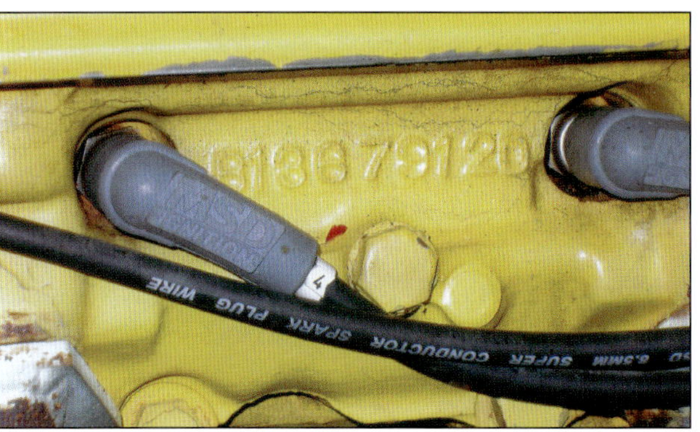

There were allegedly 28 pairs of the D head cast by the Buick Experimental Division in Flint, Michigan. The intriguing thing about these heads was the increased height in the ports to improve the breathing. The D reference had nothing to do with the shape of the ports but referred to the last character in the casting number.

Block casting number	Year	Displacement
1165165	1953–1956	322
1165752	1954–1955	264
1169334	1956–1959	322 (Chevrolet truck)
1173201	1959–1961	364
1174372	1959–1961	364
1185484	1959–1960	401
1185404	1961–1966	401
1196546	1961	401
1196547	1961	364
1340146	1963–1966	425
1345404	1959–1966	401
1346046	1961–1966	401
1349046	1961–1966	401
1354713	1964–1966	425
1354714	1964–1966	425
1364704	1963–1966	425
1364705	1964–1966	401/425
1364707	1963	425
1364714	1964–1966	401

Head casting number	Year	Displacement
1165549	1954–1956	264/322
1166349	1954–1956	264/322
1168930	1956	322
1169349	1956	322
1172889	1957–1960	364/401
1175109	1956–1959	322 Chev truck
1185485	1961–1966	364/401/425
1185485	1961–?	Also used for the aluminum heads
1190415	1962–1966	364/401/425
1196914	1959–1966	364/401/425
B1367912D	1966	Experimental "D" head
1374603	1964–1966	401/425
1376912	1966	401/425

It is reassuring for Nailhead fans that General Motors recognized the need for a motor with more torque in trucks through

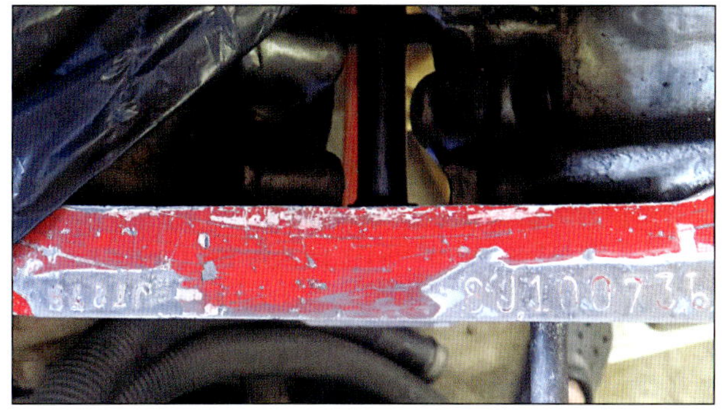

The production code number JT 278 indicates this block is a 1963 401 ci with a 4-barrel carburetor. This is a good example of how that number can help determine if a particular engine was correct for that vehicle.

1959. I have only seen a few larger trucks with Nailheads, and they were both in GMC chassis with standard transmissions behind them.

The GMC issue may have been a Canadian thing because all postwar Pontiacs and GMC trucks in Canada were on Chevrolet chassis, and most had Chevrolet engines. The only exceptions that I am aware of are the Pontiac version of the Cameo pickups and the Safari station wagons. I don't suppose that anyone has seen a Nailhead in a GMC half-ton pickup with an automatic transmission that could possibly be a 322 with the GMC 4-speed Hydramatic. It's a nice thought though.

Engine Production Codes

Buick had an easier-to-follow letter/numbering system to iden-tify the engines introduced in 1954. It started with the letter *A* and carried through annually to the letter *M* for the last Nailhead in 1966. These were called the engine production codes. You can obtain more specific information from these letters/numbers than using the casting numbers to identify different model years. Let me rephrase that, you may find that the casting numbers are actually more helpful for recognition of motors specifically from 1953 through 1959.

Unfortunately, the motors from the early years to 1959 were inconsistent with where the letter/numbers were applied (if they were even used at all). Up to 1956, the identifying digits were supposed to be on the head mating surface of the block between the number-4 and -6 cylinders, but I have seen motors without them, and they are often not legible. From 1957, the letter/numbers were known as the engine production code. That code was supposed to be located on the right front side of the top of the block (passenger's side) in front of the valley cover. Using the letters, you can determine the displacement, year of the motor, and type of carburetor(s); the numbers provide an approximate production date. The information from these was more helpful but unfortunately did not appear with consistency until after 1961.

The number at the left front side of your block in front of the valley cover is the engine serial number. It consisted of eight to nine digits, and six of those numbers were also part of the vehicle's serial number that appeared on the left front door post. Both of these numbers are of more importance to those doing a numbers-matching restoration.

The engine serial number is stamped into the left-side top of the block. Note that the center six digits are different from first two numbers and last number. Those six numbers are part of the VIN plate attached to the driver's door pillar and provide more definitive verification whether the motor is original to that vehicle.

This is the front pad of the subject motor. Note that the engine production code number is missing from the right side of the top of the block in front of the valley cover. This was not common but could usually be traced back to dealer-installed replacement blocks.

I have found that the following engine production codes are helpful for only the last five years of Nailhead production.

Year	Engine	Code/Prefix
1954	264/322	A
1955	264/322	B
1956	322	C
1957	364	D
1958	364	E
1959	364	3F
	401	4F
1960	364	3G
	364	L3G (low-compression export and regular-gas option)
	401	4G
1961	364	3H
	364	L3H (low-ompression export & regular-gas option)
	364	3HH (power pack)
	401	L4H (low-compression export)
	401	4H
1962	401 (2-barrel carb)	2I
	401 (2-barrel carb)	L2I (low-compression export and regular-gas option)
	401 (4-barrel carb)	4I
	401 (4-barrel carb)	L4I (low-compression export)
1963	401 (2-barrel carb)	JR
	401 (2-barrel carb)	JS (low-compression, regular-gas option)
	401 (4-barrel carb)	JT
	401 (4-barrel carb)	JU (low-compression export)
	425 (4-barrel carb)	JW
1964	401	KT
	401 (1 carb)	KV (low-compression export)
	425 (1 carb)	KW
	425 (2 carbs)	KX
1965	401	LR (Skylark)
	401	LT
	401	LV (low-compression export)
	401 Riviera	LW
	425	LX
1966	401	MR (Skylark)
	401	MS (race-only Skylark with Quadrajet)
	401	MT
	401	MU (Skylark with automatic transmission)
	401	MV (low-compression export)
	425 (1 carb)	MW (with Quadrajet)
	425 (2 carbs)	MZ

I have not seen any letters or numbers that differentiate between a 2- and 4-barrel carburetor on the 364 motors from 1957 to 1961. The only way that I know to identify the lesser-horsepower 364 motor with 2-barrel carburation is that they were assigned to the base model Special and identified as a series 40 in the vehicle serial number. After 1959, most of the 364s were 2-barrels. All of the 401 engines had a single 4-barrel carburetor unless indicated otherwise by the production code number. There was an exception in 1962 and 1963, when the 401 motors were only equipped with 4-barrel carburetors. After the 364 motor was discontinued at the end of 1961, the entry-level models for the next two years came with a 401 and 2-barrel carburetor.

Transmissions

Automatic transmissions for the Nailhead engines prior to 1964 were discussed in the previous chapter as far as their adaptability to a high-performance application. Today the good old-school transmission mechanics are being replaced by remove-and-replace technicians, and there are fewer people around who know how to rebuild engines. Tom Telesco is the only person that I am aware of who has a good understanding of these earlier transmissions and how to rebuild them for either a stock or performance mode. None of these pre-1964 transmissions had any interchangeable parts to the Super Turbine 400.

The tag on this transmission, although in rough condition, clearly shows that it is a 1964 BN Super Turbine "400." Rebuild parts are shared with the Chevrolet and are readily available.

The transmission identification tags are frequently weathered or damaged to the point that you cannot decipher the painted letter code. Not to worry. The code letters are also part of the transmission serial number stamped into the lower part of the tag, and they identify this as a 1965 BJ transmission.

This book is mostly about performance Nailheads, and the only transmission of choice for your high-performance application or race vehicle is Buick's Super Turbine 400. It was used from 1964 until the end of Nailhead production in 1966. It is basically a GM 400 Turbo Hydra-matic and shares all internal parts with the rest of the GM marques. The Super Turbine 400 has an identification tag fixed to the passenger-side rear of the case with one of the following letter codes: BJ, BK, BL, BN, BP, BQ, BR, BS, or BT. These codes are the key when ordering the necessary parts to rebuild that particular transmission.

The good news is that this transmission shares the bellhousing bolt pattern of all the 364, 401, and 425 engines, but the issue is that these engines are externally balanced. Swapping the Super Turbine transmission to a pre-1963 motor requires a flexplate change and rebalancing. That is not such bad news if you are in the midst of a rebuild. However, if you are swapping from one generation of transmission to another, an alternate flexplate and rebalancing enters the

picture. This certainly broadens the scope of work required for a transmission swap.

The crankshaft flange bolt patterns are the same. However, the center hub of the 1957–1962 shafts is significantly larger. If you want to adapt the Super Turbine transmission to an earlier motor, purchase a new flexplate with the correct-size center hole. New aftermarket flexplates with the correct-size center hole are available from Bendtsen's Speed Gems, Centerville Auto Repair, or TA Performance.

It may appear that you can simply machine the center hole of the later flexplates and flywheels to fit the early motors. This is not recommended.

At one time, Offenhauser adapters were reasonably plentiful, as they were the premiere aftermarket manufacturer. Buyer beware. This adapter appears to be NOS. However, take a close look at the photo. It will not fit any generation of a Nailhead as it is advertised.

Billet steel flywheels are a significant improvement to the old aluminum flywheels. The old-school aluminum flywheels were good in their day, but they were difficult to balance on an externally balanced motor (such as a Nailhead), and the friction surface on some was not serviceable. It's an important concern when buying vintage parts. (Photo Courtesy Bendtsen's Speed Gems)

First, the original 1964–1966 flywheels are a very scarce item, and the automatic-transmission flexplates are not too far behind. These are better off in the hands of someone doing a restoration. A new billet steel flywheel is much more suitable for your performance rebuild.

Second, opening up the center hole of a flexplate is not a good option for a few reasons. There is a rolled edge on the center hole of the original flexplate that is designed to carry the load of any lateral forces. The purpose of the bolts is only to retain the flexplate to the crankshaft flange, which is much the same relationship as your wheel nuts to the wheel center hole. The rolled edge of the flexplate center hole is rounded at the flywheel face to compensate as clearance of the machined radius from the crankshaft flange face to the centering hub. If you did not compensate for that radius as the center is machined out, the flexplate will not seat properly to the crankshaft flange and be under stress as it is torqued in place. It will eventually develop a crack. If you tried to compensate for the radius by chamfering the crankshaft side of the center hole, you will have sacrificed any of the load-carrying capabilities of what was originally a rolled flange on the inside of the flexplate center hole for that of a very tiny hard edge. This will eventually transfer the load to the flywheel bolts, a load that they are not designed to carry, which will potentially lead to a failure.

The bottom line is that you are building yourself a high-performance motor. Just buy yourself a new flexplate. Some of the earlier motors had the ring gear attached to the torque convertor and only used a triangular flexplate to secure the convertor. These were the same early motors that had the larger crankshaft-centering flange and required a new reproduction flexplate to work with the newer Super Turbine 400 transmission.

Bellhousings and Adapters

If you are planning your high-performance rebuild around a torque-tube era Buick with a manual transmission and are committed to that design, there are no options. You must use the original bellhousing and transmission. These were good, strong units, but it may be difficult to find usable pieces. It is much safer to purchase a new billet steel flywheel from Bendtsen's Speed Gems or have one made. The last hurdle is to locate someone to rebuild the clutch disc and pressure plate.

Buick standard transmission bellhousings from the torque-tube years can be modified to accept a Chevrolet 3- or 4-speed transmission for those who want to transplant to an open-driveshaft vehicle. Original Buick bellhousings are few and far between. The nodular steel flywheels of that vintage should not be used in any high-performance situation. Buick had a 4-speed option for the 1964–1966 Gran Sport. This is very desirable and expensive if you can find one.

The good news is that the aftermarket industry manufactured numerous standard bellhousing adapters through the 1960s. Many of those adapters and flywheels are also still reproduced today, plus there is a variety of kits available to convert to alternate automatic transmissions. Contact Bendtsen's Speed Gems or your Nailhead dealer. They will let you know what is available and may have one ready on their shelf.

When doing a conversion, it is much more practical to use a new adapter. Some of the new automatic transmission adapters space the transmission and torque converter back the distance of the Buick bellhousing flange. There is a lot of weight in the torque converter to be mounted that far off the end of the crankshaft.

It is standard practice to test-mount any flexplate or flywheel (and even more important with a convertor spaced out from the normal mounting position) prior to final assembly. Check it with your dial indicator. This measurement should be taken near the outer edge adjacent to where the pressure-plate or torque-convertor bolt holes are located. The runout tolerance must be kept at 0.003 inch or less for either of these parts. This is something that you must correct before sending the parts out for balancing.

It may be difficult to find specifications for runout of a flexplate because, as the name implies, it is designed to flex. With your initial test fitment of the crankshaft, check for runout on the main journals and thrust bearing clearance. At the same time, indicate the flywheel flange

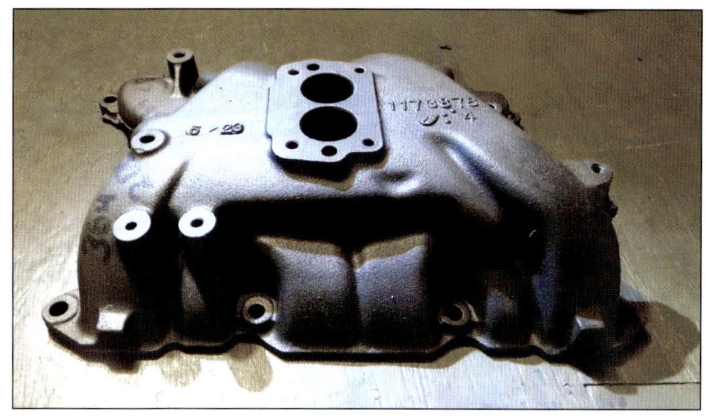

Buick made a 401 manifold for 2-barrel carburetors that was only used on entry-level models in 1962 and 1963. There was also a 2-barrel intake for the 364 engine. These are difficult to find today because most of them were discarded. (Photo Courtesy Carmen Faso)

and centering hub of the crankshaft. The tolerance here should be less than 0.001 inch. It pays to verify and, if necessary, correct your machining tolerances now and not find out the hard way during your initial test drive.

Engine Parts Interchange

Interchanging your parts from one Nailhead to another has a few good-news items and some not-so-good-news items.

Rocker Arms

Rocker arms and shaft assemblies can be used for any Nailhead. There were different production runs that began with steel rocker arms and later switched to aluminum ones. There is a sampling of rocker arms in chapter 5 that demonstrates the variation in ratios. The units that were tested in chapter 5 were the only items on hand at the time and do not cover all different production runs. It is advantageous performance-wise to use a higher-ratio rocker arm.

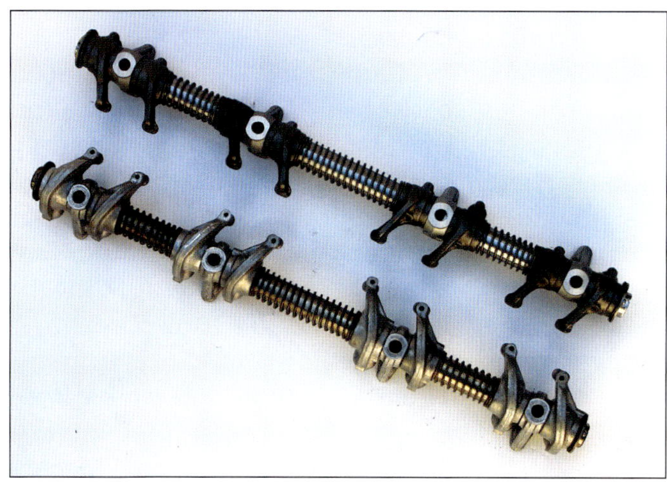

The original steel rocker arms and later-model aluminum rocker arms will fit all Nailheads from 1953 to the last motors produced in 1966. Those shown have been reconditioned and are sold in sets by Centerville Auto Repair. (Photo Courtesy Centerville Auto Repair)

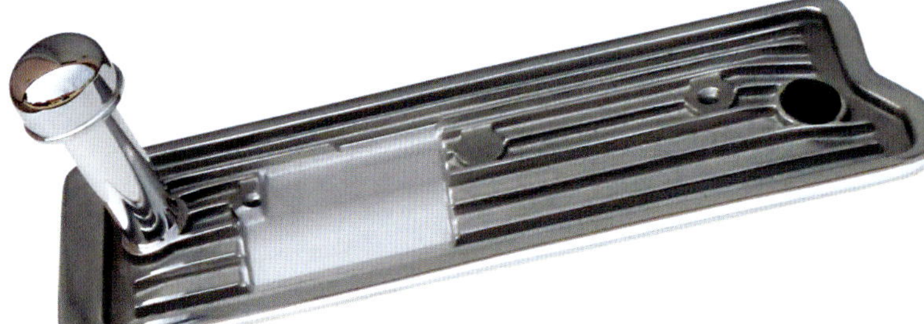

PML also makes these covers, and they fit all Nailheads. When purchasing aluminum valve covers or a valley cover (whether they are new or vintage parts), they are a universal fit. However, we don't always consider the openings required. PML offers a machining service with its products so they can be machined for fill tubes, PCV venting, or (as in this case) for clearance under the twin 4-barrel manifold. (Photo Courtesy PML Yourcovers.com)

Adjustable rockers are essential for use with all solid-lifter cams. TA Performance manufactures these rockers. They have a slightly higher ratio that will provide a little more lift and enhance your performance. (Photo Courtesy TA Performance)

This piston is for a 401 with a 4.250 bore. If you disregard the height of the piston and visualize the footprint of the dome, it is easy to understand why the combustion chamber in the first-generation heads is not compatible with next-generation heads for the 364- to 425-ci motors.

Intake manifolds for Nailheads will not interchange from one generation to another, but the exception is with the two-piece log manifolds. However, they are getting scarce. The manifold shown was manufactured by Centerville Auto Repair. (Photo Courtesy Centerville Auto Repair)

Rocker-Arm Covers and Valley Pan

Rocker-arm covers and valley covers will fit all Nailheads. If you find a good set of vintage aluminum valve covers, they will fit. Keep in mind that pre-1964 crankcase ventilation was through a vent tube or breathers in the valve covers. Those motors were vented to the atmosphere with only a fiber or metal mesh to capture oil droplets. However, we are in the 21st century and our mandate must be, at the very least, to comply with or exceed the environmental standards of today where practical.

Having said that, do not vent the crankcase of your new Nailhead to the atmosphere. Use a closed loop. Don't be concerned about any internal leakage that may compromise your horsepower. An important focus of this project is to increase the power output of the motor by assembling it to run as efficiently as possible with zero leakage from the rings, valve guides, or valve seals.

Cylinder Heads

Nailheads all had the same bore centers, valve guide spacing, and bolt patterns, but the first-generation 264- and 322-ci engines had a smaller combustion chamber and smaller ports. All the rest of the heads from 1957 to 1966 were essentially the same, although the 364 motors used smaller valves. Heads from a 401-ci motor are a straight swap onto a 364 with the benefit of larger valves, which will enhance the performance. Mounting the newer heads on the first-generation engine requires special-order pistons with domes made to conform with the smaller combustion chamber. It is costly to do that just to find out if there were any gains, and I do not know anyone who has tried to do it. I don't think there are any significant advantages because there are the Nailhead port configurations with which to contend.

Intake Manifolds

Intake manifolds should not be changed from the first generation (264/322) to the second generation (364) or to the last generation (401/425) or vice versa. You may be able to fit these by filing the bolt holes to align and grinding the ports to blend the flow, but this will have a negative effect on the intake flow. As the deck height was increased with each generation, the spacing between the heads also increased, so the result would be intake ports that are misaligned with the intake manifold.

The water crossover pipe will not interchange for the same reason as the intake manifolds. Filing the water manifold bolt holes and passages will reduce the sealing surfaces for the gaskets and become difficult to seal.

Camshafts

Camshafts can be swapped between the second- and third-generation motors. The only differences between these motors relative to the camshaft is that the last-generation pushrods are longer because of the deck-height increase. The 264- to 322-ci engines had different-size bearing journals. There are subtle differences from one OEM cam to another. It is difficult to compare the OEM cam specifications, which are rated at 0.002 lift, to aftermarket cams that are rated at 0.050 lift. Aftermarket race cams have better control over their source material and are your best choice at this point for quality compared to jobber's OEM-style cams from an unknown source. The aftermarket race cam grinder's entry-level grinds are not much more aggressive than an original Buick camshaft and don't sound any different as long as you keep a 12- to 14-degree lobe center.

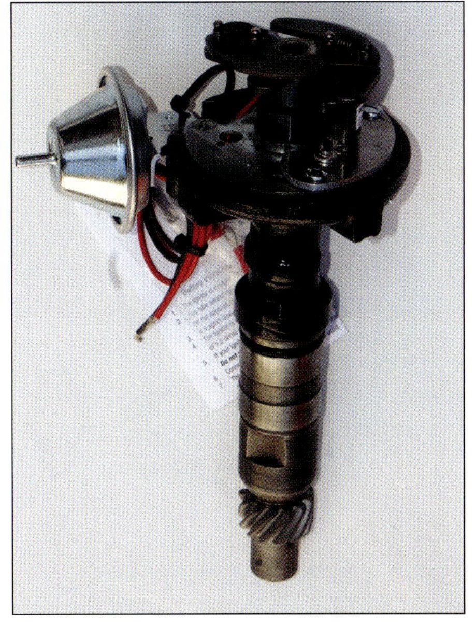

For those who want a completely original look or a sleeper that appears to be stock, this may be the distributor for you. It looks like it has an electronic module in place of the points and appears completely original. (Photo Courtesy Centerville Auto Repair)

This distributor appears somewhat similar to an original Nailhead, but it is actually an all-new unit in a billet aluminum body that comes with a magnetic pickup trigger, high-output circuit board, and a host of other upgrades. It is a ready-to-run unit that just requires being wired to the coil. (Photo Courtesy TA Performance)

This is another all-new distributor modeled after the HEI format. It comes with a high-output ignition module and a powerful 65,000-volt coil that will give you everything you need for your high-performance Nailhead. (Photo Courtesy TA Performance)

If you want to get serious about building your performance Nailhead for racing (and I assume that to be nostalgia racing), then this is the distributor for you. A Vertex is very reliable and will fit all Nailheads. Just be sure to check the oil pump shaft engagement.

Distributors

Distributors can be interchanged with all three generations of Nailheads. A strong ignition system is at the heart of any performance motor. The good news here is that there are a few different options to choose from, depending on the level of performance you want from your new Nailhead.

Be sure to check how much of the distributor shaft engages with the oil pump input shaft. There may be differences in the depth of the various aftermarket distributors, and each Nailhead generation had different deck heights. The engagement should be a minimum of 0.188 inches.

Crankshafts

Crankshafts are the same for each generation. There is an early and late version of the 401/425 crankshaft, and the difference is that both the diameter of the flywheel flange register and pilot bearing hole became smaller. The flywheel flange bolt patterns remained the same. The good news here is that all Nailhead crankshafts are a quality forged steel.

Starters

Starters from the Dynaflow era had a long nose and may require a 1/2-inch spacer to be used with an aftermarket flywheel or flexplate. The 364-ci motors began in 1957 with the starter solenoid canted downward and the mounting bolts directly opposed from each other. The 401 was introduced in 1959 with this same bolt pattern but with the solenoid canted upward. A change followed in 1963 with a symmetrically off-

There is an assortment of starter configurations to fit the different Nailheads. For originality's sake, hang onto the starter that came with your engine and set it aside on a shelf. For reliability, TA Performance has three different versions of a high-torque mini starter that will provide better starting, especially for a high-compression motor. (Photo Courtesy TA Performance)

This timing cover is a brand-new (not reconditioned) housing and comes with a new neoprene front seal. It also appears to have extra length to the left side of the flange so that it can accept either water pump. (Photo Courtesy TA Performance)

This is a new oil pump manufactured by TA Performance to fit the later motors. The company also offers a rebuilding service for the earlier pumps. (Photo Courtesy TA Performance)

set bolt pattern. The solenoid remained in the upward position.

There are starters with long nosecones and short nosecones. A standard flywheel on a Dynaflow-era motor usually requires a spacer to properly mate with a long-nose starter. Some of the high-torque starters come with dual bolt patterns, and others have a dedicated bolt spacing.

Check for fitment with the supplier before you order a starter. If you are making any changes, be sure to check for proper starter engagement with the ring gear.

Timing Covers

Timing covers are interchangeable with all of the Nailheads, but the reproduction covers will only work with the later-style water pumps. There are two styles of water pumps with long and short flanges at the inlet side; be sure it matches your timing cover flange.

Water Pumps

The short-shaft water pump is the standard unit and most commonly used in non-stock applications. A long-shaft water pump came into use as vehicles became longer to minimize the length of fan extensions—these are seldom used other than in stock applications. As mentioned previously, there is a water pump with a longer flange on the inlet side. These must be matched with a timing cover that has the same footprint. The new reproduction covers compensate for the different water pump footprints.

Oil Pans

The first-generation oil pans are rear sump. The 1957–1958 pans were also rear sump and will fit all Nailheads up to 1966 but require a rear-sump pickup that is available through Nailhead deal-

ers. The remainder of Nailheads all came with the center sump–style oil pan and will fit all engines.

Oil Pumps

Oil pumps can be interchanged from 1957 to the end of Nailhead production. The 1957 and 1958 models had a vacuum pump that ran off the oil pump, but these will only be of value to someone doing a restoration. Replacement vacuum pumps or repair parts for that pump are difficult to find or may not be available today. If you are running a combination oil/vacuum pump without sufficient vacuum for either the wipers or the brake booster, the aftermarket industry has come to the rescue again with accessory electric vacuum pumps. Similarly, any vehicle with forced induction or a radical camshaft needs one of these electric pumps to ensure that the power brakes will work properly.

DISASSEMBLY, EVALUATION, AND ESTABLISHING A PLAN

When rebuilding your own engine, there can be a lot to learn as you dismantle it, assess the parts, and determine a potential cause of failure. From the beginning, keep a camera and notebook handy as the disassembly begins. Log any areas of concern so that you can follow up on those issues. A photo gallery is very helpful, particularly when seeking advice about problem areas or if you want to revisit it yourself. It is common to have a project like this on hold for days or even weeks while waiting for parts or machine shop services. Photos can be a good refresher, and they can highlight forgotten areas of concern that can later cause a delay or become a mistake. These types of situations reinforce the need for good records.

This project's motor is a 401-ci 1964 Buick Nailhead. When the engine arrived, it did not include the transmission, carburetor, or distributor. Something it did have was a lot of grease. The motor was accompanied by an MSD distribu-

This is the motor as it was delivered. The carburetor and exhaust manifolds were in boxes. You want to do the heavy cleaning and pressure washing outside so that your work area stays clean. We will do the brunt of the cleaning outdoors.

tor and what appeared to be a relatively new or rebuilt carburetor that was delivered in a box. The owner said that the motor made a knocking noise when it was last started, and he shut it off immediately. The vehicle is a 1964 Buick Wildcat convertible and is

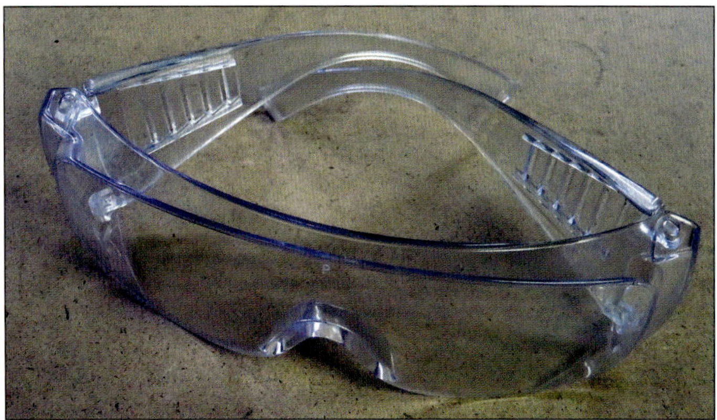

Safety glasses should not require an explanation, yet I routinely see people not using them. Every shop should be equipped with quality glasses. They fit better and will provide superior protection.

Cotton gloves can protect your hands from unnecessary cuts and scrapes. These are a must in any working automotive shop.

Nitrile gloves have a place in every workshop, whether you are working with any chemicals (such as brake clean or mineral spirits) or just performing routine jobs. They also help prevent your hands from drying out and cracking in the cold weather. The 9-mil gloves can last through several work cycles, yet they are thin enough to let you feel what you are doing.

Mono-goggles and/or a face shield each have their own uses. They are a must and provide improved protection in conjunction with your regular eye protection from abnormal airborne chemicals and particulates, especially if you are going to be doing any grinding.

currently going through a complete restoration with some safety and mechanical upgrades to improve reliability and performance. The intended use is for recreation and to attend the occasional cruise nights.

The owner wants the engine rebuilt with a little more performance, and he will possibly add a turbocharger in the future. The turbocharger suggestion will compromise some of our parts decisions for this project; particularly the camshaft profile and compression ratio. The future turbo will most certainly alter the selection of the pistons, ring package, and camshaft.

Safety

Safety supplies should normally be well stocked in your shop. Leather-faced cotton work gloves can protect your hands from cuts and scrapes. Good quality nitrile gloves provide protection from grease and oil as well as some of the nastier solvents

Dry-powder extinguishers can be used for several different types of fires. Routinely check the pressure gauges. You should pick up your extinguisher every two to three months and shake it so that the powder doesn't compact itself on the bottom.

Don't mount your extinguisher(s) in the immediate area where you most likely would have a fire. Mount the unit(s) between that area and an exit so you can safely access them in an emergency.

and brake-cleaning products. Personally, I prefer the 9-mil nitrile gloves because they can last for several work cycles.

Safety glasses are standard equipment, but whenever you grind parts or there is potential for airborne particles, a respirator and eye protection with tight-fitting goggles or a face shield are a must. When not in use, keep your dust mask, goggles, face shield, and respirators in a clean bag so that they are clean and ready to go the next time you need them.

Quality safety equipment that is kept clean and properly fitted is as important as using quality tools. The quality dust masks come with an aluminum strip to be bent into position over your nose to adjust the fit and a vent valve that helps prevent your glasses from fogging up. A cartridge-type respirator with a dust filter provides a bet-

Mount fire extinguishers strategically around your shop, particularly if you have welding equipment or may be working with any flammable materials or solvents. This carbon dioxide extinguisher should not be used for an electrical fire.

ter fit and is much more effective for protection than the paper masks. There are a variety of different cartridges available for all types of chemicals and particulate matter. Learn the proper application of the different elements for you to be able to use your respirator effectively. Using an incorrect cartridge can be as bad as no respirator at all.

Quality safety equipment is not cheap. Look after this equip-

ment so it can look after you. Write the date on the chemical cartridges as a reference to when they should be discarded. Keep a clean pair of coveralls and a work apron available in your shop and use them. You don't want to carry debris from the garage to your vehicle or into your home. It is no secret that you can burn up a lot of brownie points by bringing grease or metal turnings into the house.

Tools

Using the right tool for the job is imperative when performing quality work. Most of the tools you will use are common to most tool boxes, but they must be maintained and in ready-to-use condition. Some of your tools may be worn to the point that they are no longer safe to use or cannot perform the task they were designed to do. If so, repair or replace worn-out or broken tools before starting your project. When a job is performed with inadequate equipment, the tendency is to make do until next time, and the result will be shoddy work or possibly an injury.

A brass hammer, brass punches, and a dead-blow hammer will be required at times, but ball-peen hammers and claw hammers have no place in an engine shop. Use the right tool for the job.

You will encounter situations where improvisation is required, and some homemade tools can be a real asset for specific jobs. Quality scrapers and parting tools are not usually available when you need them. You can make these from the broken blades of industrial-power hacksaws. Your local metal fabrication shop could be a source for these blades that are made from quality steel. You can square up the end of a piece of the broken blade and sharpen it at a 15-degree angle to be used as a scraper. You can then sharpen a second one at a 10-degree angle as a parting tool, which works well when separating gasketed parts like your Nailhead water pump from the aluminum timing cover. The 15-degree scraper is too blunt for this job and could damage the parts. If you overheat these tools while sharpening, you may have to reharden them. Your local machine shop can do that or send you in the right direction. There are some informative tuto-

rials online about basic hardening and tempering of hand tools. When you are finished, generously tape the handle end or dip it into Plasti Dip to provide a safe burr-free handle. You can damage your parts and ruin putty knives when using the wrong tool for this job.

Another handy tool is a simple notched wedge that meshes with the starter teeth to prevent crankshaft rotation while tightening or loosening the harmonic balancer or flywheel.

Use a good, heavy-duty engine stand with four wheels. There are many flimsy light-duty units in the market. Don't cheap out and buy a light-duty stand; they have been known to collapse and can tip over easily!

A machined drive hub bolted to an old damper is handy to rotate the motor when removing

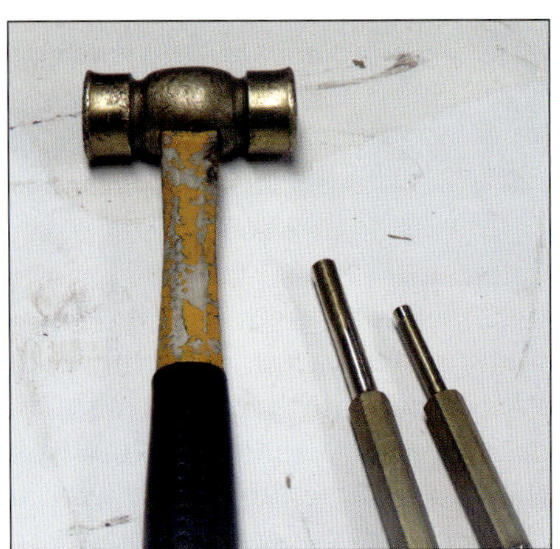

A brass hammer and punches are good for coaxing pieces into place or tapping lightly to loosen parts. The best use I get from the brass hammer is to use the rubber handle to tap pistons through the ring compressor. Most other hammers do not have a place in engine rebuilding.

Scrapers and parting tools each have their own purpose and should not be mixed up. A 15-degree edge is more durable for scraping but is too blunt to break gaskets free and may damage your parts, particularly aluminum pieces.

You can make a parting tool in the same manner as a scraper by sharpening at a 10-degree angle. These are separate tools with dedicated purposes. If you overheat either of these while sharpening, they may need to be rehardened. You can find basic tutorials on YouTube to harden and temper tools.

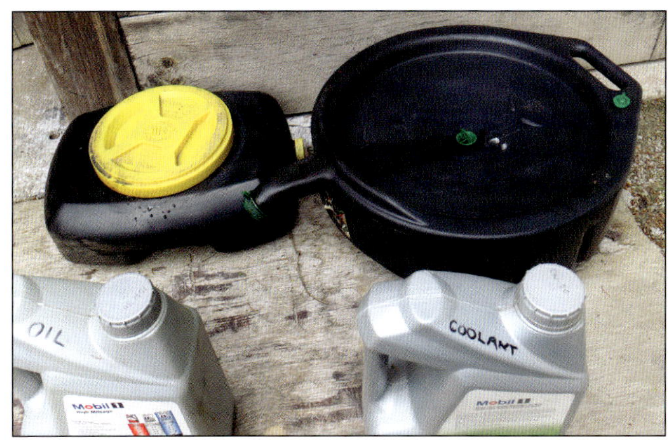

You will need a few separate drain containers and pans for oil and antifreeze-contaminated water so that they can be properly disposed of at your local recycling facility. These must be properly labeled, otherwise they may not be accepted.

or installing pistons or to mount a degree wheel.

A camshaft installation or removal tool is helpful to guide the cam into place without marking the cam bearings. A device for lifting crankshafts or heads can be easier on your back rather than trying to lift and twist around with these heavier parts. Similarly, handles will help guide the heads into place.

Aside from regular tools, a dial indicator is needed along with an impact gun and sockets, drain pans, a pry bar, puller set, snap ring pliers, and a 5/16 square dog wrench. Other items from around the shop that are needed include a few short pieces of rubber hose for the rod bolts, 2-7/16 NC x 2-inch socket set screws, a 24-inch piece of 3/8-inch round rod, and a 15-inch piece of 5/8-inch wood doweling. Be sure to have some brake clean, penetrating oil, and plenty of rags on hand. Resealable sandwich bags will keep your parts organized.

Disassembly

Mount your motor on the engine stand, and let's get started. Before you remove any parts, scrape off any heavy grease and pressure-wash the rest of the exterior. Do this outside if you have a suitable area. If not, take the motor to a car wash before mounting it on the stand. You don't want to be blasting this stuff around the neighborhood if you live in a gated community or a townhouse complex. Breaking down a motor can be a sloppy exercise.

Use large pieces of cardboard under the engine stand to keep the floor clean throughout the disassembly and rebuild process.

1 Drain the oil into a proper drain pan and store it in a properly marked disposal container.

2 Using a separate drain pan to catch coolant from the 1/8-inch drain plug on the left side of the motor, tilt the engine 45 degrees to ensure that all of the coolant has drained.

3 Repeat and drain the oil and coolant from the right side. Put these two plugs back in so you don't have vagrant drips each time the engine is rotated. Label your containers so that you can follow the proper waste disposal procedures that apply to your locality. This is where the

floor cardboard comes in handy because there are always vagrant drops of coolant or oil as the motor is first rotated in different positions. Even if you have an integral drip tray on your engine stand, the cardboard will come in handy to keep the floor clean. Have lots of containers available to keep your parts. Resealable sandwich bags are handy for storing the bolts for each piece. Be sure to label your bags and containers.

4 Remove the oil pan and leave it on the cardboard under the motor to catch any drops of oil.

Removing the pan revealed that the oil pump inlet screen was partially obstructed with thick, hard sludge. Although, there was not a significant amount of sludge in the pan or elsewhere in the engine. Either the lack of oil, the sludge at the oil pump inlet screen, or both could have caused the knocking that the owner heard as he shut down the motor.

Notebook Entry 1

Significant carbon deposits were on the spark plugs. (Our notes will be summarized later in this chapter as we investigate the cause of failure and establish a plan for correction. Think of these notes as clues at a crime scene as we forensically dissect this engine.)

A cursory inspection of your motor may help reveal some of the background of what you are dealing with. Do a more thorough inspection as you remove each part. This can tell you a lot more since each part has its own

ems

proper heat range as shown by the light coating of oil-ash deposits on the insulator.

n: Preignition or overhea... ...dition: Carbon fouled

Causes:
...rk plug too hot
...anced engine timing
...wing piece of carbon in
...mbustion chamber
...gged or partially plugged c...
...tem

Possible Causes:
1. A sticky carburetor choke
2. Faulty ignition primary circuit
3. Defective spark plug wires
4. Rich fuel mixture
5. Spark plug too cold

Remedy:
1. Clean carburetor choke plate and shaft

...tall colder spark plug

This electric impact gun can be set as high as 350 ft-lbs and gives you the brute torque required to remove the balancer retaining bolt but (and that is a big but) only if you cannot break it free with a Johnson bar. This is the only application where you may need an impact gun when working on your Nailhead. Never reinstall the damper bolt with an impact gun; use a torque wrench.

The heat range of this spark plug is a little too cold for a stock motor and that can contribute to the amount of carbon bridging over the electrode. Otherwise, it may have been caused by something as simple as a stuck or improperly set up choke.

Notebook Entry 2

An oil leak from the front seal could indicate a few things. The sealing surface on the hub of the damper needs to be checked. The seal could be worn out, but the culprit is most likely if the original rope seal is still in place.

A heavy layer of grease was apparent from the left side of the front crankshaft seal, which may mean that the seal is faulty and/or the sealing surface of the balancer is worn. Closely inspect the balancer and replace the old rope seals with new neoprene seals during the rebuild. I am not a big fan of using an impact gun because it is not very forgiving and can leave you with a path of destruction. However, the balancer retaining bolt is torqued to 200-plus ft-lbs and in some cases is installed with a locking compound. You will need to use a locking wedge in the flexplate ring gear.

5 First try using a Johnson bar to remove the balancer bolt. If it does not come free, resort to using the impact gun.

6 Remove the crankshaft pulley, clean the threads with a 5/16 NC thread chaser, and then use a gear puller to remove the harmonic balancer.

You might expect to find a lot of sludge throughout the motor when there was enough to start plugging the oil pump inlet screen. This was probably due to a lack of oil changes.

story. The spark plugs had a heavy amount of carbon—to the point that it bridged the gap of a few of the electrodes. The AC R43S plug is on the cool side of the heat range needed for a stock engine. The fouled plugs may have been an issue caused by the carburetor and/or the choke not properly set up.

A locking wedge, such as this, is reversible and can be handy to prevent rotation when you are trying to install or remove the flexplate or balancer bolts. It is also safer than jamming an old screwdriver or chisel into a tooth of the ring gear and possibly breaking it.

Remember to clean and bag your bolts as you go because you don't want to have to hunt for them later.

You should always keep a good heavy-duty puller on hand and will probably need it to remove the harmonic balancer. There are way too many cheap units in the market. Spend your money wisely on a quality puller.

This puller set is handy to have on hand (if for nothing else as a supply of grade-8 hardware sorted out and ready to use with the heavy-duty puller). Actually, the puller head pictured was bent and has since found its way into the scrap pail, which is a good example of why not to purchase cheap tools.

In this case, the balancer came off too easily and warranted a closer check of the outside diameter of the crank snout and inside diameter of the damper. The maximum clearance should be 0.001 inch or less. Check the keyway in your balancer as well. Although it is not a common problem with Nailheads, they have been known to crack in other engines.

Do a close inspection of the harmonic balancer, looking for cracks and making sure that the rubber seal between the balancer hub and counterweight is in good condition. If you are in doubt, have it Magnafluxed when the block is being checked. A broken damper is dangerous! There are sleeves to repair worn damper hubs, but you are better off replacing the worn unit with a good used or new one.

It is apparent from the excess sealant oozing from behind the timing cover that it had been removed in the past, probably to replace the timing chain and gearset or maybe just the front seal.

Notebook Entry 3

The harmonic balancer came off too easily.

Check that the crank snout and balancer are sized to spec. Balancers in general have been

Erosion, such as this on the pump inlet, is common with Nailheads and makes this housing unusable. Rebuilders used to rely on repairable cores. Fortunately, the new water pumps that are available today are based on new housings.

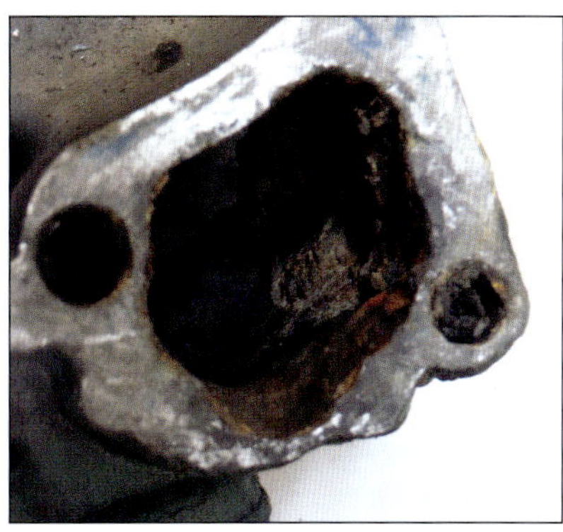

Another factor to watch for with your timing cover, as well as erosion, is pitting from cavitation in the water pump cavity. In a worst-case scenario, a failure here can cost you a motor from coolant leaking into the oil pan.

The same type of erosion on the water pump housing has also rendered the timing cover as trash. A fresh, new timing cover is a good investment for your new rebuild because the original aluminum covers usually suffer from age cosmetically over the years (on top of the corrosion and erosion issues we talked about earlier). New covers are now available through TA Performance.

known to crack at the keyway and could be the cause of this looseness.

An area of concern with Nailheads is the severe corrosion of the aluminum timing cover and water pump. The aluminum thermostat housing is also an issue. The corrosion of these particular parts is more of a problem than with other aluminum accessories because of the proximity to an ethylene glycol–based coolant. At higher temperatures, such as in your cooling system, ethylene glycol decomposes into an organic acid. Aluminum, being the more vulnerable alloy present, was the target of acidic attack.

Ethylene glycol was the standard antifreeze through the Nailhead era of the 1950s and 1960s when a little bit of corrosion was sort of accepted. This did not emerge as a significant issue until aluminum engine blocks and heads came into the picture and most of the Nailhead-powered vehicles were on the road for longer. Alternate chemical-based coolants then came into the picture, but for us the damage was done.

You may see this problem with other aluminum accessories, such as the alternator pivot bolt (but to a lesser degree). This was due to galvanic corrosion from dissimilar metals. If you combine the decomposition from acidic attack with the galvanic corrosion issue, you can then understand how the through bolts and fasteners threaded into aluminum became a problem.

When you remove these parts, test each bolt to see if it will break free and remove those that come loose at this time. Thoroughly soak the rest of the bolts with a good penetrant—particularly the four small bolts in the water pump because they are notorious for seizing. If the bolts are seized, continue to soak them with penetrant and periodically tap the heads. Soak them overnight if necessary.

Hopefully, a light tap on the head of each of these bolts is adequate to break the seal formed by the corrosion. If not, continue to reapply penetrant. A broken bolt in aluminum is very difficult to remove and could render the piece as junk. New water pumps are available and will be replaced as part of the rebuild.

Reproduction timing covers are now available and are also a welcome addition to the aftermarket. Your timing cover could also fall prey to cavitation damage behind the water pump. You can identify traces of this type of damage in a series of what looks like large pinholes. The cavitation damage is usually caused by running out of coolant. This becomes very serious because it can eventually create a passage for coolant to leak through the back of the cover and into the oil. You may also find internal wear from excessive timing chain slop on the inside of the cover. Good original covers are becoming more difficult to find.

7 Remove the fuel pump from the timing cover.

8 Remove the water crossover manifold and the thermostat housing. Note the condition of the gasket surfaces and the water ports.

9 Remove the water pump bolts and use the parting tool to make light taps at several spots around the perimeter to break it free from the gasket. Then, remove it.

Be sure to continually and repeatedly soak the timing-cover and water-pump fasteners with WD-40 penetrating oil and follow through with a light tap on the heads of the bolts to free any seized fasteners, particularly the small 1/4-inch bolts holding the water pump in place.

It's not a surprise that an old rope seal, such as this, leaks. Don't worry because new neoprene replacements are readily available. Remove the tin seat along with the old rope seal to install the new-style neoprene seal.

10 Remove the timing cover using the same approach that you used with the water pump.

Check the water pump cavity for wear and signs of cavitation, and check the water passages for erosion. This timing cover was severely eroded and will be replaced. Traditionally, you should replace your timing chain and gears with a rebuild. This set had an abnormal amount of wear for only 2 to 3 years of service; it had 3/8 inch of play!

When you have a timing chain this loose, check for wear inside the timing cover. A three-year life span for a timing chain and gearset is ridiculously short. Low oil pressure may have accelerated the wear, but I suspect that this set was a substandard offshore import.

Notebook Entry 5

Check the block and note any play in the timing chain.

Notebook Entry 6

The hardened tips on the rocker arms are worn and there were two different types of pushrods in this motor.

Get yourself a camshaft extension or installation tool. It makes life a lot easier to install or remove the cam and gives you much better control so as to not damage the cam bearings. When you are degreeing in the cam, you will have it in and out of the block multiple times with new cam bearings installed.

Some of the hardened inserts in the valve tip of the rockers are wearing, quite possibly from low oil pressure and oil not reaching the rocker-arm shafts. We have seen several instances where parts have become victims of low oil supply. This has been a good example of why you need an oil pressure gauge. Low oil pressure lights come on at less than 5 pounds of oil pressure, which is just in time to tell you that it is too late!

11 Remove the intake manifold, valley cover, valve covers, and rocker-arm shaft assemblies. Bag your fasteners and set them aside. You can use them as size samples for replacement bolts. Note that our engine arrived sans carburetor and distributor. If they were included and installed, they would be removed at this point. When the pushrods were removed, I noticed that some had been replaced with a different type.

12 Discard the lifters. They should be replaced with all rebuilds.

13 With your camshaft removal tool in place (and if necessary), use a puller to ease the timing gear off the crankshaft snout. Alternately pry or pull the gear and pull the cam until they are removed.

14 Discard the chain and timing gears. Set the Woodruff keys and fuel pump eccentric aside to be reused. The old camshaft can be sent to the machine shop with your other parts for fitting the new bearings. Not many shops have a spare Nailhead cam sitting around.

15 Reposition the wedge to lock the crankshaft rotation, loosen and undo the flexplate bolts, and remove the flexplate.

Before you start to loosen the head bolts, double check that the wheels on your engine stand are locked up and that the locking bolt or pin is in place to prevent

Get yourself a few 2x7/16-inch NC set screws to insert in the lower head bolt holes as the head bolts are removed. These will keep the head stable as the rest of the bolts are removed. This is especially helpful when you are trying to release a gasket that is partially stuck to both the block and head.

the engine from rolling over. It is a good idea to keep your foot on the lower stand to stabilize it while loosening the head bolts.

Believe it or not, this is the casting plug in the exhaust crossover in the underside of the intake manifold. This one is a good example of how corrosive the exhaust gases can become. If you leave the crossover functional, then you should isolate the carb base from direct contact with a 20-gauge stainless spacer.

These rod bearings are scored from lack of oil to the point they started to show some color from heat. They also began to shrink onto the crank journal and were only a few revolutions away from seizing and causing a catastrophic failure.

Fortunately, there was very little or no ridge at the top of the cylinders, which eliminated the need for a ridge reamer and made it easier to push the pistons out.

16 Loosen the head bolts and remove them. Leave a few bolts loose in the block and use a pry bar to break the head-to-block seal. Use a putty knife to release the head gasket from the head.

17 Try using 7/16 x 2-inch NC set screws in the lower head bolt holes before removing the last few head bolts so that the head doesn't tumble onto the floor or your foot.

18 Lift and remove the cylinder heads. Have a table or stand nearby to set the parts on as you remove each head. This way, you have a handy place to set them down and you won't need to twist or walk before doing so.

19 To take the short-block apart, rotate the motor 45 degrees, reinsert the engine-stand locking bolt/pin, and slide the damper/drive hub onto the crank snout. If you don't have a drive hub, you could have removed the piston and rod assemblies before removing the harmonic balancer. Use a socket on the

balancer retaining bolt to rotate the assembly. The heads would also have been removed earlier in the sequence. The right tool for the job will not only save you time, it will save spending money on parts that were unnecessarily damaged.

20 Before you start to remove the pistons, check to see how much of a ridge has been left at the top of the cylinders from the rings wearing in. These cylinders were fine, but if there is a ridge at the top of your cylinders, it may be necessary to use a ridge reamer to eliminate the ridge and remove the piston.

21 Turn the engine to bring a piston down to bottom dead canter (BDC) and loosen the rod bolts three to four turns. Using a brass hammer, tap on the end of the rod bolt until the rod is free from the rod journal.

22 Remove the nuts and rod cap, and install protective

There was an odd wear pattern in these cylinders. You can see light shining on the wear line at the forward side and an impression of a wear line to the left or rearward side. There was no apparent wear on the inboard or outboard cylinder walls, which leads me to believe the pistons had been rocking.

hoses over the rod bolts. In this case, the bearing insert began to shrink and grasp onto the crank journal. This is typically a sign of oil starvation.

The original pistons were knurled. I believe this would have been done when the motor was less than 10 years old because this practice was discontinued many years ago. Knurling pistons was a cheap alternative to correct cylinder wear instead of boring the block and buying a larger-size piston.

Notebook Entry 7

The crankshaft needs to be checked for size and to ensure that it is straight, especially after seeing the condition of the rod bearing.

23 Rotate the block so that the cylinder is horizontal before knocking out the piston/rod assembly.

24 Place a 12-inch piece of 1/2-inch doweling through the crankcase to the bottom of the piston head and drive the piston/rod assembly to the top of the bore so that you can grasp the piston head and pull it out. Repeat this step for the other seven cylinders.

This motor had very little ridge, and the pistons were removed easily. With a piston removed, it was obvious that this motor had been taken apart before. The stock Buick pistons had been knurled. This was a practice that was done 50 years ago as a cheap alternative to boring the block. They were attempting to fit the pistons when the cylinders were slightly worn.

We noticed at this point that the crankshaft was squeaking as it turned, which confirmed a lack of oil, and some bearing inserts were hanging on for dear life. After the pistons were removed, the crankshaft was still tight to turn. As the main bearing caps were loosened, the shaft did not free up until all but two of the bearings were removed, which is a sign that the crank may be bent. Further checking with a dial indicator showed that it was bent 0.006 inch.

25 Remove the crankshaft and set it aside.

26 Check the main bearings. In this case, they were badly worn and tossed into a scrap bucket. A lack of oil is one of the worst things that can happen to your motor. There is a succession of events that follow very quickly, and it starts with hot spots on the rod journals causing the crankshaft to bend. The rod bearings immediately shrink onto the journals, and the connecting rods start peeking out through holes in the side of your block like a bunch of prairie dogs peeking out of their holes. Fortunately, this engine didn't get past the first stage.

Observe casting flashing and inclusions from the lifter bosses in the valley.

A closer look at the lifter valley shows a sample of the significant casting flashing and inclusions on the lifter bosses that are normal in a Nailhead block. You will see many that are worse than this one. Notice the inclusion in the valley between the lifter bosses. You will need to grind down to the bottom of the root to get rid of it. Fortunately, it is not very deep.

A crankshaft lifting device is a lot easier on your shoulders. The crank will be in and out several times during the rebuild. Using this lifting device will free up one hand and provide more control and less chance of damaging the new main bearings.

27 Continue to strip the block by removing the oil filter housing and oil-pressure sending unit.

28 Position the bare block on the stand so that you can access the frost plugs in the side of the block. Using a 1/4-inch punch on one side of the plugs, drive them into the block so that they twist sideways or fall into the block. Pull them out with water pump pliers.

29 Next, take out the 1/8-inch NPT drain plugs from the bottom of the water jackets. Keep the drain pan in position under the motor because you will likely spill some coolant as you turn the block over. Repeat the plug removal on the other side of the block.

30 There are three small frost plugs in the front of the oil galleries. Use a dent puller to take out the one on the passenger side.

31 Then, use a 3/8-inch steel rod through that oil gallery to knock out the frost plug at the back end of that gallery and the access plug at the back of the block.

32 Use the rod to go through the cam bearings to knock out the large frost plug from the back of the block. Support the rod from the lifter valley so you don't damage the snap ring.

33 Remove the snap ring and put it away for safe keeping. Replacements are not always readily available.

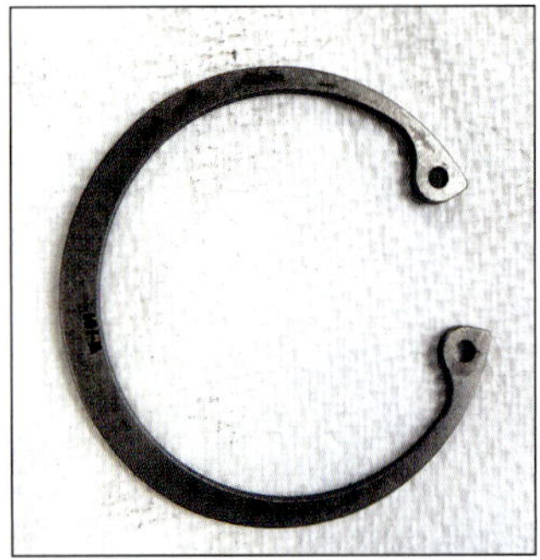

This snap ring fits on the outer side of the #5 cam bearing. It appears that the purpose is to limit rearward movement of the camshaft. However, the rear surface of timing gear does that job.

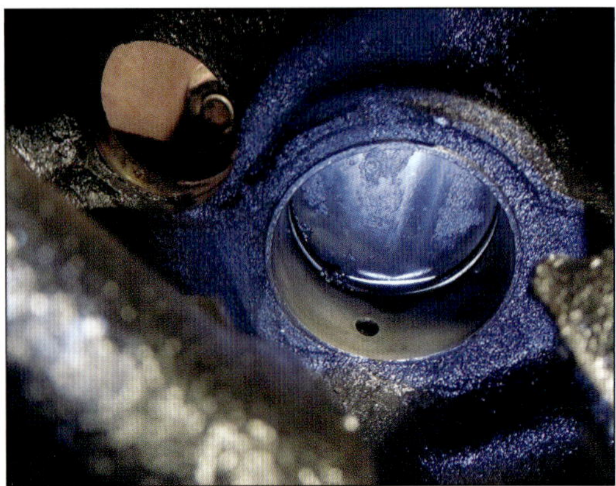

This is a view from inside the lifter gallery of the large internal snap ring and frost plug in place at the rear of the #5 camshaft bearing. This frost plug is part of the frost plug kit. This kit and the internal snap ring are readily available from TA Performance.

There is sludge buildup at the rear of the oil galleries that feed both banks of lifters. It is normal for sludge to accumulate here because this is the end of the oil passage and there is no flow. It does reinforce the need to access all areas of the block for a thorough cleaning.

The plugs at the rear of the oil galleries that have been exposed to the elements since the motor was new are usually difficult to remove or are seized. They can be removed with a little persuasion. If you have a seized plug, use an oxy-acetylene torch with a small tip and heat only the plug with the torch.

Heat the plug (not the block) until it shows some color. Shut off the torch.

Melt some candle wax on the plug as it cools.

Wait until after the plug has cooled. It can be removed easily with a 5/16-inch square dog wrench.

34 The last of the oil gallery plugs are the two 3/8-inch NPT plugs at the rear of the left and center oil passages. You will need a 5/16-inch square dog wrench to take out these plugs, but bear in mind that these have probably been in the block for 50-plus years. If they come out easily, you are lucky. Save these plugs; they will be put back in.

35 Use the 3/8-inch rod from the rear of the block to knock out the frost plugs at the front of the main oil gallery and the left lifter bank. The block is now ready to go out for cleaning.

Evaluation and Establishing a Plan

Let's establish a plan from our notes.

Notebook Item 1: Carbon

You can correct this by using the correct spark plugs and having the carburetor set up properly. New rings will resolve any carbon fouling from leaking rings.

Notebook Item 2: Oil Leaking from Front Seal

You can fix this easily by upgrading the old rope front and rear seals with new neoprene seals. The sealing area of the hub is clear of wear marks and measured at 1.999 inches, which is correct.

Notebook Item 3: Harmonic Balancer Appeared to be Loose

You need to check the inside diameter of the balancer hub, which should be 1.438 inches. The outside diameter of the crankshaft snout should be 1.437 inches. Both were within spec. There are no signs of a crack in the keyway area of the hub. A test fit on the bench seemed normal. Send the balancer out and have it Magnafluxed as a precaution.

Notebook Item 4: Erosion

Erosion in the timing cover, water pump, and thermostat housing are common with Nailheads. In this case, all three pieces are ruined. The immediate solution is to replace these items with new reproduction pieces.

The primary cause of the corrosion was an acidic attack from the organic acids created by overheating the original ethylene glycol coolant. The first corrective action is to only use aluminum-compatible antifreeze solution when the motor is reinstalled.

The secondary cause was from galvanic corrosion. Powder coating is not conductive and will help insulate the fasteners from the aluminum. Anti-seize on the threads of the bolts will also help. As much as you may like to use stainless steel hardware, regular grade-5 fasteners are less likely than stainless steel bolts to initiate corrosion in this application.

These steps are only considered to be helpful and are not an end-all solution to the problem. To completely eliminate the corrosion of dissimilar metals, they would need to be completely isolated from each other, which is not practical in this situation.

Notebook Item 5: Sloppy Timing Chain

You can easily replace this with a quality timing gear set from one of the Nailhead-specific dealers such as Carmen Faso, Centerville Auto Repair, or TA Performance.

Verifying the distance between the crankshaft and camshaft centerlines is an area that is seldom checked. The likelihood of this being a problem is slim; I have only encountered it once. This distance is not a published number that I have been able to find, so I took the measurements from what I am certain to be a virgin block. The measurement I have is 3.374 inches between the cam bearing and main bearing openings with the bearing inserts removed.

The reason that I make an issue of this is because every automotive machine shop I have dealt with has been adamant that every engine block must be align bored or honed. About 25 years ago, I was having machine work performed at a reputable race engine shop. I could not keep timing chains in that block for more than three or four races. It was to the point that the sloppy chains wore a hole in the vintage Weiand front cover. We finally found the cause: the camshaft-to-crankshaft center line was 0.004 less than another block. I really believed the cause was a machining error. Of course, the response was, "You will just have to do another block." Needless to say, I did another block—but not at that machine shop. Subsequently, I have not had a Nailhead block align bored since. This is not to say that you shouldn't check.

Have your crankshaft ground and straightened before beginning the block machine work. Install the crankshaft with #1 and #3 bearings with a light coat of 20W oil and torque to spec. Then, use a dial indicator and check the #5 main journal for runout. This must be zero. If there is any reading at all, return the crankshaft to the grinder. Remove the crankshaft and reinstall it with all five main bearing inserts and caps torqued in place. If it spins freely by hand with no resistance, there is no reason to align bore or hone that block. It may be kudos to Buick machining or the stability of the skirted block design, but I have not come across an unsatisfactory block to date.

Notebook Item 6: Rocker-Arm Hardened Tips with Excess Wear

I did not make note of which valves had the different pushrods. Regardless, new rocker arms are a normal rebuild item. When rebuilding a 55-year-old motor, there is probably no record of the history behind it: whether the block or heads have been resurfaced, how much material was removed, and what current machining is required.

After your machine work is complete, mock up the block and heads with the gaskets in place and rocker arms. Use an adjustable pushrod to measure with the new camshaft and lifters in place to determine if stock or custom-length pushrods will be required for correct preload.

Notebook Item 7: Bent Crankshaft

The root of this problem was a lack of oil. The rod journal overheated to the point that there was some discoloration, which is enough to warp the crankshaft. A new oil pump and pickup are also a normal part of the rebuild. The crankshaft also needs to be turned and straightened. The crankshaft was picked up by John from Canadian Chromeplating and Crankshaft Inc. This is a routine job for him.

Notebook Item 8: Casting Flashing

Use a die grinder to remove the flashing and relieve any inclusions to erase any sign of the faults.

Final Observations

There were a couple of observations from the disassembly that you may find interesting but were of no real consequence to the rebuild.

First, the production code number was missing from the passenger side at the top of the block. In the early Nailhead years up to 1960, it was common for either the production code or engine serial numbers to be misplaced or missing altogether. From 1962 onward, these numbers were very consistent. This is a 1964 block. From that alone, I suspect that it is a factory replacement block.

The second issue is the wear pattern from the rings. It appears that the cylinders had excessive wear and the pistons were knurled to compensate for the extra clearance. This allowed the pistons to rock, causing the rings to create a wear pattern fore and aft of the cylinders. As the piston rocked, the rings lost their edge on the IB and OB surfaces. Consequently, there was very little wear pattern from the rings in the inboard or outboard walls of the cylinders.

I do not believe that this could have been done at a Buick dealership. They probably would have taken the easy way out and replaced the short-block assembly or (more likely) a new long-block through warranty.

This is a best-guess interpretation of what we saw while breaking the engine down. It will not have any effect on the rebuild.

The Plan

Sonic tests and head cc'ing are discussed in chapters 5 and 6. However, that information is essential and needs to be available as soon as it is completed to establish a plan. You need to do a sonic test on the cylinders to ensure that there is no serious core shifting and that there is adequate material to bore out the cylinders. Once you confirm cylinder thickness, the machine shop can take the block out to a standard bore size. In this case it's the big-block Chevrolet standard bore of 4.250 inches, which has a good selection of ring packages. Given the intended use of this vehicle, we decided to use a Total Seal 1/16 x 1/16 x 3/16 ring package.

The owner confirmed his intention to add a turbocharger in

the future, which will require the use of forged pistons. To do this, we need to discuss the project with a piston manufacturer and confirm the bore size, stroke, deck height, combustion chamber cc's, piston dome size for the desired compression ratio, ring package, camshaft duration, valve lift, and whether the vehicle is going to be raced or used on the street. Only then can we proceed with the order.

Piston manufacturers require this information for any non-stock application so that they can custom design a piston to be suitable for the project and provide adequate dome thickness and valve pocket material.

Once the availability of the bearings, gaskets, seals, frost plugs, timing gear sets, rocker arms and shafts, water pump, and oil pump are confirmed, place the order with your supplier. We sourced these parts through Carmen Faso. Prep work can now begin on the block so that when the pistons arrive, they can be sent with the block to the shop (we used Forrest & Forrest Racing) for the machine work. Rings can be ordered as a package with pistons or through an alternate supplier.

There are a few different companies that have cams for the Buick Nailhead. I prefer a dual-pattern grind with longer exhaust duration and a wider lobe separation of 112 degrees for any Nailhead regardless of the performance level. The owner wants the motor to sound like it has a racing cam. I discussed this with Jerry at Schneider Cams, and we settled on his suggestion of their 270-80H grind. The cam and valve springs were ordered from Schneider.

The carburetor can be sent to a shop (we used Al at Moffat Carburetion Specialties) for flow testing and setup.

For the naturally aspirated version, you can use 0.018 steel-shim head gaskets. Once the motor has been broken in with carburetor and the owner is ready to proceed with the turbocharger, we can change over to the 0.042 copper head gaskets. O-ring grooves were cut into the block during the initial machine work, so you only have to install the stainless O-ring wire and replace the head gaskets to switch over to the turbo. This lowers the compression ratio enough to allow us to run up to 7 pounds of boost.

Onward to the workshop and then the machine shop.

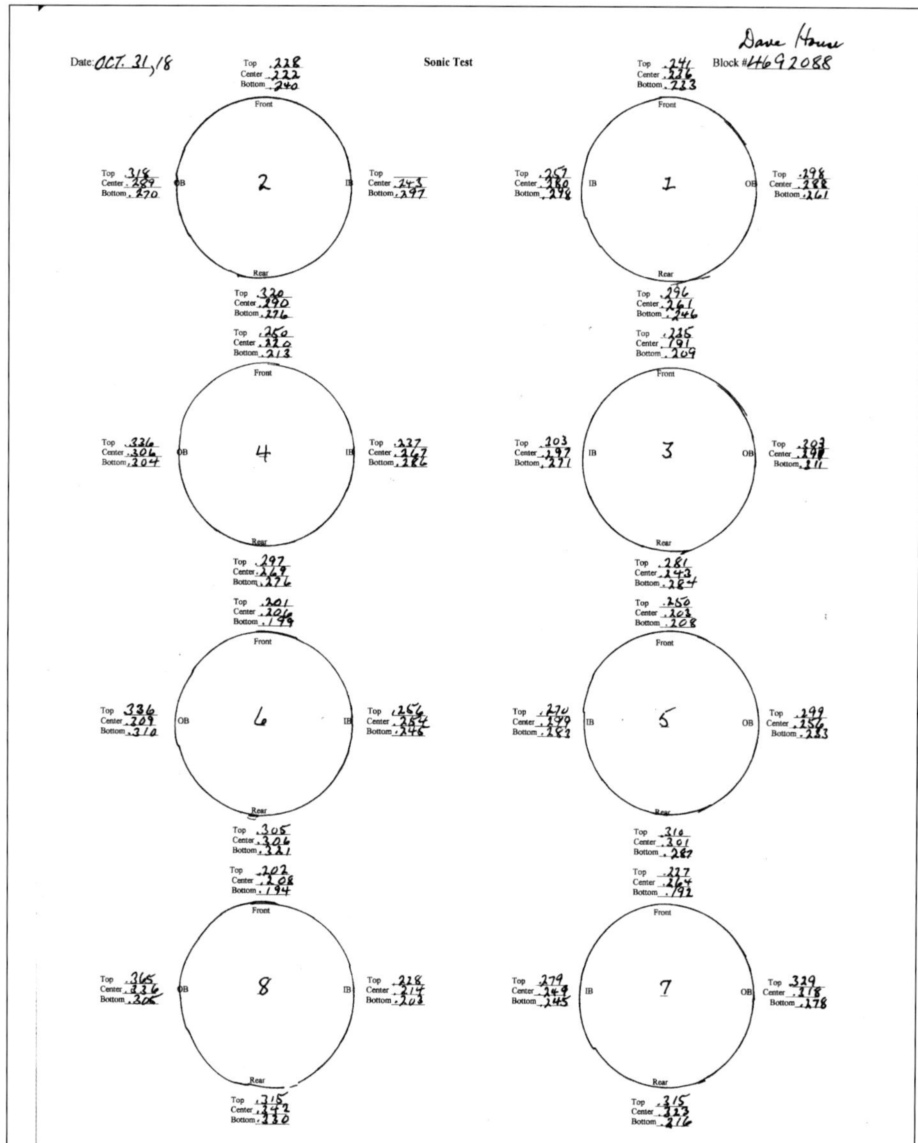

A sonic test is necessary for any rebuild and can reveal why that block may or may not be a good candidate. An area of concern with a Nailhead is the outer block thickness at the bottom of the water jacket. This is a dormant zone with little or no coolant flow and is prone to corroding.

CYLINDER HEADS

Performance Porting has done all of my head work for the past 20 years, so this chapter begins with an introduction from Bill Bonnell from Performance Porting and what he has learned from his experiences.

I have known Bill Bonnell for more than 50 years from when we were in the same car club. We have been friends ever since. After Bill left the club in the early 1970s, he bought a flow bench and pursued performance head work, porting in particular. When I was doing the heads for the first race motor, I ground away everything that I didn't like and polished the port. Bill looked at what I did and pushed me aside in disgust. He has been preparing my heads ever since.

For this discussion, we are referencing heads for the 401 to 425 motors. Nailheads received their name by the fact that their inline valves looked like nails put in line vertically. All other V-8 engines have the valves at various angles closer to perpendicular to the engine bank.

In general, heads are one of the main ingredients in a motor that can greatly influence performance. Buick's production cars from 1953 to 1966, for which these motors were destined, were large, heavy vehicles and not quite the muscle cars of later years. Although, hot rodders and performance enthusiasts always have had different ideas. In the muscle car era of the 1960s to the mid-1980s, motor performance was thought of in terms of cubic inches, valve size, and compression ratio. Today, you still have those standards as well as intake runner cc's, CFM, and the valve guide angle in the head.

The information supplied here is meant as a guide for a performance street engine. Race engines incorporate a higher degree of input in both materials and design.

Porting has always been one of the processes that hot rodders use to increase performance of their engine's heads. In general terms, it refers to physically altering the intake and exhaust ports of the head. If done properly, this will increase the CFM of both the intake and exhaust ports, which will increase the horsepower output of the engine. If not done correctly, it can have a reverse effect and reduce the CFM, reducing power output. Have a realistic approach on this. The age-old saying "You can't turn a sow's ear into a silk purse" comes to mind, meaning that there are limitations. *Bigger is better* is not always the way to go. Remember that shape is as important as size.

Can one do this porting him/herself? Absolutely. However, first a word of caution: safety should be the first concern. Safety glasses and dust masks go a long way to stay healthy and be able to drive your car.

Intake ports in these heads are different than most because they are consistent in height and width throughout their length—think of a square tube. This was for velocity. These are not like Chevrolet, Ford, or Mopar heads in any way (or even later Buick heads for that matter). While

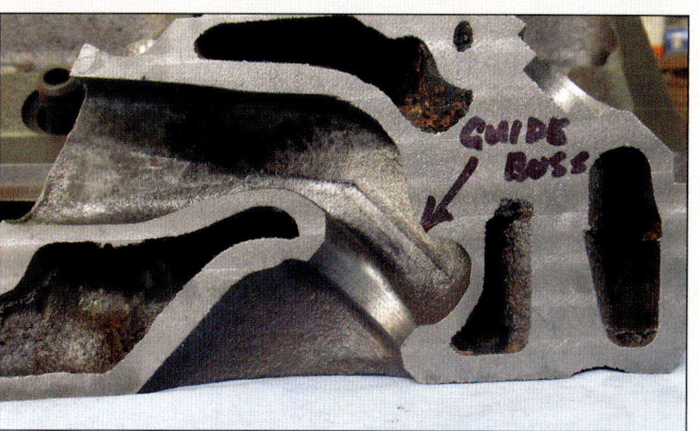

A side profile of the exhaust port from start to finish shows you how much of a challenge you are facing. Trying to improve the flow through this type of port is difficult enough due to the limited access but also because relieving some areas could actually hinder the exhaust flow. Notice how quickly the port transitions from the area below the valve head to the bowl area and around the short-side radius (SSR) to the port. This is a good example of something best left for an expert.

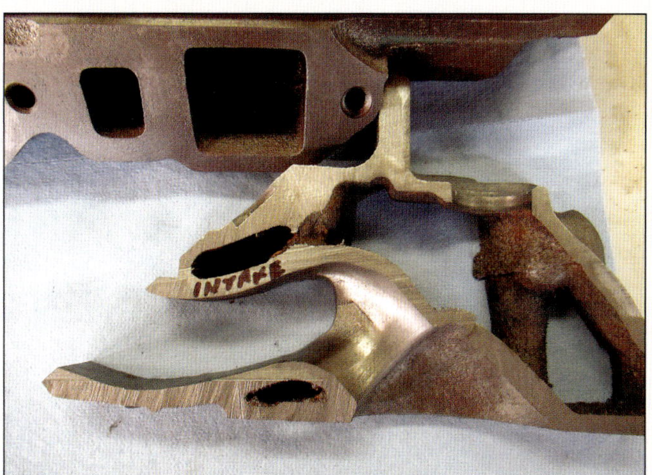

A side profile of the intake port from the intake flange to the valve seat shows what you have to work with when porting a Nailhead. This side view also shows how shallow the port really is compared to what you see when looking at the cross-sectional view from outside of the flange.

Bill uses an assortment of shaft-mounted discs such as this as a guide to remove material from the short area immediately below the valve seat to the bowl. The seat area and below are coated with layout dye, and the disc is used to identify the high spots. The shafts are machined to fit into different valve guides, and the discs are machined to 85 percent of the outside diameter of the valve head for that particular head. Beyond that, you are re-countering shape into the bowl area.

flow is measured in CFM, velocity is measured in feet per second (ft/sec), which is the speed that the air moves. Velocity is a necessity for a street machine that needs low-RPM torque to move from stoplight to stoplight. On a race car, low-RPM torque is not as important. Remember, we don't race flow benches, we race cars.

Nailhead exhaust ports are a nightmare for a head porter. Once you see a cut-up or mold of these heads you will understand. Don't expect huge gains in flow numbers when porting a Nailhead exhaust, but every little bit helps.

When porting, opening up the throat will help the airflow. The throat is the area below the valve seat for about 0.200 to 0.300 inch. Below that is what is referred to as the bowl. The normal way to do this is to measure your valve head diameter and use a percentage of that number to open the throat. Normally 85 percent of the valve head diameter is used for performance street machines. Be careful on how far you go. Buick engineers were generous in the water capacity of these heads. A sonic tester is of great value when porting.

The short-side radius (SSR) is the tight curvature of the port just past the valve that leads to the port floor. After you have done the throat, blend the SSR into it, keeping a smooth curvature to the top of the SSR. Do not attempt to rework the SSR unless you have a flow bench or access to one. This is the easiest way to screw up any set of heads. The opposite side of the SSR is the long-side radius. Blend this to the throat as well. Take out any imperfections left in the port from the process of casting the head. Sharp edges in the port produce turbulence that hinders airflow.

Now, let's look at the valves and guides. Valves in all Nailheads had 3/8-inch-diameter stems. The largest-diameter valve available was 1.875 inches for the intake and 1.5 inches for the exhaust. Guides are extremely important in any valve job. If it is worn too much, you cannot get a good valve job. They have two important functions. One is to position the valve so that it hits the seat in the same place every time (so it produces a good seal). The other is to cool the valve head through heat dispersion from the valve stem to the guide. Porting a head when the guides are bad is a complete waste of time.

Many people want to put Chevrolet 1.94-inch-diameter valves in the intake to

The short-side radius is barely visible in the upper left corner of the intake port in this photo. It is almost inaccessible around into the port. Imagine how much more difficult it is to access the exhaust.

Access to a flow bench is invaluable to verify your porting. Bill has several pieces of different heads he has kept over the years as a reference to which modifications produced positive or negative results.

increase the CFM. Installing larger valves will increase low-lift flow but does little for middle to top end flow without porting. It also shrouds the valve more on the cylinder wall side, which actually reduces the flow. This can be done by an experienced machine shop because it requires changing the guides from 0.375 inch to 0.341 inch. The smaller-diameter stem of the valve means that there is more room in the bowl for air to flow to the valve, but it is not a cheap fix.

A better idea for a street cruiser is to cut the 3/8-inch valve guide down in the bowl area to almost the guide boss. This can be done in both the intake and exhaust bowls. Stainless steel valves in the correct size and length can be found at SI Valves in California. OEM-style valves are still available through your machine shop.

A quality valve job is important. All Buick production heads came with a single-angle valve job, and the seats are very wide, usually from 0.100 to 0.120 inch. On a Nailhead, the seat angle is 45 degrees.

In the performance world, we generally do at least a minimum of a three-angle valve job. This means taking the 45-degree seat and adding a top angle of 30 degrees, which narrows the 45-degree seat. Adding a bottom cut of 60 degrees narrows it more. Finish it off by taking a 70- to 75-degree cut to blend the seat into the bowl area. This is cheaper and more effective for airflow than changing the stem size of valves. The finished seat width should be in the 0.060-inch range for the intake and 0.080 for the exhaust. The extra seat area for the exhaust provides more heat dispersion from the valve head to the seat. Air flow can bend up to 15 degrees without losing either flow or velocity. That is why you see valve angles with no more than 15 degrees change from one angle to the next. Today, a performance head shop will probably change the top and bottom angles a bit. It is more important that you do the porting before doing the valve job.

Back cutting valves has long been done on production valves to increase airflow. In general, if you have an original Nailhead-type valve, this can help on the intake. In most Nailheads, the exhaust is a tulip valve. Back cutting these is a waste of time.

Do you need hardened seats? The valve seats were integral on cast heads, meaning they were cast into the heads. They were then hardened

Nailhead exhaust ports are vulnerable to porting mistakes, particularly at the boss for the head bolt in the two center exhaust ports of each head. A sonic tester is very helpful to determine the amount of material with which you have to work. The reading here should be taken at several spots. Do not reduce the thickness below 0.188 inch.

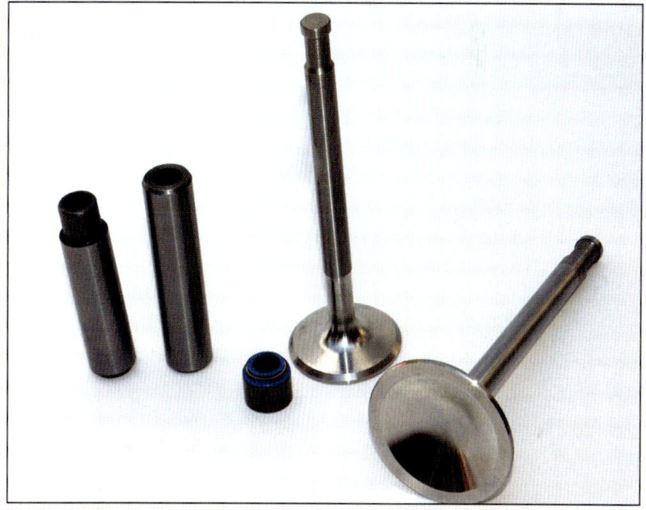

Centerville Auto Repair carries replacement guides and seals as well as sets of new valves. Note that the intake guide is pre-machined for the positive seal in the photo. (Photo Courtesy Russ Martin)

by flame hardening. In the 1960s, we used leaded gas, which acted as a cushion for the valves. Leaded gas was discontinued after the mid-1970s. Engines with heavy spring pressures suddenly developed seat recession, especially on the exhaust. The solution was to install hardened seats. This meant that the seats had to be cut out and replacements pressed in. This should never be done on a Nailhead because you will very likely hit the water jacket. The good news is that Nailhead spring pressures are not that great.

A better solution is to use a lead alternative for the first few fill-ups with a fresh set of heads and taper off to none. Likewise, trying to cut the spring seat for a larger spring can lead to hitting water and/or interfere with the pushrods. Look for a better spring with the same or slightly smaller outside diameter.

As mentioned previously, you are limited by the head's design as to what you can use for valve springs. OEM springs are still available through most machine shops. Do not try cutting the spring seats in the head for larger diameter springs. You will have interference problems with the pushrods rubbing on the spring shims or the bottom of the spring itself, or worse yet, you may hit a water jacket. Look for a better spring with the same original dimensions. OEM springs are still available through your machine shop, or for better springs, investigate what is available through cam companies or Nailhead parts dealers.

Buick Nailheads all used a shaft-mounted rocker-arm system. They are a very rigid design. Although they don't have roller tip rockers, they are very efficient. GM's modern LS engines that produce much more horsepower also don't use a roller tip. All you really need is a good oiling system.

Buick did not use valve seals until 1966, and then they were only on the intake. The reason for not putting a seal on the exhaust was because when the valve was open, it was pushing gases out of the combustion chamber, and no oil could run down the stem into the exhaust port.

There are three types of valve seals: O-rings, umbrella, and positive. The O-rings are placed in a grove in the valve stem below the keepers. They cannot be used on Nailheads because the stems are not cut for them. That leaves both the positive and umbrella types. These fit between the inner spring and the valve stem. Space is of great importance. If the inner spring hits or rubs against the seal, it will destroy the umbrella seals because they are too large. That leaves only the positive type. The valve guide must be cut for these to seat against. There has been a huge improvement in valve seals since their inception with resistance to heat being the most important.

TA Performance has a complete line of new valve springs that are specifically made to spec for all levels of Nailhead performance. These springs are made with the correct OD and installed spring height, and they will handle up to 0.650-inch lift, which is more than you would ever need for a Nailhead. (Photo Courtesy TA Performance)

Positive valve seals are the only ones to use with the Nailheads. They should only be used on the intake guides. If you think you need an exhaust seal, it is more likely that you need to replace both the guide and the valve.

This head and its companion became the borrowed heads. The original exhaust porting job broke into the #3, 4, 5, and 6 head bolt holes. It is a common mistake with an amateur trying to improve Nail-head exhaust ports. You need to closely monitor inside the port with a sonic tester. This set can be rescued by installing sleeves through the corresponding head bolt hole, but it is still only a repaired head at best.

The D heads came with improved taller ports. The exhaust ports are readily recognizable as the extra height brought the top of the port flange to the same level as seat area of the head bolts. You need to use caution and a sonic tester when trying to clean up the port adjacent to the spark plug.

Thanks, Bill. After what he has said, it is not a surprise how the perceived shortcoming of the Nailhead family of motors for street performance or racing came about. The restrictive breathing and consequently their limited RPM potential were not impressive. It was a popular misconception that horsepower and RPM numbers were the ultimate barometer to measure the capabilities of your motor. While those are important factors (and good numbers to use for bragging rights at the coffee shop), the real workhorse in that equation is torque. The Balchowskys, Ivos, and Kernahans were successful at racing Nailheads in the early years because they learned how to manage and work within the torque curve of these engines. Unfortunately, there were no aftermarket heads made for these motors to correct the breathing limitations that would have extended their competitiveness.

Buick's Experimental Division in Flint reportedly did produce about 28 sets of what we refer to as the D head. These were an improvement but certainly not a solution to the problem.

Experimental Heads

This was not a D-port head like the Chevrolet big-block that you may be familiar with. Instead, it was an iron head with taller ports and identified by the letter *D* following the casting number. We had a set of these heads on loan from a friend who donated them for temporary use on the roadster. Now, mind you, this particular set had a pretty crude porting job and had seen better days. They were bead blasted, and the valves and seats were cleaned up and reseated. On the flow bench, we found that they did not perform any better than properly ported and race-prepped stock heads.

We may have been able to clean up the ports and possibly produce better flow numbers, but you would not want to spend a lot of money on a set of heads that you did not own. It was not only about the cost of restoring these heads. The real obstacle was that these heads were not a simple head for a head swap. It required changing out the intake and exhaust header flanges to better match the taller ports. The heads were returned to our friend.

Unfortunately, he passed away a few years ago, and almost all of his Nailhead stuff disappeared a short time later. Nonetheless, a set of these heads would be a really neat find, especially if they included the companion intake and exhaust manifolds that came from the experimental division. I have seen a few variations of intake manifolds that were made

Aluminum heads are few and far between. The casting numbers for these are the same as an iron head production that ran from 1961 to 1966. I believe the aluminum version was cast in the early years of that production run. Note that the machined surface of the exhaust flange appears wider than an iron head, and the port appears a bit narrower.

I apologize for the poor quality of some of the vintage pictures. These parts are no longer available to be photographed. This head is from a pair of ported aluminum heads that Carmen Faso had many years ago. Notice how much the port flange was reduced when they were ported. This is the second of three sets produced. (Photo Courtesy Carmen Faso)

to fit these heads but only one style of exhaust manifold.

There were purportedly three sets of aluminum heads produced at the Flint plant, and there was a rumor that a few more sets were made without water jackets during the night shift. Assuming that those production numbers I heard are correct, it is a safe bet that you will never see a pair of these heads. If you are fortunate enough to find a pair, they will certainly not be cheap.

These heads had an early casting number and noticeably smaller ports. I would be very hesitant to do much modification to them particularly in the 3 to 5 and 4 to 6 exhaust ports because there is not much material separating them from the head bolt holes.

I heard all the rumors about early General Motors aluminum castings that emerged from the 215 V-8 blocks and heads that were done at Alcoa Aluminum. It

This rig is easy to make using leftover Nailhead parts. It frees up one hand to guide a head into place without it sliding around and marking the fresh machining on the mating surface.

Nailheads are definitely not lightweights. I am sure we all cannot afford to buy that elusive last set of aluminum heads. Do yourself a favor and make a pair of handles to move them around.

was said they have impurity and porosity issues and it can be difficult to do a weld repair. Assuming these were cast at the same location, it would certainly not be worth taking a chance on trying to port something that is irreplaceable. There were no records (of which I am aware) of these parts being cast at the experimental plant or of any quantities. Whatever rumors you hear, add a dollar or two, and it might get you a cup of coffee. However, I have seen a dated photo of a pair of these heads that Carmen Faso had several years ago. More recently, I saw a second pair belonging to another friend that were virgin heads that had never had valves in them.

Porting

I have heard a lot of positive comments and posts on websites about the quality of head work that has come out of Pro-Tech Racing in Fresno, California. Recently, I contacted Mike Lewis and had a very interesting discussion with him about porting and specifically Nailheads. Mike's business is head porting and complete head rebuilding, plus some parts specific to Buick Nailheads. The unfortunate part is that geographically Mike lives in Fresno, which is about 3,000 miles west from where I live. Shipping a pair of head castings that far and across the border would be cost prohibitive. He sent some photos of what he refers to as the Buick Nailhead Stage 4 Porting package. As you can see from the photos, he has done some very impressive work.

Mike Lewis from Pro Tech Racing has an excellent reputation for the quality of work he has done with Nailhead intake and exhaust flows. He doesn't stop there, as evident when he polished the combustion chambers. It may be difficult to visualize without a valve in place as reference, but it appears that he may also have removed material from the sides of the combustion chamber to relieve the shrouding of both the exhaust and intake valves. (Photo Courtesy Pro Tech Racing)

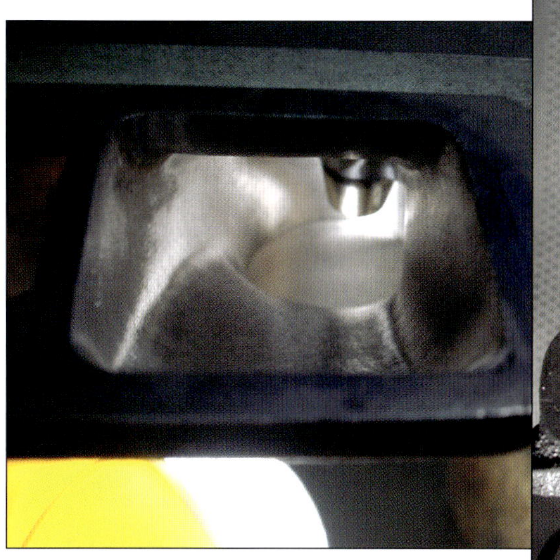

This is a good photo of the intake ports that highlights how shallow they actually are. Notice the bronze guides have a tapered nose in the port to enhance flow, and the tops for both intake and exhaust valves are machined to accept positive valve seals. (Photo Courtesy Pro Tech Racing)

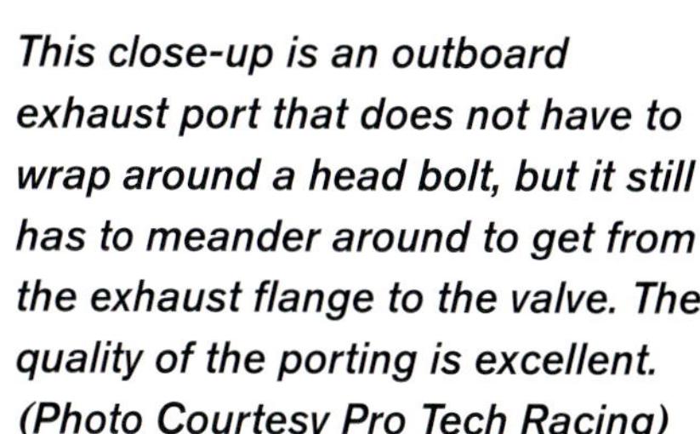

This close-up is an outboard exhaust port that does not have to wrap around a head bolt, but it still has to meander around to get from the exhaust flange to the valve. The quality of the porting is excellent. (Photo Courtesy Pro Tech Racing)

The rocker shafts that came with the project motor were showing a lot of wear on the hardened tips and appeared like they had been hammering on the valve stems. This could have been caused by low oil pressure or pushrods that were too short.

New rocker arms and shafts are a must when rebuilding a Nailhead. These pieces were sourced through Carmen Faso. Be sure to oil the inside of the new rocker with an assembly lube and shafts as you are assembling them.

The early version steel rocker assemblies are in the background with the later-style aluminum rockers in the foreground. These are sold as an assembled set as pictured here by Centerville Auto Repair. (Photo Courtesy Russ Martin)

These aluminum rocker assemblies are the Cadillac option for a high-performance Nailhead. They are adjustable, with roller tips and trunnion bearings and have the best ratio. The only drawback, if you can call it that, is they will not work with taller valves. (Photo Courtesy TA Performance)

Rocker Arms and Shafts

Any time you are rebuilding a Nailhead or just doing a valve job, replace the rocker arms and shafts with new parts. These are available from all of the Nailhead-specific dealers. Stock rocker arms are being used with this rebuild. The new rockers and shafts used here were purchased from Carmen Faso. Before installing the rockers, use a hone stone to debur the oil holes and the bolt holes for the shaft stand bolts and test fit the new rockers. They should slide on easily with no resistance but not have a sloppy fit. Thoroughly wash the shaft before assembling.

When you put these pieces together, rub some assembly lube on the inside of each rocker arm as you install it on the shaft assembly. Later, as you are installing the new shaft assemblies, add a dab of assembly lube to the top of each valve stem.

Prior to the initial startup, run up the oil pressure with an electric drill and continue to do so until you see oil oozing from the #7 and #8 exhaust valve rocker arms. You have to do this for quite a few minutes after getting oil pressure. These two rockers live in the last house on the block and consequently are the last to get any lubricant.

Bill Bonnell spoke about stock rockers, but there are some options in that area. Buick made adjustable rocker arms for the first-generation 322-ci Nailhead and again for the second-generation 364-ci motor. These were known as the "export" rocker arms. Gotha made adjustable rocker arms for the hot rod and race car market in the 1950s

From left to right are the early steel rocker, aluminum rocker, Gotha adjustable rocker, Buick export adjustable rocker, Tom Telesco's aluminum roller rocker, and TA Performance aluminum roller rocker. These were the rockers that I had available at the time for testing to verify the ratios.

The rocker pictured is an early cast unit. Surprisingly, it performed better than both the Gotha and Buick Export rockers by opening the valve an extra 0.014 and 0.018. The shortfall of the steel rocker is that it is heavier; however, Buick's newer aluminum rockers have been known to break under stress.

These test valve springs are used for a number of setup operations when preparing the heads. These extra light ones I find easy to work with when checking piston-to-valve clearance. Once you have everything in position, you can easily push the rocker arm with a finger and read from the indicator.

and up into the 1960s. Neither of these are readily available today.

More recently, TA Performance and Tom Telesco stepped up to fill the need, and both now make adjustable aluminum roller-tip rockers. The units from TA Performance are fully rollerized and come as a complete assembly on a shaft with fiber spacers in lieu of spring separators. Tom Telesco has altered Buick's original rocker-arm geometry to increase the ratio for those wanting extra-high lift. These are sold as sets or individuals. The shafts are sold separately and the rockers need to be reamed to fit the new shafts. They are assembled with aluminum spacers in place of the springs in an effort to stabilize any side-loading caused by Buick's offset geometry.

I tried them in the Bonneville car, but the machine work for the adjusters was inconsistent in relation to the shaft and resulted in different valve openings. Also, the adjuster threads were cut too loose, so valve lash had to be adjusted after every run. We upgraded to 7/16 adjusters by using a jig to hold the rocker while cutting the new threads to get them all in a standard position. Even with the oversize threads it was necessary to have a 0.003 undersized tap made to attain the correct thread fitment with the new adjusters. They work fine now, but I would not recommend them for street or endurance applications.

I have heard various claims about the ratio of different Nailhead rocker arms, so I tested some on my own using a stock Buick cam with 0.263-inch lift at the lobe. The aluminum roller-tip rockers were checked with the adjuster fully retracted and then extended three full turns. Note that TA Performance does not recommend for its rockers to be adjusted more than one full turn from the retracted position. I did not check the Buick Export or Gotha rockers with the adjusters set in different positions because I did not expect much variation from those units with the stock geometry. As for stock Nailhead rocker arms, I checked an early cast unit and a later aluminum one. I suppose that General Motors made different batches of these and there may some variations. However, expect the numbers in the chart below to be representative.

Rocker type	Max. lift at the valve	ratio
Early cast rocker	0.409	1.55:1
Later aluminum rocker	0.405	1.54:1
Buick Export adjustable rocker	0.391	1.49:1
Gotha adjustable rocker	0.395	1.50:1
TA Performance roller rocker	0.439	1.67:1
TA Performance roller rocker (extended three turns)	0.426	1.62:1
Telesco roller-tip rocker	0.439	1.67:1
Telesco roller-tip rocker (extended three turns)	0.478	1.82:1
Note: TA rocker adjusters are perpendicular to the shaft and there is minimal ratio change. Telesco's rocker adjusters are canted away from the normal perpendicular resulting in an exaggerated ratio.		

I came up with a few surprises. The stock rockers showed up better than I had expected. I had higher expectations for both the Buick Export and Gotha units, being that they were supposedly high-performance parts. However, they had lower ratios than stock rockers. I have heard that both the Buick Export and Gotha rockers were made with different rocker-arm ratios, but I only have one version of them.

For a street-performance application or race motor, my first choice is the TA Performance rocker. The increased valve lift with the better ratio becomes an important asset. Our poor old Nailheads need all the help we can give them when it comes to airflow. Also, this unit is adjustable, has beefier construction, and is fully rollerized with a trunnion bearing and roller tip, which makes it more suitable for street use. I would not discount the Export or Gotha rockers, but availability could be an issue.

Machining

For this particular rebuild, the owner wanted to have the engine powder coated, which requires the castings to be ground smooth. After the grinding of the exterior casting, the heads were sent to Performance Porting for a complete reconditioning, including a street porting job and flow testing. Bill has done several sets of Nailhead heads from street to all-out racing over the years and is very familiar with how to get the most out of them. The heads will be resurfaced with a minimum cut because we did not want to increase the compression or have to remove more material from the tops of the pistons.

A primary concern when working with a 60-year-old motor is to determine if the castings can be salvaged with new machined surfaces. The important issue with Buick heads is whether any pitting from corrosion is severe enough to render them as scrap.

The next concern is the valve seats. If the seats in the heads need to be cut excessively, it will seat the valves too deep. These are also scrap. This is a fine time to look for another set of heads. I would only consider replacing Nailhead seats if it was an exercise to restore something rare like one of the D heads. It is too easy to hit the water jackets when trying to cut out the old seats, and they will probably end up leaking anyway.

Another thing to avoid is machining the valve spring pockets. This was an old-school practice to get a little more room for taller springs. The primary concern is that this increases the interference between the bottom of the valve spring and the push-rod. There is not enough material beneath the spring pocket. Check

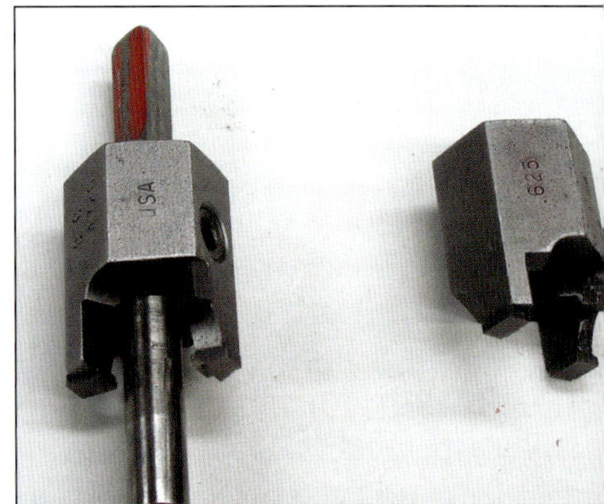

There are different sizes of cutters available for alternate seals. You need to purchase quality tools to get quality results.

You can use these cutters with a hand drill at a slow cutting speed, and apparently many people do. Be careful and be like a carpenter: measure twice, cut once.

You need to cut only the intake valve guide to fit the positive seals. Be sure you have the correct-size cutters for your seals. You need to have precise control with the depth of cut taken to fit the seals properly. Your machine is only as good as the operator. If you are not experienced with these procedures, it would be wise to take this job to a professional shop rather than ruin your new guides or, worse yet, ruin a head.

The Neway valve seat cutter kit is for hand-cutting the seats and comes with 15-, 30-, 46-, 60-, and 80-degree cutters. A motorized version is also available. The cutters are really versatile and will fit almost any size valve seat.

for clearance. If you are using shims under the valve spring, and particularly if you have 5/16-inch pushrods, you may have to notch the outer spring shims to clear the pushrods.

On first inspection, these heads have had a previous valve job. The guides were worn, and the valve stems were tapered. New steel guides were installed, and then only the intake valve guides were cut for positive seals. Bill ordered a set of new SS valves.

Over-cutting a valve seat can quickly ruin a head. Remember, Nailhead valve seats should not be replaced. You need to use soft hands when cutting each different angle, as they cut quickly. The primary 45-degree cut should be 0.100 to 0.125 inches wide, and you should test fit your valve with layout dye. The subsequent 30-, 60- and 75-degree cuts are made to blend the flow, but each cut is proportioned to center the valve seat contact in the center of the valve. You also need to control the seat area width as Bill mentioned in his preliminary discussion. This is a procedure best left for the professional.

A rack is helpful to organize all of your valvetrain components, including the retainers and springs, shims, seals, and even the keepers as well as the valves to keep them ready for assembly. A simple rack can be made from material left over from another project. Be sure to seal the wood to help control dust particles.

You need to check the installed height of your valve springs. Corrections can be made using shims to reduce the installed height back to the specification for the spring or using offset keepers to increase the installed height. Keep a chart with valve spring height, spring pressure at the installed height, and pressure at the open position.

Valve Spring Pressures

Intake #	..Installed Ht.	shims	Corrected HT.	. Seat pressure .	Open ht.	Open pressure .
			1.600		1.140	
1	1.614	.015	1.599	116		248
2	1.616	.015	1.601	114		244
3	1.609	.015	1.594	113		244
4	1.612	-.015	1.597	110		236
5	1.608	.015	1.593	114		245
6	1.612	.015	1.597	116		247
7	1.614	.015	1.599	113		240
8	1.612	-.015	1.597	114		242

Exhaust #	..Installed Ht.	shims	Corrected HT.	. Seat pressure .	Open ht.	Open pressure
			1.600		1.140	
1	1.601	/	1.601	114		244
2	1.620	.030	1.590	115		245
3	1.621	.030	1.591	112		242
4	1.619	.030	1.589	116		244
5	1.614	.015	1.599	114		243
6	1.604	/	1.604	115		244
7	1.608	.015	1.593	108		233
8	1.612	.015	1.597	112		243

A complete record of all the clearances, torque numbers, and specifications of your engine build should be kept on file for your own information and future reference. In this particular instance, valve spring pressures can be verified if an issue develops with your valvetrain.

These were checked for trueness, and each valve was set into a dedicated slot in the valvetrain rack. We are using a Schneider cam and valve springs with this rebuild. Check the springs for seat pressure, open pressure, and for coil bind. Record these numbers for future reference.

There are three types of replacement valve guides that can be used: bronze, bronze liners, or cast. Although they cost a little more, the solid bronze guides are preferred because they have much better wear characteristics. Buick combustion chambers were machined during the production process, and the volume from cylinder to cylinder is usually pretty consistent. Any variations that you encounter are most likely due to previous valve jobs and the depth of cuts taken to reseat the valves.

Once the new valve guides are installed, it is time to cut the seats. Each head is set up and properly squared so that each seat is cut the same exact same amount with each of the three cutters and will have a minimal effect on the combustion chamber volume.

At this time, mock up the valves with the spring retainers and keepers and substitute a valve spring micrometer for the spring. Adjust the micrometer to check for the installed height of each spring. Log this information, along with the previously measured spring pressures, for all 16 valves.

Resurfacing the heads is a standard procedure with any rebuild, so you have a level platform to start. Both heads must have the same amount of material removed. The amount of material to be removed depends on what is required to restore the worst head mating surface. The second head will be milled the same amount. This needs to be done as early as possible so that you can confirm the combustion chamber volume. This number is an integral part of the equation to determine the piston dome volume required to achieve the desired compression ratio. This will be part of the information needed to order your pistons. Keep in mind that every 0.005 inch that is cut from the head surface will reduce the combustion chamber volume by about 1 cc. With the set of heads for the project motor, the combustion chamber volume averaged 127.5 cc plus or minus 0.1 cc.

Once the heads have been resurfaced, and only after the porting is complete, valve seats can be cut for a three-angle valve job. One head will then be mocked up with lightweight test valve springs and used to degree in the camshaft. This is a good opportunity to check the piston-to-valve clearance. The heads can then be prepared for powder coating.

Powder Coating

When the engine block, heads, and other cast parts are to be powder coated, it is imperative that the castings are free of any oil contamination and the powder does not get inside or onto any of the freshly machined surfaces. The oil pan, valve covers, and other sheet metal parts have been sandblasted and, along with the cast pieces, are washed with metal preparation solution and thoroughly rinsed with hot water. Do this before the parts are assembled so you can dry them quickly, especially the machined surfaces.

The easiest way that I found to protect the internal areas is to prepare all the external parts, bolt them together, coat them as a closed unit. Use an old timing cover at the front of the block, or mask that area off with paper and tape, and turn some wooden plugs to fill the crankshaft and

The motor is almost ready to go for powder coating except for the installation of an old timing cover. Balls of newspaper are stuffed into the intake and exhaust ports; there is not enough heat in the baking process to ignite the paper. The frost plug openings are closed off with machined wooden plugs.

Whether you to paint or powder coat your new engine, the preparation of the metal is the same. After the surfaces have been thoroughly cleaned, use a metal conditioner, such as this product from B&G Restorations, to clean and etch the metal. The added benefit of this product is that it leaves an iron-phosphate coating that enhances adhesion of paint or, as in this instance, powder.

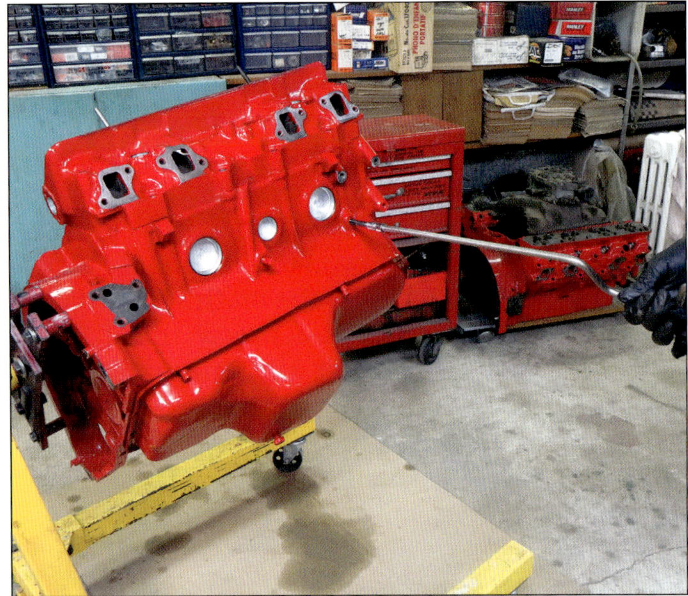

Some bolt holes were left exposed so that the coating would cover all the exterior surfaces. Any threaded holes will need to be cleaned out with thread chasers. The exhaust flanges were left exposed and the mating surfaces would be dressed and trued later.

Using a machined stop to set up your valve spring tester is the only way to get accurate and repeatable information. You need to make separate stops for the full open position of the valve and the basic installed height of your springs. If you are going to be working on various motors, you will need quite an assortment of these stops.

All valve springs need to be tested to ensure consistency. Those that are out of spec need to be replaced. This information, combined with the installed height of your valve springs, will also assist with determining which shims to use. If a spring has a little less tension than the others, you can shim it to the low side of your spring installed height.

Valve spring shims may be required to help bring spring pressure up to par or bring the installed height back into range if it is too high. The shims are available in 0.015-, 0.030-, and 0.060-inch increments to correct the spring height.

frost plug openings. Rolls of paper are adequate to protect the head bolt holes. Break the porcelain off of the old spark plugs and screw the plug base into the head. Put 1/2-inch-long pieces of tubing under the head of the bolts on the oil pan, valve covers, etc. This allows the powder to cover all of the exposed surfaces.

The first step is to pre-bake the whole assembly to ensure that any oils are drawn out of the castings. Let it cool down. Wipe it down using the metal preparation solution again, followed by a cloth soaked in hot water. Be selective about how much water you use.

Offset keepers are also available to either increase or decrease the installed height of your springs. If you do not maintain the correct installed heights, you cannot maintain the pressure to control your valves. If you try to use taller valves in a Nailhead, clearance between the spring retainer and the rocker arm may become an issue, especially with a high-lift cam. A negative-offset keeper can help resolve that issue.

Don't allow water to soak into the seams. The heat from curing the powder may cause some of the machined surfaces to lose that fresh new look, although for some reason this does not seem to affect the cylinders as much as the deck surface.

When the motor is returned from the powder coater, most of the parts can be set aside until needed. There is not enough temperature used in the curing process to have any ill effect on the machine work, but all the parts (especially the castings) will need a thorough cleaning before assembly.

Final Assembly

Prior to assembly, there are some important measurements that need to be recorded and/or verified, if you haven't done so already. It will save you some aggravation to have a rack to hold the intake valve seals, valves, shims, springs, retainers, and keepers in an orderly fashion near the work area. From this point on, the valves, shims, springs, and retainers will be kept separate in the rack according to the assigned valve position. The valves should have been set into the rack in that dedicated location as they were being cut.

The new valve springs need to be tested to confirm the pressure at the base installed height and at the maximum opening level. The basic installed height of Nailhead valve springs is 1.600 inches; 1.140 inches is the maximum opening height per the camshaft specifications. You can also measure the amount of valve opening when you are set up to degree in the cam. At this point, I took the

easy way out and went with the advertised lift.

Log each valve position with the spring pressures measured. As each one is tested, set it into the rack at the intended installed position. Use a valve spring micrometer to check how well the actual installed height of each valve corresponds to the specified height of 1.6 inches. Record this along with your spring pressures. You may need to correct the installed height, and this is where your shims come into play. Record what size of shim is required with each spring. The shims are available in 0.015, 0.030, and 0.060 thicknesses, so you can get the spring height to within 0.010 of the 1.600-inch target.

There are instances where you may need to use offset keepers

There are some poor-quality valve spring compressors in the market today. The solution is to purchase a quality compressor. However, even some of those are not strong enough if you are using excessive valve spring pressure. If you are fed up with buying substandard tools at high-quality prices, make your own like my friend Bill.

It is not uncommon to have interference with Nailhead valvetrain components if you alter any one factor. In this case, there were no geometric changes, and the retainer clears the rocker arm. However, look toward the inward side of the rocker shaft stand and notice that it appears to interfere with the retainer. A further check showed 0.035 clearance. I have had to machine a flat on the inboard side of the shaft stand when using the taller 1.700 valves.

The pushrod appears to be larger than stock because of the close-up in this picture, but it really is the factory 0.250 OD. Higher valve spring pressures require stronger pushrods that are usually 0.312 OD. You can see from this picture that there is very little extra room here, and as the rocker arm swings through its cycle, the pushrod moves up and down and the clearance diminishes. Often the pushrod opening needs to be opened up when using a higher-lift camshaft.

to alter the valve spring retainer height to accommodate different spring pressures or provide extra clearance if you are getting close to coil bind. They can also provide extra clearance if the retainer is close to interfering with the rocker arm. These keepers come in either 0.050-inch positive or negative offsets and should be used as a set so that all the valve stems are relatively the same.

You need to have a sturdy stand that can hold the head in a few different positions for reassembly because you will need both hands. Work on a wooden or rubber surface so that it will not damage the newly machined head mating surface or the freshly coated parts. Keep a small container of grease within reach. A dab of grease works just fine to hold

Check your pushrods for scuff marks about 1 inch from the top. Remove the spark plugs and turn your engine over manually, stopping at regular intervals to check for the lack of clearances. Frequently, the shims under the valve springs are the cause of the scuffing and can be resolved by notching the shims as seen in the photo. If there is adequate clearance through the rocker-arm cycle, yet there has been recent scuffing, the pushrods are probably flexing and should be replaced by stronger pieces.

the spring retainer keepers in place while assembling the heads.

From your notes, add shims as required with each spring and valve. Set up a head in your stand in a position that you find comfortable. I prefer starting with the guide tipped up about 30 degrees from horizontal so the valve will stay in place.

Push the seal onto the intake guide and slide the first valve into place through the guide and seal. Then, use the valve spring compressor to hold the shim, spring, and retainer in line with the valve stem as you compress these parts together with enough room to insert the keepers. Put the keepers in locking grooves on the valve stem. Release the compressor and repeat for the remaining valves. When complete, tap each valve stem with a brass dead-blow mallet to ensure they are sealed.

Whenever you make any changes with the valvetrain, whether it is a higher-lift or longer-duration camshaft or different height valves, check to see if other clearances have been compromised. The more aggressive the camshaft you select will require an appropriate increase in valve spring pressures. This additional loading may necessitate going to 0.312-inch tubular pushrods to prevent flexing and the subsequent erratic reactions in the valvetrain. The pushrod holes in the heads were marginally big enough originally and left little room for the larger pushrod size or extra movement. You can drill these holes out to 0.562 inch. However, you are taking a significant chance because there are not

Checking your pushrods for straightness should be done on all of your used rods and even the new ones. The testing is really quite simple: roll the pushrod on a flat surface. Any irregularities will show up right away. Don't even think about trying to straighten a bent pushrod because it will bend much easier the second time; just replace it.

The Schneider camshaft came with an extreme-pressure lube and a cam card for reference when dialing in the new camshaft. We are all familiar with using the high-pressure lube on each lifter face and camshaft lobe. It is also important to put a dab of this on each valve stem when you use stock non-roller rocker arms.

any means to check the material thickness through each of the 16 pushrod holes before you start drilling. This could buy some side clearance and a bit more room under the pushrod, but it does not provide any additional room between the pushrod and the valve spring. If opening up these holes is necessary, it should be done before the porting and machine work is started.

It is time to bag up your heads and move on to assembly.

PREPPING THE BLOCK, MACHINE WORK, AND PREASSEMBLY

For this stage of work, I want to reemphasize the importance of good eye, hearing, and respiratory protection. Although you may not opt to grind the block for powder coating as we are going to do, these items are essential to grind away casting flashing and inclusions from the lifter valley.

Hearing protection is necessary in a variety of jobs. It is primarily necessary during this rebuild when you are grinding the casting or prepping the external block surfaces. There are numerous activities in a workshop that generate enough noise to necessitate hearing protection, such as operating machinery, compressors starting up, or breaking in your new motor.

Quality respirators are not cheap, but neither are your lungs. There are several types of chemical cartridges as well as those that only filter out particulate matter. Be sure to use the correct respirator for each situation. You should wash your mask regularly and keep it in a bag in a clean area when not in use.

Additional Tools Required

Both 90-degree and straight die grinders will be needed to correct the casting flaws previously mentioned. You will need a variety of die grinder bits and a supply of sanding rolls to finish smoothing the casting. Other tools needed include a dial indicator with short and long probes on a magnetic base, a sonic tester, a set of NC thread chasers plus 1/8 and 3/8 NPT taps, a degree wheel, a crankshaft drive hub, a cam installation handle, intake and exhaust valves with test springs and retainers, adjustable pushrods, and an assortment of block cleaning brushes.

Prepping the Block

As noted during disassembly, this block appears to be a very good candidate for a performance rebuild. However, appearances can be deceiving.

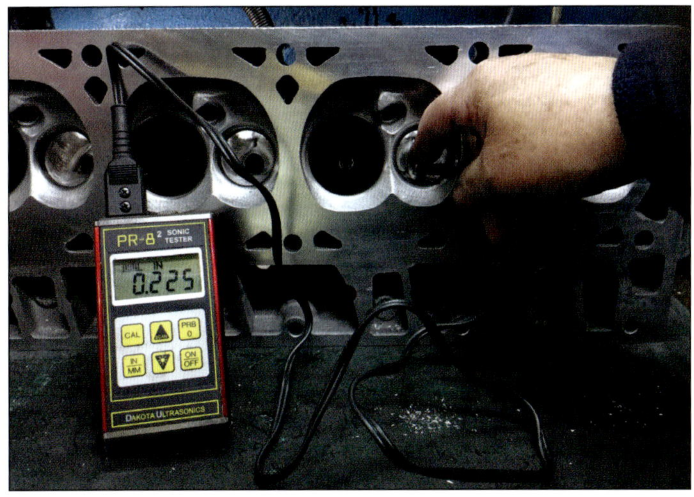

A sonic test is necessary for any rebuild and can reveal why the block may or may not be useable. An area of concern with a Nailhead is the outer block thickness at the bottom of the water jackets. This is a dormant zone in the cooling system and is prone to corroding. A sonic test will also determine whether there has been any core shifting and if there is adequate material to bore the block. The tester in the photo is being used to check the material thickness in an exhaust port.

Flashing and casting inclusions such as this are normal in the lifter valley of almost all Nailhead blocks. Fortunately, this is the only area where you see it this bad, and it is reasonably easy to remove.

Sonic Checking

A sonic test must be performed on any engine block before spending money and time on any further preparation. Sonic testing sounds high-tech, but it really is straightforward and not difficult to do.

The unit works by sending an inaudible ultrasonic sound wave into a material with a known density and measures the wave reflected back to the unit. It uses this information to calculate the thickness of the material tested. If you have access to a tester, you can do this testing yourself and can spend the additional time doing random checks in multiple spots. The kits have become more affordable for home use, or you can have this done at your local machine shop.

Do not skip over this step. It is absolutely necessary to determine if the core shifted during production to created inadequate cylinder material for boring. This becomes even more important in old engine blocks because of the potential for corrosion in the water jackets that compromises the integrity of the cylinders or the block itself. Pay particular attention to the lower outboard side of each cylinder, about 3/4 inch above the bottom cylinder edge, to catch the water jacket area.

Also check the exterior of the block along the lower portion of the water jacket. This is a stagnant area in the cooling system and it is not uncommon to find corrosion starting here. The thickness of the outer-block surfaces should be reasonably consistent of 0.125 or more. The areas to be concerned about here are abnormally thin spots that may be porous or can start to crack from pressure in the cooling system.

Follow a set pattern of your test area in the cylinders and record the readings. Usually these checks are done at the top, middle, and bottom of each cylinder at four quadrants (fore, aft, inboard, and outboard) to verify the material thickness. The cylinder wall thickness may range from 0.200 to 0.300. Your concern with the cylinder-wall thickness is that an after boring measurement is an absolute minimum 0.100 in a normally aspirated motor. In the case of this particular rebuild for a turbocharger, the minimum is 0.125 after boring.

Die Grinding

Once satisfied with this information, grind the flashing away at the lifter gallery and smooth over any casting inclusions. It is best to do this type of work outside or in a partitioned area with an exhaust fan.

Nailhead Buick blocks are generally good for not having any vagrant casting flashing except when you look at the lifter valley, where it can be anywhere from bad to worse. The casting inclusions and ragged edges can be easily ground away and smoothed

---

Whether you are prepping the casting surfaces or removing flashing, do this in an area away from where you want to do clean work. This could be outside or an indoor area that is well ventilated. It is not only the work area that you want to protect but also your ears, eyes, and lungs.

Even though the block is going out to be cleaned, you should minimize dirt and grinding debris by keeping old valve covers, oil pans, etc., in place to block out any extra foreign material from getting into the oil passages. The more trash that gets into these areas increases the chance of them being missed during the cleaning process.

I am sure many of you were resentful when governing agencies began outlawing the old, hot-tank chemicals when there were no effective alternatives in the market. But if it were not for their intervention, we might not receive this quality of block cleaning today. This is by far superior to the older practices.

It is unfortunate how many people take things for granted, especially when it comes to protecting their eyes and lungs. It is necessary in so many aspects of this job. Later in life, you will be grateful (or regretful) of how well you cared for these priceless assets.

Most of the block preparation is complete. Do not use a tap drill; the holes are close enough to the tap drill size. Tapping the oil galleries at the front of the block must be done very carefully depth-wise to ensure you do not obstruct the oil passages that are fed from these primary galleries.

The block and heads are ready to go for powder coating. You need to protect the interior from overspray, so what better way than preparing and installing the valve covers, valley cover, and oil pan? The water crossover casting and the intake manifold are coated separately. Wooden plugs, broken spark plugs, and paper towels are also used to isolate the inside of the motor from vagrant powder.

over. This should be done with any kind of rebuild to ensure that you don't get pieces breaking off into the oil pan and the oil pump, which would be catastrophic.

There is a concern with high-performance and race motors about oil return flow to the pan. Some people prefer to paint the inside of the block to enhance the return flow, but you may want to rethink this practice. There is potential for the paint to come loose and plug the oil pump pickup screen.

You can take a more effective approach by grinding the interior of the block and head castings with die-grinder bits and then smoothing the surfaces with sanding drums. This not only improves oil return flow but also (equally as important) relieves stress and surface tension from the castings.

You can take this a step further by grinding and then finishing the exterior of the block and heads with sanding drums. This will reveal casting inclusions that can develop into a crack and should be ground away to sound material beneath. It also provides a good base for painting or powder coating the castings. If you prefer to powder coat your parts, even the block and head castings can be done, and it is much more durable for something that is routinely disassembled.

If you find any irregularities, which are usually behind the starter, you can smooth them out and have a closer inspection for casting flaws or exterior corrosion. This is a common problem area for corrosion or the beginning of cracks.

While you have the die grinder out, check the transition of the oil passages to and from the block and the oil filter housing. Make a pattern from the face of the oil filter housing, transfer this to the block flange, and trace the inlet and outlet openings. If there are any obstructions, blend the oil passage just enough to eliminate any flow restrictions.

Tapping Gallery Plugs

Next, tap the oil galleries to 3/8 NPT so you can install threaded plugs in the three oil galleries behind the cam gear at the front of the block, rather than relying on the original-style press-in plugs. I have not had a problem with the original type of plugs, but I feel that the NPT socket plugs are a more positive solution and cheap insurance.

It is not necessary to use a tap drill. If you do need to drill, it must have a limiting collar to

The pipe plugs can be shortened by threading into the mandrel on the right and mounting in the lathe to be shortened. It can then turn it around in the lathe jaws to remove material from the inside as required. Use your vernier caliper as a depth gauge to measure the socket relative to the overall length.

prevent hitting the #1 and #2 exhaust lifter bores. You could ruin a block if you drill too deeply and go into the lifter bore. The best option is not to drill.

The rear of the main oil gallery and left lifter gallery are already tapped to 3/8 NPT, but the rear of the right lifter gallery had a frost plug and should also be tapped. You need to use an extension for the tap and have to be very careful not to thread too deep and interfere with the #7 exhaust lifter bore. You can actually watch for the tap as you are cutting the threads by looking down the lifter bore. You should have adequate threads cut well before you see the tap.

Now for the three more difficult front oil gallery plugs. You can use either hex or square-socket 3/8 NPT plugs. Machine the exterior side of each plug so the socket recess is 0.188 deep; then, if necessary, machine the interior face to reduce the overall plug length to 0.312. As you are tapping each hole, hand-fit the plug that will be used for that oil gallery, but only go as deep as you need to fit it flush with the face of the block.

Check the position of the oil passages relative to the face of the block. If you go too deep with the plugs, it may cut off or reduce the oil flow to either of the rocker-arm shafts or, worse yet, the oil flow from the main oil gallery. Obstructing any of the oil passages could be a critical mistake. If you have any concern about doing this yourself, do not hesitate to have this done at a machine shop.

Selecting a Machine Shop

Selecting a machine shop can be a challenge depending on where you live. When I started in the car hobby, multiple auto parts stores were in the area, almost within walking distance for those who lived in the city. Many of them had their own machine shop in the back of the store. However, most of these automotive parts suppliers have disappeared at an alarming rate and been replaced by franchised outlets. There is only one survivor left in my city with a population of 500,000 people.

Motors last much longer today, and in most cases, it is more economical to replace them with a new crate engine than to rebuild the original motor. Consequently, automotive machine shops that remain today survive mostly by specializing in race engines or restoration projects. The selection narrows even further when you are looking for someone who is familiar with and has had experience with Nailheads. You should also research the quality of their workmanship and reliability, although I expect the less reputable shops would have disappeared as the market shrunk. The bottom line is when you find a dependable machine shop that gives you quality work, stick with them.

This crankshaft suffered from a lack of oil. Fortunately, it is not damaged too badly and should be corrected by being straightened and ground. It will be sent to Canadian Chromeplating and Crankshaft Inc. with a request to grind the journals for 0.002 clearance.

The next step is to deliver the block with main caps, rotating assembly, and torque plates to Forrest & Forrest Racing. They will send the block and heads out to be baked and shot-blasted. When it's returned, it will be Magnafluxed, which is a process that can detect any cracks in the component. This is an important and final test to ensure this is the right candidate for your project.

For several years, it has been difficult to get parts cleaned effectively due to the restrictions on the chemicals available for use in the old hot tanks. However, this baking/shot-blasting process is far superior to any of the old school techniques and is environmentally friendly because it is not reliant on chemicals. The heads will be sent to Performance

The new forged pistons from Ross were ordered with 0.927 pins. The full-floating piston pins makes it necessary to resize the top of the rod and press in the undersize bushings. A secondary advantage of full-floating pistons is that you can assemble them or take them apart in your home shop.

Paul is using a quality dial bore gauge to check the inside diameter number of the main bearing inserts to verify they are 2.490 inches. The crankshaft main bearing journals were turned 0.010 under to 2.488 and were also miked to confirm the size. It is essential to have the main caps torqued to spec for accurate readings when you are taking this measurement.

The new bushings need to be taken out to fit the new piston pins with 0.0005- to 0.001-inch clearance. When you assemble these after balancing, be sure to coat the pin and the inside of the piston boss and rod bushing with assembly lube.

Porting for a street-performance valve job.

Once you are satisfied that you have all the right basics to begin, you then need to determine the piston specifications. (This process was detailed at the end of chapter 4).

Connecting Rod Preparation

Nailhead connecting rods and crankshafts are forged and strong enough to tolerate a mild turbocharger application. The rods will be resized, fitted with 0.927 bushings for full-floating piston pins, and have ARP bolts installed. We ordered the ARP part number 125-6001 rod bolts, but they required excessive pressure to press them in. Comparing the shank size of the stock Buick rod bolt of 0.3906 on a thin, knurled part of the shank compared to the actual shank of the ARP bolt at 0.3915, we found that the original Nailhead rod bolt shank was 0.0009 smaller than the new ARP pieces. Forrest & Forrest reduced the ARP shank to 0.391 to reduce the interference fit of 0.0005.

With the new bolts pressed in, the rods will need to be resized. According to Mike at TA Performance, it is good practice to have your machine shop spot-face the seat area for the rod bolt nuts as the ARP nuts may have a slightly different footprint than the stock Buick rod nuts.

As an aside, a local sprint car racer ran Nailheads on alcohol very successfully from the late 1950s until 1969, when he switched to big-block Chevys. He started with a factory short-block assembly, opened up the main clearances, used stock rods and oil pumps, and added aftermarket cast high-compression pistons and a roller cam. He doesn't ever recall having a crankshaft or rod failure. He did recall that the pistons in that era were ridiculously heavy by today's standards, like maybe 900 to 1,000 grams each, and had to be replaced after every 10 races.

Align Boring

There is one operation that most machine shops are adamant that they must do, and that is align boring, or line boring, depending whom you ask. I have yet to test a Nailhead block that needs this procedure. However, you should never assume anything. Check your block. If you have a machine shop nearby, have them do the check to satisfy them and yourself about align boring. Install your new main bearings in the block and torque down the caps. Use a dial bore gauge to verify the bearing inside diameter (ID) at each main journal and make note of the reading. After the crank has been ground, mike and log the outside diameter (OD) of each journal. These numbers must be consistent. In this case, the main bearing ID was 2.490, and the crankshaft journals were 2.488.

Remove the bearing caps and leave #3 and #5 bearings in place. Use a lint-free cloth to wipe each of the main journals and then wipe the bearing inserts with a lightweight oil. Keep in mind that all of the main and rod bearings have to push in with a little snap. If they are loose at all, there is a problem. If the bearing has lost its snap, it must be replaced. If the bearing cap or saddle is somehow out of spec, it must be resized.

Reinstall the crank and torque #3 and #5 caps again. The crank-

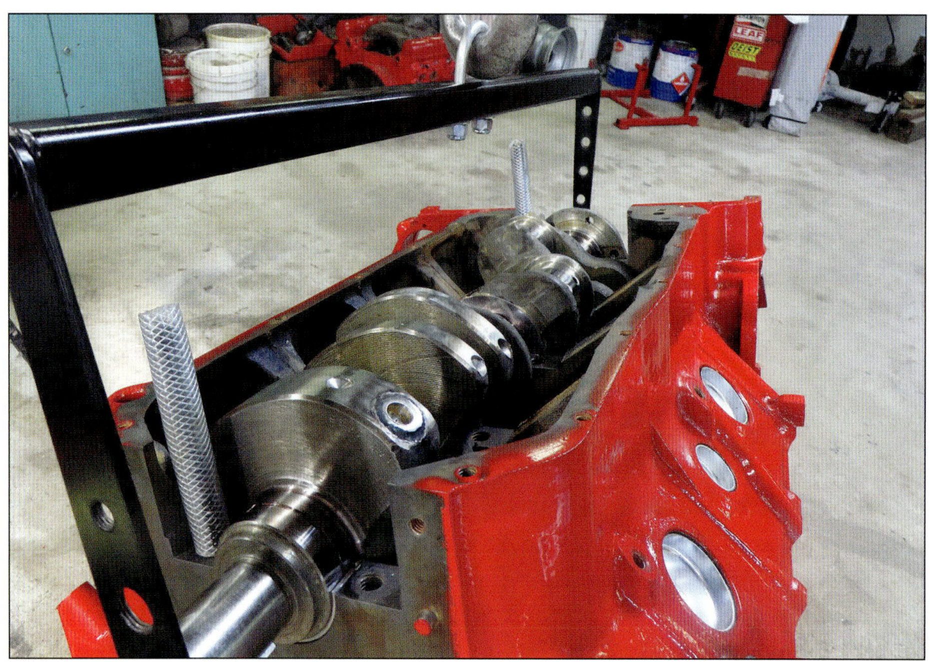

Lowering the crankshaft into position is a lot easier and less likely to cause any damage to the main bearings when you have a free hand to guide it into place. Any damage at all to one of your bearing inserts is just cause to replace it. The fit of these inserts is too critical to even think of trying to repair a damaged piece.

You need to measure your new pistons to verify the outside diameter. This may be an old habit that is hard to break but is a good habit to retain. You never assume anything. With the quality control in today's manufacturing, there are seldom any errors.

shaft should spin freely by hand. Use a dial indicator on #1 journal and check for runout. This number must be zero.

Now remove the crank, install the rest of the bearings with a light coat of oil, wipe each main journal clean before you replace the crankshaft, and retorque all five bearing caps. The shaft should spin freely by hand with the same feel as it had when you spun it with only #3 and #5 caps secured. If everything works, the block does not require align boring or honing.

If you felt a difference of resistance while turning the crankshaft, check to see if it is straight. Any amount of runout will have to be corrected by your crankshaft grinder. If there is any resistance at all there, you will need to have the block align honed. Once you are satisfied, remove the crankshaft, wipe the journals and inserts clean, bag up the main bearings and crankshaft, and set them aside until you are ready to mock up the block to check deck height.

Piston Assembly

Once the new pistons arrive, check and record the size and cylinder number of each piston as a reference for honing the cylinders to size. With the computer-controlled machinery in today's world there is seldom any variation in size or weight; but, you should always check. New 0.927 bushings were ordered for the connecting rods, pressed in and reamed to fit the new piston pins.

After you install the new ARP rod bolts and ream the wrist pin bushings to size, you will then need to have the rods checked for

We are using steel-shim head gaskets with this motor. Here is a good use for the fiber head gaskets that came in your gasket set: as spacers under the torque plates. Remember, you need to remove the metal sealing ring around the cylinder before they mess up your boring or honing operation.

If you have a custom set of torque plates made, they should be thicker with counter-sunk bolt holes. It makes it easier to mount the boring bar without relying on precision-ground spacers. The spacers present an extra step and a potential for error.

The torque plates are tightened to the same specs as the head bolts with gaskets in place to duplicate normal stress in the block. Although not visible in this photo, the main caps were replaced and torqued to spec. Use Buick torque specifications here unless you have ARP bolts to fit here.

The boring bar was manufactured by the Van Norman Company in the early 1930s. It was purchased with the assumption that it would need an overhaul. A pleasant surprise was that it had double bearings throughout and required very little refurbishment. This is a testament to the quality of equipment produced by that company during that era.

The Van Norman Honing Machine has been updated electrically to operate a preset number of strokes so each cylinder gets the same number of passes with each of the different honing grits. This ensures that the amount of honing can be replicated from one cylinder to another.

straightness and then resized. You can now carry on to temporarily assembling the #1, 2, 7, and 8 pistons and rods.

The first step is to thoroughly clean your vise and attach aluminum or plastic jaw inserts to hold the connecting rod while you install the piston and wrist pin. Because this is a temporary fitting, you only need to apply a light coat of oil on the rod bearing inserts and wrist pins. If you have a swivel-base vise, rotate it 90 degrees and keep a catch tray beneath the vise to capture any droplets of oil.

Set the #1 rod in the vise with the top sticking out with enough space to fit the piston and the outboard or numbered side of the rod facing you. Position the piston on top of the rod with the valve pockets away from you and slide the pin into place. Set the bearings into the rods and put the rod cap back on. Hand-tighten to ensure the inserts don't fall out. Bag the four piston assemblies and set aside until you are ready to mock up the block to check out if the deck is not square.

Boring and Honing

The block is fitted with torque plates and fiber head gaskets in preparation for the boring and honing operations. Remove the sealing rings of the fiber head gaskets, as they can wreak havoc with the honing machine. Both the block plates and the main bearing caps should be torqued to spec to simulate normal preload conditions. The cylinders were bored to 2.245 and the block was then moved over and mounted in the Van Norman honing machine.

When honing the block, Paul followed a sequence starting with the #5 cylinder, then #1, then #7 and finishing at #3. A similar format was used with the left bank by honing in order from #6 to #2 to #8 and finishing at #4. The purpose of this practice is to avoid honing beside a freshly honed, warm cylinder with a cold cylinder on the opposite side.

The cylinders were honed to size with three grits of honing stones and then finished with a brush hone. This last stage of honing with the brush will knock the heads off from the last

Even with the controller setup on the honing machine, Paul used the dial bore gauge after each phase of honing to verify how much material was removed. The quality of the finish is consistent from cylinder to cylinder and is much superior to the old-school handheld drill approach.

The brush hone is used for the final finishing passes. This will clean off some of the peaks left from the last honing grit and help reduce the break-in time required to seat the rings.

280-grit hone and help reduce the break-in time.

Deck Height

Remove the block plates and main bearing caps in preparation to reinstall the crankshaft and mock up the block with pistons in #1, 2, 7, and 8 holes. We need to determine the deck height and check how square the deck is relative to the crankshaft. Bring the #1 piston to TDC and use a depth gauge to measure the deck height at the front of the cylinder directly above the piston pin. Note the reading.

Do the same with the #2, 7, and 8 cylinders, and you now have established a reference of

The deck height is the distance from the piston head at TDC to the deck surface. You must take the measurements for the deck height at several quadrants of each cylinder to establish a baseline for setting up to deck the block.

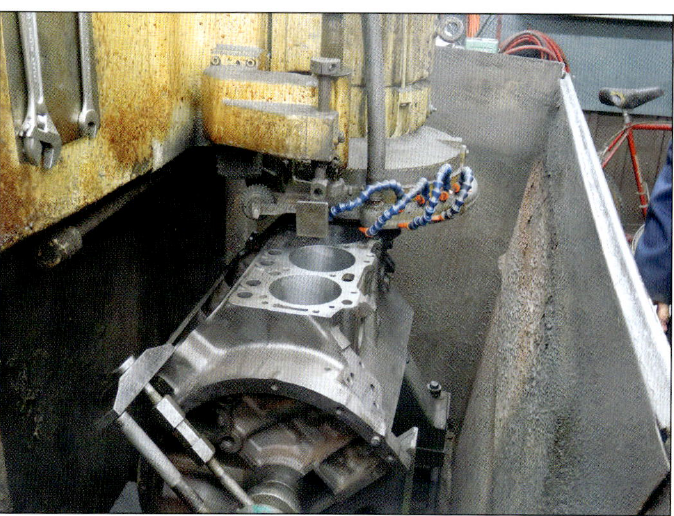

Once the block has been set up with reference to the baseline measurements, the decks can be cut at consistent heights with each other and will be perfectly square to the crankshaft. Each cylinder will then have the exact same volume.

Until we get a TDC marker permanently set up, Paul will verify it for each different measurement. If you have a head in place and don't want to keep removing it, you can verify it with an extended probe on your dial indicator through the spark plug hole or set up your indicator on the #4 cylinder to verify #1 TDC.

Verifying the cylinder volume with a burette is the most reliable method to get an accurate reading. The calculation to determine cylinder volume takes in many factors and consequently has more chances of an error. You do not want to make a mistake here and try to correct your compression ratio by removing material from the piston dome using erroneous data.

how square the deck is from front to back and left bank to right bank. This will be your guide to decking the block square with the crankshaft. Remove the rotating assembly and move the block over to mount in the decking mill. With this particular block, the variation was less than 0.004 and only a minimal cut was required to square up the decks.

Compression Ratio

Verify the volume of the combustion chamber so that you can calculate the compression ratio and determine how much material (if any) needs to be removed from the piston dome to obtain our target compression ratio of 10.1:1. You will need to reinstall the crankshaft with the #1-cylinder piston assembly. You can calculate this volume with known values, such as how the heads have been cc'd to 127.5 cc's. The bore, deck clearance, piston-dome volume, and gasket bore size and thickness are also known values, but the burette method is more direct with less chance of error. You need to convert all your measurements to either metric (cc) or imperial (ci) to do your calculations, but do not change from one to the other or you will get incorrect data.

Use the crankshaft drive hub with the degree wheel and a piston stop to locate top dead center (TDC). Set the motor at TDC per your timing indicator. Seal around the piston top to the cylinder with thin strips of 0.003 brass shim stock to hold the piston from rocking, and then seal around that area with grease.

Install the #1 intake and exhaust valves with lightweight test springs, and then use a smear of grease on the seats to seal the valves. Install the head using a gasket the same thickness as the ones that will be used. It should also be torqued and sealed with grease.

Rotate the block to a 45-degree angle so the spark plug hole is the uppermost part of the #1 cylinder. Then use a 100 ml burette with a colored solution (automatic transmission fluid works well) that is easy to read and note the cc's required to fill the combustion chamber to the bottom of the spark plug threads. Record this number as the combustion chamber volume.

Calculate your swept volume as bore x bore x stroke x 0.7854. Next, divide your swept volume by your target compression ratio of 10.1 to get a target combustion chamber volume. Then, subtract this number from your original calculation of combustion chamber volume; this will be how much material you need to remove from your piston domes.

Remove the brass shims and replace the head with the piston mocked up in place to check the piston-to-valve clearances once you get the camshaft set up.

When replacing the #2 through #5 cam bearings, be sure to use a guide bushing in an alternate cam bearing to ensure the bearing goes in straight. The primary concern is that the oil supply holes are at the six o'clock position and properly aligned with the feed hole coming up from the main oil gallery.

The #1 cam bearing is the heart of oil distribution for the remainder of your engine. The feed from the main oil gallery is obviously important; however, it is critical to get the correct alignment of the oil outlet channels located at 10 and 2 o'clock to ensure you get correct oil flow distribution to both the right and left lifter bank rocker-arm shafts.

It is easy to make an extension handle for your camshaft that helps guide your cam into place with minimal contact with the bearings. The longer it is will make it more user friendly and provide better control. This one has different threaded sections for different camshafts.

As you get set up to install and degree the camshaft, you will need a means to monitor the position of the crankshaft. You will need a drive hub with a hex drive to attach to your harmonic balancer as a means to turn the crankshaft over as well as an adjustable degree wheel to fasten to the drive hub. Add a temporary pointer to identify the crankshaft position.

The block has returned from powder coating. We attached as many accessories as we could to keep the powder from getting into the machined surfaces, but we also had these parts prepared so they are finished as well. Any open mounting holes will need to have the threads chased again.

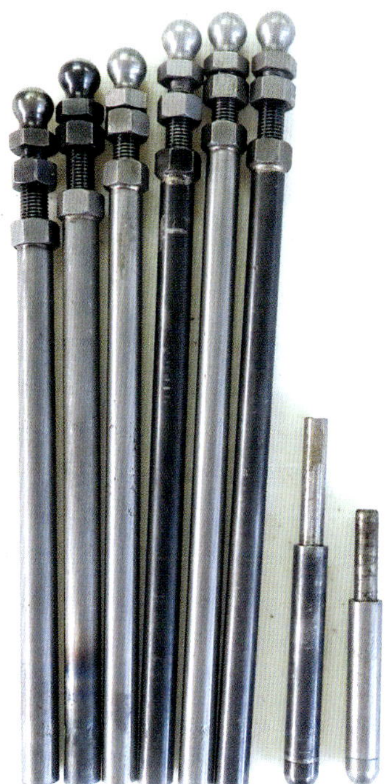

A set of adjustable pushrods in varying lengths and two lifters are filled with a solid material to mimic the height of your hydraulic lifters. These are necessary to determine the correct lengths for your pushrods and test different rocker-arm ratios or to degree the cam accurately. These pushrods have been modified to use for test purposes only.

The test pushrod is adjusted to zero clearance to proceed with set up. You will need a second lifter and pushrod for the exhaust valve. These were sold in sets as a cheap alternative to purchasing adjustable rocker arms. They only fit with the adjuster down, and the intake manifold had to be removed to reset the valves, but back in our youth we had lots of energy and no money.

Installing the cam bearings is relatively routine work when you have the correct mandrels, but be sure that all the bearings are properly aligned with the oil feed passages from the main oil gallery. The #1 cam bearing can be misaligned by being installed backward. It must also be aligned with the main oil feed as well as the passages to the left and right lifter galleries. Misalignment of the front bearing is one of the most common mistakes made with Nailheads. Be sure to have an old camshaft and a bearing scraper or reamer on hand to fit the new bearings. These usually need some fine tuning for the cam to turn freely. Check your new cam to be sure it also turns freely.

Checking Piston-to-Valve Clearance

Prepare to degree in the camshaft for the purpose of checking the piston-to-valve clearance. You will need an adjustable pushrod, cam installation handle, dial indicator, degree wheel, drive hub for the crankshaft, two low-tension valve springs, a top dead center stop, and a temporary timing mark.

1 Mount the degree wheel on the drive hub and set the timing indicator so it can be easily read.

2 Since the head is already in place on the right bank, install a piston assembly in #4 and bolt the top dead center (TDC) stop over that cylinder. With a Nailhead, the flat bar portion of the dead center stop is adequate as a stop on the piston dome.

3 Turn the crankshaft clockwise until the piston dome rests against the stop.

4 Adjust the degree wheel to 0 degrees. Then, turn the crankshaft counterclockwise until the dome hits the stop again. Let's say the pointer now indicates 62 degrees after top dead center (ATDC); reset the degree wheel to half of that number (31 degrees ATDC).

5 Tighten the degree wheel and turn the drive hub clockwise and it should stop at 31 degrees before top dead center (BTDC). You may want to repeat this step just to verify that you have TDC, then remove the TDC stop.

6 Install the camshaft keyway in your new cam with Loctite 609 retaining compound unless you are planning to use offset keyways, in which case apply the compound when you are finished.

7 Test fit the camshaft and crankshaft gears a few times so that they slide on and off with some effort but not sloppily. You may have to deburr the keyways with a hone stone, but you do not want these to fit loosely.

8 We are using a timing set from Carmen Faso with multiple keyways in the crank gear that allow you to advance or retard the cam up to 8 degrees. Install the new cam at zero degrees.

9 Continuing with the low-tension setup valve springs, you will also need a couple of solid lifters or you can make one by filling an old hydraulic lifter with solder to support the pushrod disc at the normal relaxed position. Put lifters in for the #1 intake and exhaust valves with adjustable pushrods, the rocker-arm shaft, and rockers.

10 With the lifter setup on the base circle of the cam, set up your dial indicator with enough travel to measure total valve lift on the #1 intake retainer and set to zero.

11 Adjust the pushrods to zero lash and turn the crankshaft slowly through one cycle, stopping frequently to readjust the pushrod.

12 When you are content that the lifters are on the base circle, reset the dial indicator back to zero.

When you take your readings from the valve retainer, you must multiply the specified 0.050-inch reading by the ratio of that particular rocker arm. We are using the later-year cast-aluminum rocker with a 1.54:1 ratio and will take our measurements starting at 0.077-inch lift. (Refer back to chapter 5 where different rocker arms were tested. They do vary, and it becomes more important to have correct numbers at this stage in the game.)

It is more accurate to read lift directly from the lifter if you have an extended measuring tip, but not everyone has one. However, you are setting this up for the purpose of checking piston-to-valve clearance. It is more convenient to leave the pushrod in place and take your measurements directly from the retainer.

13 Turn the crankshaft slowly until the indicator reads 0.050 at the lifter (or 0.077 inch if you are reading from the valve spring retainer). Using 0.050, the reading is 2.5 degrees BTDC. Continue turning the crank until the reading peaks. This number, 0.447, as read directly from the valve spring retainer, is your maximum intake valve opening. If your peak reading came from the lifter, it would have to be multiplied by your rocker-arm ratio to determine the maximum valve lift.

14 Continue turning the crank slowly until the indicator returns to your original 0.050 reading, which is now 31 degrees ABDC. Add your readings of 2.5 BTDC plus 180 degrees plus 31 ABDC, which equals 213.5. Divide the total open degrees (213.5) by 2, which equals 106.75, and subtract 2.5 degrees BTDC, which equals the lobe center of 104.25 ATDC. The lobe center position you are looking for (as per the cam card) calls for 108 degrees ATDC. The cam should be advanced 3.75 degrees in this position.

15 Remove the cam and reinstall it 2 degrees retarded from the initial position and repeat the process. The intake opened at 0.5 degrees BTDC and closed at 33 ABDC, which totals 213.5 degrees open. Divide by 2 and then subtract the 0.5 BTDC. This gave us a lobe center 106.25 degrees ATDC. It's better but not good enough.

16 Repeat the process again using the 4-degree retarded keyway. The 4-degree setup gave us an opening of 1.5 degrees ATDC and closing at 35 degrees ABDC. Things change a little with the calculations because the opening occurred ATDC. You

start with 180 degrees minus 1.5 degrees and then add 35 degrees, which gives you 213.5 total degrees open. Divide the total degrees open by 2, which equals a 106.75 lobe center. Because the opening came after TDC, you have to replace the 1.5 degrees ATDC to determine the relationship of the lobe center to TDC. The cam is now set up with a 108.25 ATDC lobe center.

This setting of 4R will be our setup number. As mentioned previously, this setup was primarily done to determine the piston to valve clearance. This will also give you a starting point for the final assembly, but you should repeat the degreeing process again to verify the cam position as you do the final assembly. A side benefit to this is you get an actual reading of your total opening of 0.447. Keep in mind that you will lose up to 0.030 due to compression of the hydraulic lifters.

Once we have established a correct pushrod size, we can install a piston and rod assembly and check the piston to valve clearances. You also need to set up a dial indicator on the valve spring retainer and check total lift.

The primary purpose for setting the cam in the proper position is to check the piston-to-valve clearance.

1 Leave the dial indicator set up at zero degrees on #1 intake valve retainer with the valve closed.

2 Slowly rotate the crankshaft until the intake valve begins to open and stop at 10 ATDC. Make note of the reading on the indicator.

3 Tip the rocker arm by hand until the valve hits the piston and check the indicator reading again. The difference is your piston-to-valve clearance at this particular position.

4 Move the crankshaft to 15 degrees ATDC and repeat the above readings. Repeat the measurements again checking at 20 degrees ATDC. You now have the clearances for the intake cycle.

5 Reposition the dial indicator to the exhaust valve retainer and set it up again at zero degrees with the valve closed. At this point, you want to take your readings as the valve is closing but at 20, 15, and 10 degrees BTDC at the end of the exhaust cycle. Be certain that the readings you have are the differential of the retainer measurement to the reading at piston contact.

Remember, the indicator reading from the valve closed at zero degrees to piston contact is not a relevant number. The absolute minimum clearances that you are looking for are 0.060 on the intake and 0.090 for the exhaust.

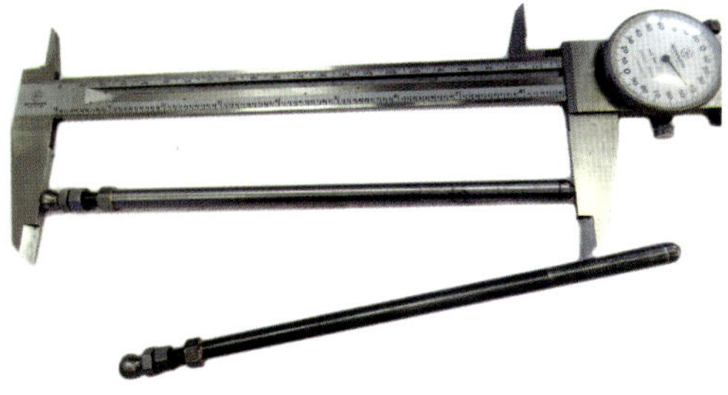

Each time a block is decked or the heads are milled, the preload on the lifters is increased, and you ultimately need a new set of pushrods. The easiest measurement for length is from ball tip to ball tip as in the photo. You also need to specify the outside diameter of the ball. Some manufacturers have an alternate way to measure the length. The safest approach to ordering new pushrods is to email a picture with your order.

Intake ATDC

10*	15*	20*
0.108	0.115	0.128

Exhaust BTDC

20*	15*	10*
0.105	0.135	0.155

These readings are well within tolerances and there is no need to cut the valve pockets any further.

Pushrod Length

The next issue you need to resolve is the correct pushrod length. Considering the machine work that was completed here in addition to the unknown past of a 60-year-old motor, this is a good opportunity to check the pushrod length required for your new motor. Remove the rocker arms and shafts.

Measure the length of the adjustable pushrods as they are

You can fit that old piston to your ring filer so it will slide back and forth and stay straight to the abrasive wheel. Machine a 0.080 recess in the bottom side with a 0.050 larger inside diameter than the largest anticipated bore size. Remove the extra 0.040 from the outer ring and leave two segments to act as guides over the tail of the ring filer.

You will need a small fine-grit hand stone to give the filed rings a light touch to remove any possible burrs that will impede ring movement. Keep in mind that this is only a light touch of the upper and lower sides and not the face of the ring.

If you have an old piston that is large enough, you can make use of it as a ring holder. This makes it a lot easier to hold onto the ring and keep it square when file fitting your rings.

To get an accurate measurement when fitting rings, they must be square in the bore. This is another use for one of your old pistons. Machine it so that it slides down 1 inch into the cylinder and will set the ring at that depth. This helps ensure consistent measurements.

removed and compare it to a stock pushrod. The difference in these readings is 0.060 inch, which is at the upper limit for the amount of preload you want to have on your lifters. That is fine for now; however, with the transition to the turbo and the thicker 0.042 copper gaskets, new, longer pushrods will be necessary due to changes in head gasket thickness. You can now disassemble the block and remove the rotating assembly in preparation for balancing. The next step is to file fit your piston rings.

Piston Rings

You will need a piston ring filer, feeler gauges, and a ring-setting tool. Calculate the gap required by the manufacturer's instructions for your particular

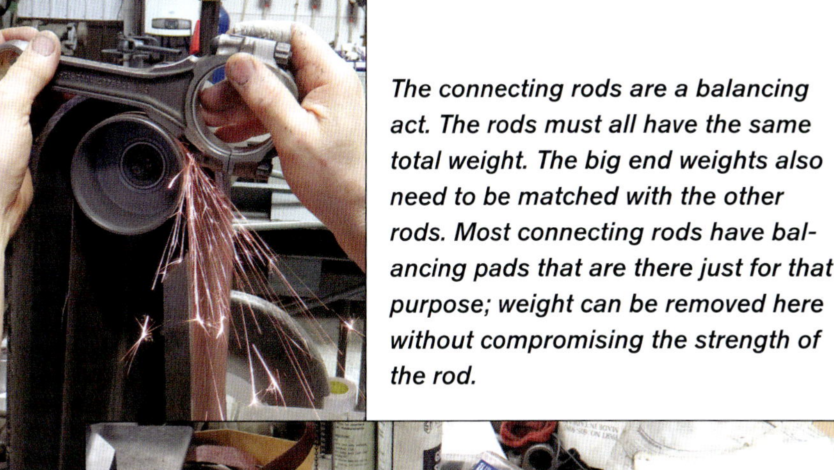

The connecting rods are a balancing act. The rods must all have the same total weight. The big end weights also need to be matched with the other rods. Most connecting rods have balancing pads that are there just for that purpose; weight can be removed here without compromising the strength of the rod.

The balancing act continues. This scale has been set up specifically to weigh connecting rods with a fixture made up to weigh the small end only while the big end is suspended from another unit. The scale will be zeroed to account for the weight of the fixture before the rods are set up to be weighed.

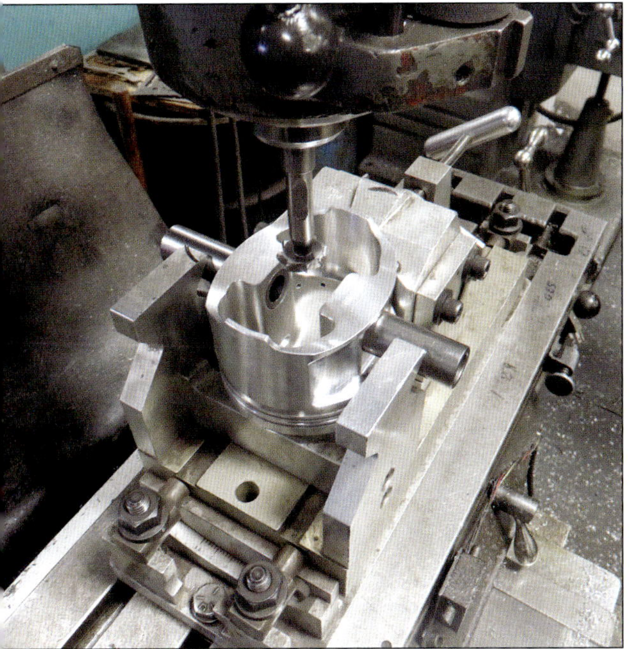

Nailhead pistons are notoriously heavy (in the 700-plus-grams range). You don't get any of that 450- to 500-gram stuff here. Glen is machining any excess weight he can find from this piston. Don't expect any miracles here.

The weight of each piston, a set of rings, a piston pin, and the weight of the small end of a rod are all part of the calculation of the bob-weight to be added to each rod journal of the crankshaft so it can be balanced. Glen is using the previously collected data to assemble one of the four counterweights.

bore size and application for the top and second rings. The ring gaps should be checked about 1 inch down the bore using a ring-setting tool to keep the measurements consistent.

After the top and second rings are gapped, use a small hone stone to very lightly deburr the top and bottom of fitted ring ends. Do not touch the sealing surface of these rings. Clean the rings and store them in a resealable sandwich bag numbered for the cylinder to which it was fitted. One complete set of rings will go with the pistons for calculating balancing weight.

You can now disassemble the #1, 2, 7, and 8 rods and pistons and remove the crankshaft.

Engine Balancing

You will need the crankshaft, harmonic balancer, connecting rods, pistons and pins, a set of rings, rod bearings, the flexplate or the flywheel with the pressure plate, and attaching hardware.

Each piston and pin are weighed with a set of rings and the weight recorded.

The connecting rods are weighed at both the small end and the big end, and then they are ground so that the small and big ends of each weigh the same and the total weights also match.

These numbers are also recorded and (along with the piston, piston pins, and ring weights) are used to calculate the required weight to be added to each rod journal as the crankshaft is spun.

Some engines are internally balanced, and the crankshaft can be spun and balanced at this stage with the harmonic balancer installed to simulate the finished installation. The weight adjustments will be made at the crankshaft counterweights. The flexplate or flywheel assembly will be balanced as separate unit. Other motors, as is the case with the Buick Nailhead, are externally balanced and require all the components to be balanced as a unit.

This becomes an obstacle if you decide to change from an automatic to a standard, replace a cracked flexplate, or have your clutch assembly serviced. When working with a motor for a street-driven vehicle, many shops will assume a) that if the motor had been previously balanced, the weight adjustments would have been made at the crankshaft; and b) that the weight built into the replacement parts is close enough to the factory tolerance of plus or minus 15 to 20 grams and will not be a factor. That may be fine for a grocery getter, but in a performance or race engine, you never assume anything. The whole motor will have to be torn down so the rotating assembly can be removed and be rebalanced as a unit.

There is an alternative when you are building a motor. Glen at Forrest & Forrest Racing has been able to modify the crankshaft counterweights to balance the crankshaft assembly internally, and then balance the flexplate or flywheel and clutch assembly pieces as a separate unit. This makes subsequent servicing of the flexplate/flywheel or changing drive units much more user-friendly.

Preassembly

Balancing is the last phase of machine work. We can now complete putting the pistons and connecting rods together and have them ready for final assembly.

1 Head back to your vise with the protective jaws and catch tray. Set up the #1 rod as you did for the temporary fitting, but this time thoroughly coat the rod bushings, wrist pin, and pin bosses with assembly lube. Remember to keep the outboard (numbered) side of the rod closest to you and the valve pockets on the opposite side. If you get this mixed up, you are really going to be upset. You will find out why after you start working with the spiro locks.

2 With the wrist pin inserted to contain the piston, reposition the rod 90 degrees in the vise and tilt it away from you at a 45-degree angle. The wrist pin receiver groove will be facing up.

3 With this motor, the pistons were machined to accept spiro locks, which can be installed with a tool or by hand using a couple of small screwdrivers. Two locks are required at each end of the wrist pin. Start by springing the clip apart, but be careful not to bend it.

4 Set one end into the receiver groove and rotate the clip counterclockwise as you slide the clip into place.

5 Once you have about 3/4 of a complete coil in the groove, use a small screwdriver to roll around the rest of the clip until it is all in the groove. Push the clip to the inboard side of the groove and repeat to install the second spiro lock. Follow up with a blunt object like a 1/2-inch punch to roll around the inside of the clips with some outward pressure to ensure they are properly seated.

6 Turn the piston and rod over so the opposing receiver groove is facing upward and repeat the above installation with the next two locks.

7 Continue to assemble the remainder of the rods and pistons. This is not the most user-friendly part of this job, but the proper fitting of the spiro locks is another critical phase of rebuilding your Nailhead.

While degreeing the cam, you may have noticed the snout of the new cam had a little larger chamfer than a stock Buick cam. This left insufficient material to act as a register to seat the fuel pump eccentric. This is an area that you need to be aware of while rebuilding your own Nailhead. In this case, we machined 0.040 from the outer face of the of the cam gear, which allowed for more of a register on the cam snout and better contact with the cam keyway for the fuel pump drive.

When the timing gear was attached to the front of the camshaft, it was apparent that there was not enough of the cam nose and keyway sticking out to act as a register for the fuel pump eccentric. An electric fuel pump is part of the plan for this motor, but you should not discount the future use of a mechanical pump.

The balancing is completed and the parts that were returned from the machine shop need to be cleaned, bagged, and ready for assembly.

The remaining parts are prepped, bagged, and ready for assembly. This includes all of the necessary fasteners for each part so that the assembly can go uninterrupted. The water pump fasteners are freshly powder coated in an effort to minimize corrosion and have them ready to go.

ASSEMBLY

Before starting the assembly, your shop or assembly area will need a final cleaning, and all your parts (including the block) should be cleaned and bagged or wrapped up. Don't leave the parts cleaning until you are assembling them because this will only stir up more dirt. Don't trust that your new parts are clean out of the box.

Wash all of your parts in hot water with Dawn dish detergent, rinse them off in hot water, and immediately blow-dry them. Use a lint-free rag to wipe down the parts with a light film of oil (particularly the machined surfaces) and bag them up until they are ready to install.

Use a break-in oil that has a content of zinc, or you can treat with a zinc additive to wipe down these parts. You will also use this oil for engine assembly in areas that do not require assembly lube. You can give the block a similar treatment, except use brushes to clean out the oil galleries again and then use a pressure washer to flush the detergent out. Your final flush will be with brake cleaner so that you quickly back blow them dry to ensure that they are clean.

Once you have completed the pressure washing and blow drying, move back inside to a clean area to avoid airborne contaminants. You need to work quickly with the block to prevent rust from forming and do a final and more thorough wipe-down with clean oil.

A thorough block scrub down is your starting point before assembly. All of the internal passages, including the lifter bores, get scrubbed with a stiff nylon brush powered by a drill and blown through with the power washer.

A power washer is used to flush out all of the soap solution, including the internal passages, and then immediately blown dry before rust starts to form. The cylinders are wiped down with oil as soon as possible using a lint-free cloth.

A variety of different-sized engine brushes from 1/4- to 1-inch diameter are needed to access the main oil galleries, oil passages to and from the oil filter, lifter bores, and the small oil feed lines that run up from the lifter oil gallery through to the block deck, and finally through the head to the front rocker-arm bolt hole. This last passage is easily missed.

After the block has been blown dry, flush each of the oil galleries with brake cleaner. The 1/8-inch discharge tubes will fit into the small passages as well as the larger oil galleries.

Don't try to flush all the oil lines at once or the brake cleaner will dry up and not be as effective. As you flush a portion of each oil passage and the brake clean is still wet, feed the back blower and blow it clear of any remaining contaminants. You can blow out the smaller lines with a blow gun. It may be necessary to wash the block again and repeat this process if there were foreign contaminants blown around.

If you are lucky, you will find cans of brake cleaner, such as this, that will accept a 1/8-inch plastic tube. They are no longer available in many areas, and the nozzles do not interchange with the regular cans. They are very handy for feeding the tube through the internal passages for that last flush.

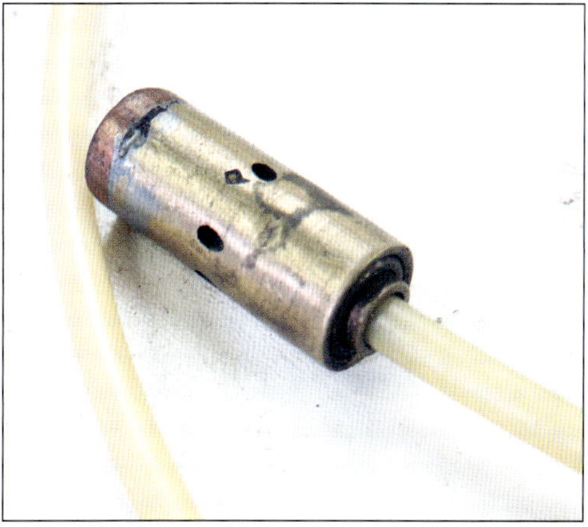

You can make a back blower, such as this, from airbag fittings with push-lock fittings. Solder the end closed and drill four to five 0.125-inch holes at a 45-degree angle. The body needs to be turned down to less than 0.400 so it can fit through the three main oil galleries. This back blower is an effective way to give a final cleaning of the oil passages.

You may or may not have the luxury of a dedicated engine-assembly room. An HVAC air filter or an air purifier system will help keep your shop clean by reducing particulates and odors, but that does not preclude the necessity of a thorough cleaning of your workshop prior to engine assembly.

Start off by vacuuming all the floors and shelving areas as much as possible. Then, run a large exhaust fan and blow off everything from all the nooks and crannies. This appears to be clean, but it sure stirs up a lot of airborne particulates. After everything appears to have settled, vacuum again, blow it out again, and let the fan run for another 15 minutes.

Keep all the doors and windows closed to maintain your clean status quo. There are times you may want to lock the door to limit traffic and stop the door opening and closing from the "Watcha doin'?" visitors.

Fasteners

Before you get into further cleaning and assembly, you need to think about the hardware you are planning to use. The wrong grade of bolts and improper tightening procedures are a significant cause of engine and chassis parts failure. (This issue could be a standalone topic for new book by itself and a complete lesson in Engineering 101.) Whether you are rebuilding your new Nailhead or doing other day-to-day projects in the shop, you need to focus on some frequently neglected or overlooked concerns pertaining to the nuts and bolts that you are about to use in this undertaking.

Over- or under-tightening nuts and bolts is dangerous and is an area where many of us err. I am sure you have seen someone hook a couple of closed-end/open-end wrenches together for some extra leverage. Or you have likely seen others use their torque wrench as their best Johnson bar because it is the longest wrench in the tool box. If nothing else, it probably affected the calibration.

Stressing any tool beyond the intended range is abuse! There are people who tighten a bolt with their torque wrench until it reaches the intended torque or clicks and then give the wrench a little extra push. This can be a dangerous practice. You hate to disappoint your friends, but you should let them know that they are not smarter than their torque wrench or those who prescribed the tightening specifications.

THE IMPORTANCE OF PROPER ROD BOLT STRETCH/TORQUE...

Whether measured by stretch or by torque, properly installing a rod bolt is essential for trouble-free performance. If a bolt is installed without sufficient clamp load, every revolution of the crankshaft will cause a separation between the connecting rod and rod cap. This imposes additional stretch in the bolt. The stretch disappears when the load is removed on each revolution, or cycle. Over time, this cycle stretching and relaxing can cause the bolt to fail due to fatigue, just like a paper clip that is bent back and forth by hand. To prevent this condition, the bolt's clamp load must be greater than the load caused by rotating assembly reaching top dead center.

A properly installed rod bolt remains stretched by its clamp load and is not subjected to the cyclic loads imposed on the connecting rod. A quality bolt will stay stretched this way for years without failing. The important thing is to prevent the bolt from failing due to fatigue by tightening it to a load greater than the demand of the engine. Protect your bolts – tighten them as recommended.

You can measure the actual stretch of rod bolts through use of a stretch gauge, or a micrometer for that matter. Prior to installing the rod, measure the length of the bolt in an untorqued state. Write this length down. You can make a chart similar to the one shown on this page to keep track of the data. When you tear the engine down for maintenance, again measure the length of each rod bolt – being careful to keep everything in the proper order. If any of the rod bolts have taken a permanent set and have stretched by .001″ or longer you should replace the fastener IMMEDIATELY! The stretching is a sure indicator that the bolt has been compromised and taken past its yield point.

In other types of bolted joints, this careful attention to tightening is not as important. For example, flywheel bolts need only be tightened enough to prevent them from working loose. Flywheel loads are carried either by shear pins or by side loads in the bolts; they don't cause cyclic tension loads in the bolts. Connecting rod bolts, on the other hand, support the primary tension loads caused by engine operation and must be protected from cyclic stretching. That's why proper tightening of connecting rod bolts is so important. *See pages 25-26 for recommended stretch and torque values.*

Friction is a challenging problem because it varies so much, and is extremely difficult to control with most commonly known lubricants. The best way to avoid the pitfalls of friction and the known variables associated with different lubricants is by using the stretch method. By using the stretch method and removing the friction variable, clamp load can be controlled and repeated. Each time a new bolt is torqued and loosened, the friction factor gets smaller. Eventually the friction levels out and becomes constant for all following repetitions, making it necessary to tighten and loosen a new bolt several times before final installation, when the stretch method cannot be used. The number of cycles depends on the lubricant. Most lubricants require, 5-7 tightening and loosening cycles to level out the friction before final installation. However, with the introduction of ARP's new Ultra-Torque fastener assembly lubricant, cycling a new fastener before final installation becomes a "thing of the past." *See page 126 for more information on ARP Ultra-Torque® fastener assembly lubricant.*

A rod bolt stretch gauge is one of the most important tools a serious engine builder can own. It's valuable in properly setting up a rod for resizing, obtaining the proper clamp load when installed. See page 127 for more information.

Rod Bolt Length Monitoring Chart							
Rod #1		**Rod #2**		**Rod #3**		**Rod #4**	
Inside Bolt		Inside Bolt		Inside Bolt		Inside Bolt	
In	Out	In	Out	In	Out	In	Out
Outside Bolt		Outside Bolt		Outside Bolt		Outside Bolt	
In	Out	In	Out	In	Out	In	Out
Rod #5		**Rod #6**		**Rod #7**		**Rod #8**	
Inside Bolt		Inside Bolt		Inside Bolt		Inside Bolt	
In	Out	In	Out	In	Out	In	Out
Outside Bolt		Outside Bolt		Outside Bolt		Outside Bolt	
In	Out	In	Out	In	Out	In	Out

29

800-826-3045

The ARP catalogue has a lot of good information that explains in layman's terms about bolt stretch relative to applied torque, identifying different causes of fastener failures, etc. This page only deals with rod bolt stretch. You can pick up a catalogue or view it online. (Photo Courtesy Automotive Racing Products)

Anti-seize is absolutely essential for a vehicle that will race on the salt flats, but it is good practice for your daily driver and street rod. There are different grades of anti-seize available depending on the application and the type of metal fastener used.

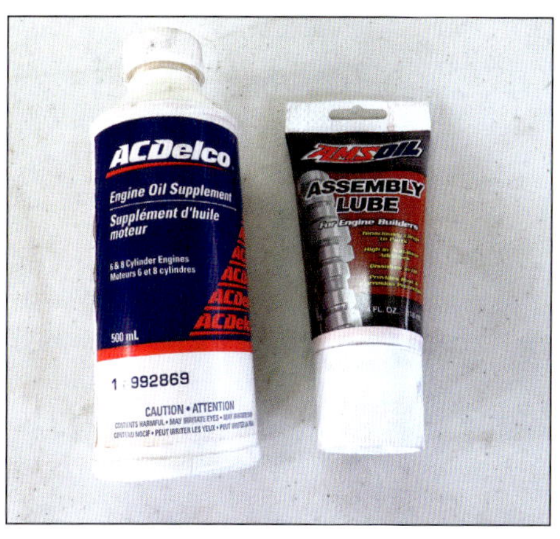

Assembly oil is used to soak your pistons, rings, timing chain, gears as they are being installed, and other areas of the block you want to wipe down to prevent oxidation. Assembly lube needs to be applied to your bearings during the final assembly. Don't be stingy when applying either of these. It is your lifeline at initial start-up.

Few people have their wrenches recalibrated, especially those who abuse them. This should be done routinely; the cost is negligible. The quality ones can be recalibrated for no charge by returning it to where it was purchased. Otherwise, you can do it yourself by following a YouTube video.

Smaller fasteners that require an inch-pound wrench are seldom tightened to any spec. It is preferable for you to have more than one torque wrench with differing ranges. Generally, a torque wrench is the most accurate in the middle of the tightening scale. As you approach the upper or lower range of that wrench, the accuracy diminishes.

There is a wealth of information in the ARP catalogue about fastener selection and torqueing practices in laymen's language. Read this and refer to it regularly. The ARP articles make good reading for anyone who is reading this book or into cars in general.

Impact wrenches should only be used in a select few applications when working on your motor. You have probably seen charts for pneumatic impact guns relating air supply pressure to a specific torque number. They are useless. These are not torque wrenches, nor do they or their electric counterparts produce a reliable tightness. You will find that tire shops are the best bad example of impact wrench usage, yet the tool manufacturers have convinced the governing agencies that these tools can be used reliably to torque wheel nuts. Most franchises only give their personnel a cursory training about proper tightening procedures and very few enforce good work practices when it comes to tightening wheel nuts. We have all seen way too many broken wheel studs over the years. One is too many. Broken wheel studs kill people. Over- or under-tightening any fastener with your Nailhead rebuild can have serious and costly implications. You need to put a lot of thought into fastener selection and application through each step of this project.

You may have heard complaints from fellow car enthusiasts about stainless steel fasteners galling, being difficult to disassemble, and not practical for automotive use. To be successful when using stainless bolts, you need to know what grade they are. Lubricate the threads with a nickel-based anti-seize and tighten them to a prescribed torque for that particular grade of bolt. Don't use just any anti-seize, it must be nickel based. Over-tightening SS bolts and/or not using a proper thread lubricant is what causes threads to gall up. Ask your fastener supplier for a torque chart that includes the different grades of bolts to have the information at your fingertips.

You cannot assume that socket-head or stainless steel fasteners are a better grade of bolt; they are usually only grade 5. Ask your supplier for the specific grade required when purchasing bolts. Grade-8 fasteners should only be used with hardened-steel washers. Utility washers will compress and not maintain your torque settings. Better yet, it is good practice to toss out all of your Grade-2 utility washers and replace them with hardened washers.

You may think that this fastener rhetoric has strayed from the topic of this book, but the moral of these comments is very basic. Whether it is the quality of

---

Once you have your parts cleaned and ready for assembly, bag them up. It is good practice to keep them that way or you may have to clean them again. You do not want that kind of interruption while you are trying to focus on assembling your new Nailhead.

You should take care when removing or installing the cam rear retaining snap ring. These are available through any of the Nailhead dealers, but when you need one at the eleventh hour, you will not find a replacement at your local parts store.

bolts, nuts, parts, or tools you buy, or the quality of your work practices, all of these will combine to affect the outcome of your Nailhead rebuild. If you let any one of these fall into mediocrity, the final product will be mediocre. As the level of performance you want to build into this motor increases, the quality of the parts and practices you input must also increase. Let's move on to assembling this beast.

Short-Block

The pistons, pins, and connecting rods have been cleaned, assembled, and bagged up after balancing so they are ready to be installed. You will need the aluminum or plastic jaws in your vise again and use a pair of ring-installation pliers.

1 Have your rod bearings and rings cleaned and lay them out on a clean, dry surface.

2 Take the #1 connecting rod and install the bearing inserts into the connecting rod and the rod cap. The inserts must snap in place. If they fit loosely, the rod size must be rechecked. If this is the correct size, the bearing insert should be replaced.

3 Secure the cap so that the inserts can't come out, and

mount it in the vise with the piston end facing upward.

4 Install the oil rings first. Use your ring-installation pliers to set the compression and top rings. Be sure to align the ring gaps as per the ring manufacturer's directions. Ring pliers

With each phase of the rebuild, you want to have all of the parts, tools, sealants, and lubricants required for that portion of the job laid out in order of assembly. Your tools also need to be clean and ready for use. In this case, lay out all your plugs in order, particularly those that have a dedicated location.

are not expensive, easy to use, and have much less of a chance of ruining a ring. Bag up this piston and continue with the remainder of the pistons. Set them aside when they are ready for installation.

5 Start by visually checking the alignment of the cam bearings; particularly that the front one has clear passages to the lifter galleries.

6 Install the three oil-gallery plugs in the front of the main oil gallery and the two lifter galleries. Be sure to use the thin plugs. They should fit flush with the front face of the block. Check that they do not obstruct the secondary passages to the lifter galleries or to the heads.

7 Screw in the right lifter gallery rear plug and be sure to install the freeze plug in the back of the block.

8 Next, install the rear main oil gallery and left lifter gallery plugs with a petroleum-compatible pipe dope. You can use that same sealant to seal the two 1/8-inch pipe drain plugs at the center of the water jackets on each side of the block.

9 Next is the internal snap ring behind the rear cam bearing. Some of these have a sharp edge on one side that should face outward.

10 Install the frost plugs with a light coating of shellac-based sealant such as Permatex Aviation Form-a-Gasket. It is easier to install these plugs using a correct-size mandrel so the plugs go in square, particularly on the shallow plug at the rear of the cam. Because of the narrow lip on that plug, use a center punch at three different quadrants to stake it in position. Install the plugs with the outer lip flush with or slightly below the outer block surface.

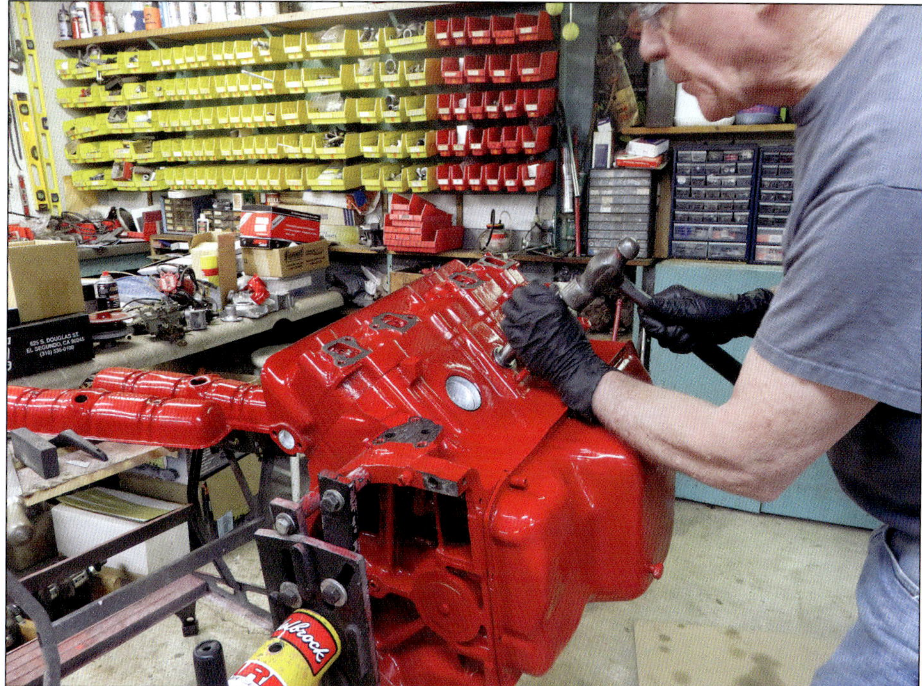

A good driver helps keep the plug square to the hole. Only drive it in deep enough so that the top edge of the plug is at the bottom of the bevel. This is one of the very few applications to use a hammer while working on your motor.

11 Put in the upper halves of the main bearings with a very light coating of oil on the bearing surface only. Check that the back side of the thrust bearing lips, the #3 bearing cap, and the block where they fit are clean before they are installed.

12 Lower the crankshaft in place and secure it with the #3 and 5 bearing caps.

13 Mount a dial indicator with the tip riding to the front of the #1 journal. Rotate it slowly to verify the crankshaft is not bent. In this case, the reading was less than 0.0001.

14 Install the rest of the main bearing caps with a light film of oil and torque to spec. The crankshaft should spin freely by hand. It is good practice, especially since the crankshaft had to be straightened anyway, to indicate the flywheel flange for lateral and radial runout and also the snout of the crankshaft for runout. These readings should both be less than 0.001 inch.

The easiest way to install frost plugs is to use a dedicated mandrel to fit different-sized plugs. The mandrel should be 0.040 inch smaller than the inside diameter of the plug. Use a good shellac-based sealant to install the plugs to ensure that there will not be any leakage.

Dropping the crankshaft in by hand is a good way to damage your bearings. Use a couple of 4x1/2-inch NC studs with rubber sleeves threaded into the #1 and #5 main bearing cap bolt holes as guides. Lowering the crankshaft into place with the lifting device will free up one hand to help guide it into position.

A dial indicator is the best way for you to measure thrust bearing clearance. Feeler gages are not very accurate here and may scratch the bearing. Pry the crankshaft back and forth to get your reading.

If the clearance is below specification, tap the shaft back and forth with a dead-blow hammer two to three times and measure again. This may be enough to seat the thrust bearing and give you more clearance.

15 Firmly tap the front and rear of the crankshaft with a fiber dead-blow hammer to seat the thrust bearing.

16 Reposition the dial indicator with the tip riding on the front of the counterweight at the #1 journal. Pry forward on the counterweight and reset the dial indicator to zero.

17 Pry rearward and record the difference; this is your thrust bearing clearance.

18 If the clearance is less than 0.004, remove the dial indicator and firmly tap the crankshaft fore and aft two to three times as you rotate it. Replace the dial indicator and check the thrust bearing clearance again; it should be between 0.004 and 0.008. In rare cases, it may be necessary to sand the thrust bearing to get the clearance required. Hold the bearing halves firmly together so they stay flat on 600-grit sandpaper on a dead-flat surface. Then, slide them back and forth twice. Thoroughly wash and install them to recheck the thrust clearance. You may have to repeat this to get the required clearance. Take it in small steps as you cannot undo excess clearance.

19 Next, remove all five bearing caps and lift the crankshaft out of the way. New neoprene rear main seals and the #5 cap side seals are readily available from any of the Nailhead dealers. Don't even think about trying to use the old rope seals that may have been included in your gasket set.

20 Install the upper half of the rear main seal in the block with the lip facing inward and lightly coat the seal lip with oil.

21 Coat the upper bearing insert surfaces with assembly lube and lower the crankshaft back in place.

22 Put a tiny dab of Ultra Black gasket maker to each end of the new rear seal and add a liberal amount of the assembly lube on each main bearing journal.

23 Install the lower seal halfway in the rear cap with the seal lip facing inward and wet the seal lip with a thin film of engine oil.

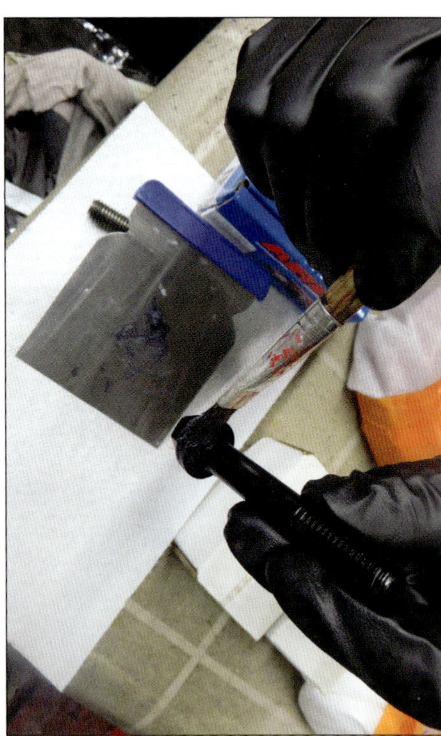

When applying ARP thread lubricant, be sure to thoroughly coat the threads and the underside of the bolt head. You may find it easier to squeeze the lubricant on a palate and apply it with a brush. You will not waste as much and can get more accurate coverage.

Plastigauge

The main bearing journals were miked at 2.488, and the bearings were checked with a dial bore gauge at 2.490, which would give you 0.002 main bearing clearance. Verify the clearance with Plastigauge. Even though you had sent your crankshaft out to have it turned, you need to check the clearance; do not assume it is correct. Keep a record of the clearances at each journal. Proceed as follows to check with Plastigauge before coating the bearings with the assembly lube. It is available to check different amounts of clearance; the 0.001 to 0.003 range is the most common for automotive applications.

Remove the #1 bearing cap and wipe most of the oil from the bearing and all of the oil from the journal, place a 1/4-inch piece of Plastigauge on the journal away from the oil hole, replace the cap, and torque to spec. Do not turn the crankshaft.

Remove the bearing cap and measure the clearance using the paper gauge supplied with the Plastigauge package and record the clearance.

Use a plastic spreader and clean all traces of the Plastigauge material from the journal and the bearing insert, then wipe the journal and insert with lacquer thinner to remove any traces of the foreign material. Do not use metal or any hard scrapers that may mark the journals or bearing inserts.

Repeat this with the next four main bearings. The clearance we are looking for is 0.002. We had specified both the main and rod journals to be ground 0.002 under when John took the crank. ■

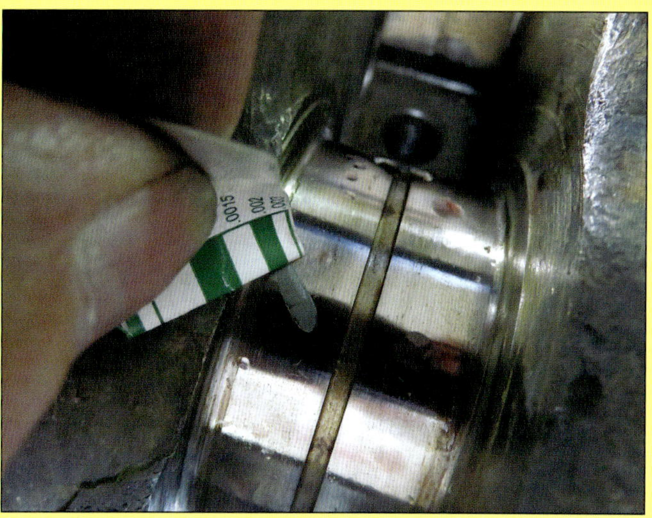

You can read the clearance from the scale on the package. In this case, it appears that the clearance is slightly less than 0.002 inch, which was calculated from the measurement of the bearing inside diameter minus the main bearing outside diameter.

Plastigauge can be very useful to check your bearing clearances. You only need a 1/4-inch-long piece. Put a light film of oil on the bearing so the Plastigauge will stick to the journal and not the insert.

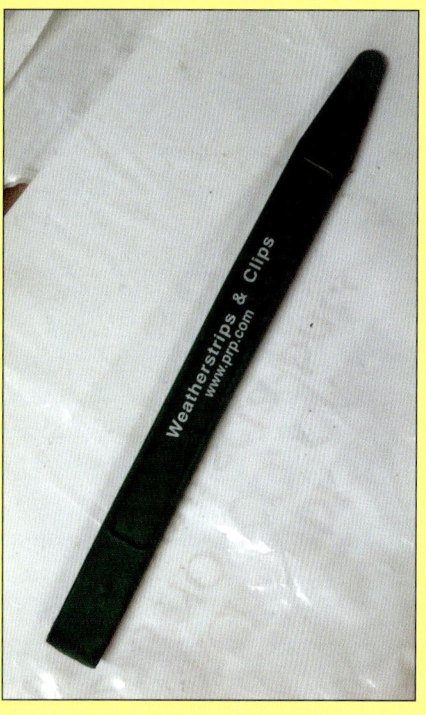

Never use any metal object to remove the material from the journal or insert. Even with a plastic scraper, such as this one, you need to be gentle. Wipe the area clean with lacquer thinner when finished and thoroughly coat the bearing with assembly lube before replacing the main cap.

When using ARP products, use their thread lubricant or thread sealant (if required) and their torque specification for that particular bolt or stud. That number is probably different from factory specifications and only applies to original bolts and without the ARP lubricant.

24 Coat the threaded portion of the ARP main cap bolts and the underside of the bolt head portion with ARP lubricant.

25 Bolt all the bearing caps in place starting with 50 ft-lbs on each bolt for the #1 cap, then the #2 cap, and turn the crankshaft by hand. Then, tighten to 80 ft-lbs and finally to the ARP specification of 100 ft-lbs.

26 Coat the side seals for the #5 main cap with Ultra Black and slide them all the way down until flush with the pan rail. Tap the nail into place to lock it.

27 When the black sealant has started to set, trim it off flush with the pan rail. The crankshaft should still turn by hand but with a little more resistance than before the rear main seal was in place. To install the pistons, use the Amsoil Assembly Lube again, as well as your break-in oil, ring compressor, Plastigauge, and rod bolt rubber sleeves. You will find that the non-adjustable ring compressors are more user friendly than the old-style adjustable units.

28 Position the engine stand with the block at 45 degrees and rotate the crankshaft to BDC for the #1 cylinder so that we can start with the #1 piston assembly.

29 Install the rod bearing inserts and leave the cap off.

The clearance between the head of the Buick bolt and the oil pump is adequate, but the ARP main bolt with the hardened washer interferes with the oil pump body. This can be corrected, but check the height of the stud to the right. There is no way that it could be made to fit under the oil pump.

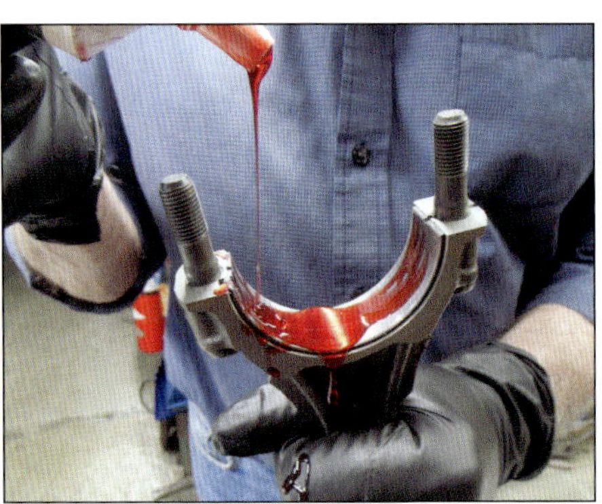

Apply a generous amount of assembly lube to the rod bearing insert prior to installation. Do not add the assembly lube to the cap insert until after you have checked clearances with Plastigauge. Remove any traces of the Plastigauge material from the bearing and the rod bearing journal before you complete the assembly.

The more you handle your pistons by cleaning them or just putting them in or out of the bag will cause the rings to move around in the ring lands. Check that the orientation of the top and second rings corresponds with the manufacturer directions prior to soaking them in oil.

Slide the piston and rod assembly into the ring compressor, wobble it around so that the rings are properly in place in the ring lands, and push the piston dome down with your thumbs until it is even with or below the top of the ring compressor.

Using rubber sleeves to protect the crankshaft from the rod bolts is a common old-school remedy. Fuel hose is simple. It works and will not deteriorate when exposed to petroleum-based products. Some generic hose will break down and leave particles that you don't want.

You need something forgiving to tap down the piston without damaging it. This is where the rubber handle grip on your hammer comes into play. These may be forged aluminum pistons, but they are still vulnerable.

30 Slide the rubber sleeves onto the rod bolts.

31 Check the orientation of the top and middle rings to verify they are positioned according to the manufacturer's guidelines.

32 Use a lint-free rag to wipe the cylinders down with oil.

33 Just before you slide on the ring compressor, thoroughly soak all the rings with your break-in oil, and then slide the ring compressor up onto the piston as you work the piston around until the rings are all captured in the compressor and the piston dome is below the top edge.

34 Put some assembly lube on the connecting rod bearing insert and slide the assembly down the top of the #1 cylinder. Be sure the valve pockets in the piston dome are facing inboard toward the camshaft.

35 Line up the connecting rod square to the rod journal and use your non-dominant hand to guide it in place as you tap it down. Use the rubber handle end of a hammer to tap the piston down. Be careful to momentarily hold the handle in place after each tap so it will capture the ring compressor when it comes free. Don't let the ring compressor ring fall to the floor. Once it is damaged, it is junk.

36 You are still supporting the end of the rod with your non-dominant hand. Use the hammer handle to catch the aluminum compressor ring and set it aside to a safe place. Continue to tap the new piston assembly down the bore until the bearing is seated on the crank journal.

37 Wipe a thin layer of oil on the rod cap insert and place a small piece of Plastigauge on the bearing insert. Be sure that it is not aligned with the oil hole in the crankshaft. The oil film will hold it in place until you install the cap. It should stick to the shaft and not the softer bearing material.

38 Tighten the rod bolts and torque them to spec, as done earlier when checking the main bearings. Don't rotate the crankshaft.

39 Remove the rod cap, check the clearance with the supplied gauge, and record the measurement. Use a plastic tool to clean the squished Plastigauge from the journal and wipe it clean with lacquer thinner. In spite of the oil on the bearing, you still need to use extra caution and clean the rod cap insert.

40 Assuming the clearance was correct, thoroughly coat the bearing with assembly lube and replace the cap.

41 Coat the rod bolt threads and the underside of the

rod bolt nuts with ARP assembly lubricant and tighten them to 30 ft-lbs, and then again to 50. When using ARP fasteners, always refer to their tightening techniques and required torque. Their specifications are very specific. In this case, it is 50 ft-lbs, while the factory manual calls for a range from 40 to 50 ft-lbs. Always follow the torque specified by the bolt manufacturer (in this case ARP specs).

The single-size ring compressors are a big improvement from the old one-size-fits-all units. As with any quality tool, you have to take care of it. As you tap in the piston and the top ring enters the cylinder, there is nothing to contain the loose compressor. When you get close to the piston leaving the compressor, keep the hammer handle in contact with the piston dome to catch the compressor.

42 Carry on installing the right-bank pistons. Then, roll the block over with the left-bank cylinders canted up at 45 degrees. Lock it in place.

43 Install the four remaining pistons following the previous procedures with one additional step. After you finish installing the companion piston and rod assembly, check the rod

side-play clearance by simply pushing the rod back and forth on the crankshaft journal to confirm there is clearance. Then use a feeler gauge to determine the clearance and record it. The connecting rod side play has nothing to do with retaining oil pressure and is not a critical measurement as long as you can feel lateral movement and the rods do not interfere with each other.

When using ARP main cap bolts, they have a taller head plus the thickness of the washer. In this case, the rear main bearing bolt interferes with the oil pump casing. If you machine 0.075 from the bolt head and file 0.050 from the pump housing, it will fit with a thinner hardened washer. The main bearing cap bolts were retorqued and will now fit the oil pump in place.

The side clearance checked out fine. You may notice that there are studs in the main caps; however, these were replaced with ARP bolts, as there was not enough clearance for studs under the oil pump housing or with the baffle in the center sump pan.

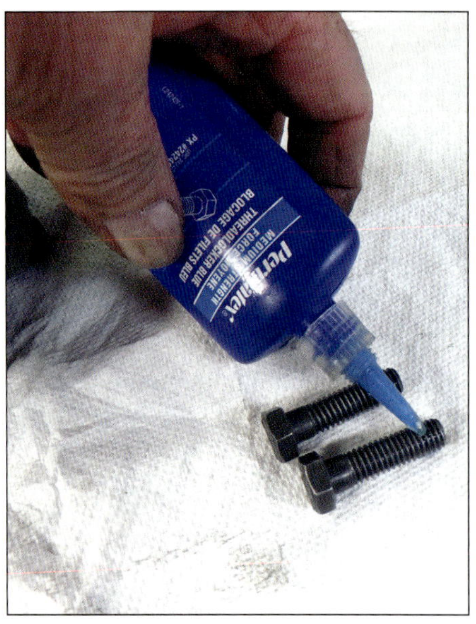

There are applications where you should use Loctite as you assemble your motor. One of these is the oil pump mounting bolts. For a race motor, I tack weld the pickup tube to the mounting flange as well. There is a lot of harmonic vibration that goes on inside a race engine crankcase.

44 Treat the pump flange bolts with Loctite and torque to 35 ft-lbs.

45 Paint the oil pan flange on the block with a good shellac-based gasket sealant that will hold the oil pan gasket in place should you need to remove it at a later date.

46 Install the oil pan and torque the bolts to 17 ft-lbs. This is out of range for most 1/2-inch-drive torque wrenches, so you need to use a 3/8-inch-drive torque wrench with a lower range to tighten these bolts. Keep in mind that if you are working at the lower or upper limits of the range for your torque wrench, chances are that it is not accurate.

The studs will act as guides when you install the heads so that they can be easily slid into place (as opposed to sliding the head around and searching for the dowel pins). They will also help keep the head gaskets in place.

Once the heads have been lowered into position and a head bolt has been screwed in, the guide studs and lifting device can be removed.

This ARP lubricant is also a sealant and should be used whenever a fastener hole is open to the cooling system. You can then be confident that there will not be any leak-back and that the fastener will be correctly torqued.

Cylinder Heads

1 Before installing your heads, check that the sealing surfaces on the block and the head are clean.

2 Use a couple of 2-inch locating studs as guides to fit the heads into position so that you don't have to slide the head around to find the dowel pins. These studs do a better job of keeping the gasket in place and protect the gasket and piston domes from damage with the head sliding around. Use the thin steel shim head gaskets for a bit more compression at this stage. They also seal better than the fiber head gaskets that come in most gasket sets.

3 For peace of mind, you can put a small dab of gasket sealant around the oil passage that feeds the rocker shafts. If you are using a fiber head gasket, you should definitely use a sealant around that oil passage.

4 As with all the other ARP fasteners, thoroughly coat the threads and the bottom side of the head of the head bolts with their Ultra Torque thread lubricant.

5 Be aware of the three center head bolt holes that go into the water jacket and that the corresponding bolts must be installed with a thread sealant. ARP has a lubricant that is also a sealant. Apply this to the threads of these three bolts and the regular lubricant under the bolt heads. It is essential to use this product to seal the three center bolts to maintain consistent torque.

6 There is a sequence to follow when tightening the head bolts starting with the center of the middle row and going in expanding clockwise circles until all the bolts are tight. Repeat that cycle with each different torque stage starting with 30, then 50, and finally to 70 ft-lbs. You can find a few alternate head bolt tightening sequences on various websites, such as Chilton or Motors Manuals, etc. What they have in common is they all start in the middle of the head and work outward. Each of these has its own merits, but the most important factor is that you follow one particular pattern and that all the bolts are torqued evenly.

When you torque the head bolts, follow a particular sequence and torque the bolts down in different stages to get even pressure across the head. Once you are finished, follow up with a second click (not a click with an extra push) to ensure all the bolts have the same torque.

Schneider's Extreme Cam Lubricant is absolutely essential in today's world of non-zinc lubricants to ensure the cam lobes and lifters can be broken in properly. Do not shortchange the cam lobes, but if you have some left over, apply it to the top of each valve stem. As you install the pushrods, put a dab of assembly lube on both ends.

This multi-keyed gear provides a lot of options to ensure the cam is indexed properly. In this case, you use the 4-degree retarded position with the 4R keyway slid onto the crank, and the 4R etched into the gear becomes the point to align with the cam gear. I have used this timing set for several years in the race car and is the most reliable of all the different sets I have tried.

This is a complete TA Performance multi-position timing gear set. Note that the cam gear keyway, the alignment dot on the cam gear, and the alignment dot on the crankshaft are in line with each other. When the cam is properly indexed, the alignment dot on the cam gear will be at the 6 o'clock position and aligned with the 4R etched into the crankshaft gear when the crankshaft is at TDC. (Photo Courtesy TA Performance)

When setting up to verify the intake opening point, the adjustable pushrod must be adjusted to zero lash on the base circle of the cam. You must use a solid lifter to do this test accurately. A hydraulic lifter will start to collapse, and you will get erratic numbers.

The cam has been reinstalled according to the 4R setting that we established in the test setup in chapter 6. However, you can never assume anything with engine assembly. Check that the valve openings correspond to the previous setup.

Camshaft and Valvetrain

You test installed the cam in chapter 6 to check for piston-to-valve clearance and to degree the cam to establish the correct keyway position in the crankshaft sprocket for the correct cam timing. For the final installation, you will need the cam installation tool, Schneider's Extreme Cam Lubricant, a drive hub with the degree wheel, a solid lifter, an adjustable pushrod, and a dial indicator.

1 Wipe some assembly lube in each of the cam bearings.

2 As you insert the cam, thoroughly coat each lobe with Schneider's Extreme Cam Lubricant.

3 When the cam is almost in, coat the bearing journals with assembly lube.

4 Finish installing the cam with the keyway at the 6 o'clock position.

5 Using the drive hub, bring the crankshaft to TDC.

6 Slide the cam gear halfway along the installation tool with the timing chain hanging loose and the timing indicator also at the 6 o'clock position. Set the crankshaft gear in the chain with the 4R keyway aligned with the crankshaft keyway.

7 Slide the chain and gear assembly all the way into position on the crankshaft and camshaft.

8 Set up a rocker-arm shaft on the left bank with a solid lifter and adjustable pushrod on the #1 intake lobe.

9 Test the fit of the pushrod by turning it between your fingers at several positions to verify zero clearance on the cam base circle. Adjust it to be loose enough to spin with your fingers but not be sloppy. This will be your base length to compare with stock-length pushrods and determine if new pushrods should be ordered.

10 Mount your dial indicator on the valve retainer set at zero with the valve closed. When monitoring the valve opening and closing from the valve retainer, the actual 0.050 reading should be taken at 0.077 lift.

11 Rotate the crankshaft through a complete cycle to verify the #1 intake opening at 1.5 degrees ATDC and closing at 35 degrees ABDC.

12 Once you have confirmed that the cam is indexed in the correct position as determined from the original setup, carry on bolting the fuel pump eccentric onto the front of the cam. Use blue Loctite on the retaining bolt and torque to 65 ft-lbs.

Even if you do not plan to use the mechanical fuel pump, the fuel pump eccentric is necessary to hold the cam gear onto the camshaft. This is another situation where you need to use a locking compound on the threads. If a mechanical pump is to be used in the future, the eccentric needs to be properly secured.

As insurance, add a liberal coating of cam lube to the face of the lifters prior to installation and use the remainder of Schneider's Extreme Cam Lubricant to coat each valve stem. Coat the pushrod ends with assembly lube when you are ready to install them.

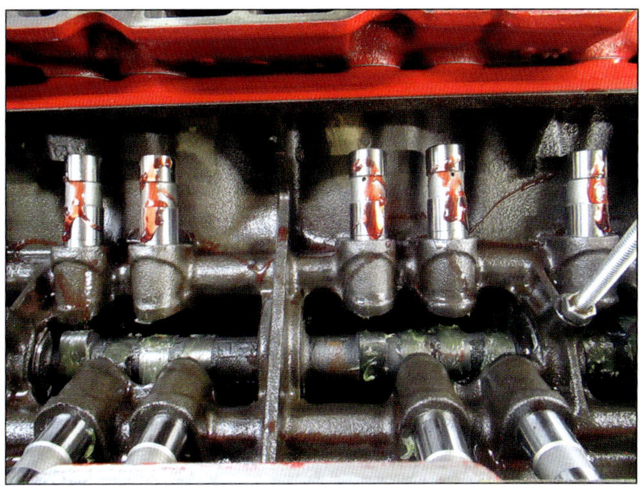

After the lifters are set in position, add a coating of assembly lube and slide them around as you push each one down onto the cam lobe. These should get lubricated when you pre-lube the motor, but it is good insurance to get some there now.

As with all the other bolts that are torqued, apply ARP thread lubricant to the threads and under the bolt heads to ensure even pressure on the rocker-arm shaft.

If you use the factory-style rocker arms that slide back and forth across the valve stems, they will also benefit from the assistance of Schneider's Extreme Cam Lubricant on the valve stems. If you use roller rockers, assembly lube is the correct lubricant here.

When you install your rocker arm shaft assembly, it is a good practice to feel how the pushrods go into the rocker arm sockets. You are doing this blind because of the Nailhead rocker-arm geometry. When you use a higher-lift cam, this becomes even more important. Verifying that the pushrods are in place by feel is the best approach.

Don't forget to install this deflector under the positive crankcase ventilation (PCV) valve location. It is difficult to visually check if your pushrods are seated in the rocker arms, but if you leave it off, a lot of oil is going to be sucked away by the PCV valve. This is not an environmentally responsible thing to do.

13 Remove the rocker shaft with the test lifter and pushrod and reapply some more cam lube to the #1 intake lobe and to the face of the new lifters.

14 Add assembly lube to the lifter bodies as you slide them into place.

15 Put a dab of cam lube on the top of each valve tip and pushrod.

16 Apply ARP thread lubricant to your rocker-arm shaft bolt threads and under the bolt heads. Fit the new shafts into place on the heads, ensuring that each pushrod is in the rocker-arm socket.

17 Start tightening the shaft bolts evenly and visually check that the pushrods are in place. You may want to use a mirror to get a better look. It may be easier to use your finger under each rocker to feel for the pushrod position.

18 After the bolts are tight but not yet torqued, remove the two center bolts on the right bank and install the deflector shield that goes under the PCV valve. This will prevent excessive oil from being sucked away with the vapors.

19 Continue to torque these bolts to 35 ft-lbs. If you are using a solid-lifter camshaft and/or adjustable rocker arms, leave the deflector shield off and cap the hole. Mount your PCV valve in the valley cover, but you must have a means to restrain oil droplets. The pre-1959 valley covers had deflector shields with steel-wool arrester material to capture those oil droplets. All you need is a rubber bushing to adapt the PCV valve to the old blow-by tube fitting.

20 It will be easier to remove and replace the valve covers by installing 5/16 national coarse studs in the heads. You may need different lengths depending on which valve covers you use. Studs don't work with the valley cover as you have to remove the intake manifold each time you need to remove the valley cover. Use a good, strong gasket cement and only apply it to the sealing surface of the valve covers so the gasket stays with the cover when it is removed. You do not need to replace it each time you pull the cover off. Fasten the covers down with 10 ft-lbs using a 1/4-inch-drive,

inch-pound torque wrench at 120 in-lbs to tighten.

Apply assembly lube to your new timing chain at alternating positions and different intervals to ensure that the chain is well soaked and will not be dry before the engine is started. Just before you install the timing cover, make sure that the oil defector is in front of the crankshaft gear.

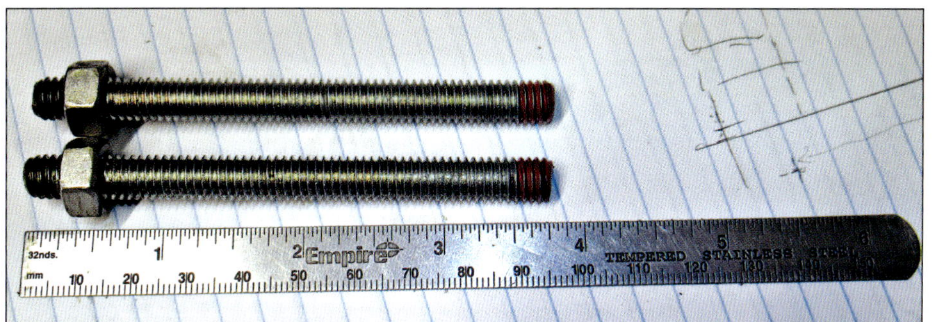

Use studs in place of your valve cover hold-down bolts. You will find it so much easier to drop the valve cover back into place. You will appreciate this even more with a solid-lifter motor where you routinely need to adjust valves. Use an appropriate-length of 5/16-inch NC all-thread rod and lock them in place with thread locker and a jam nut.

If you get your valve cover studs cut at the right length, it makes for a cleaner look and is easier for you to guide the valve cover into position. Be careful not to catch the gasket on one of the studs as you move the valve cover on or off.

Corrosion between the aluminum timing cover, the water pump housings, and the bolts that hold them in place is a serious concern with the later Nailheads. Powder coating the fasteners is not the solution, but it may help to somewhat to isolate them from the aluminum castings.

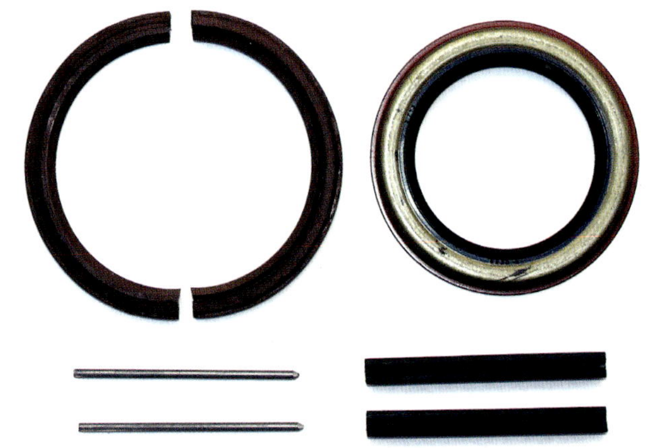

We no longer have to rely on the old-fashioned rope seals for the rear main bearing journal or the front seal in the timing cover. Some of the newer gasket kits may come with these seals or you can get a complete set from Nailhead dealers such as Centerville Auto Repair. (Photo Courtesy Centerville Auto Repair)

We were fortunate to have a good original timing cover on hand. Good originals are becoming scarce. It is reassuring to see a quality replacement from TA Performance. (Photo Courtesy TA Performance)

Many of the water pump housings fell victim to the same type of corrosion that occurs with the aluminum timing covers because they are in direct contact with coolant. These fasteners were also powder coated as a preventative measure. (Photo Courtesy TA Performance)

Timing Cover

1 Knock out the tin ring that held the old rope seal in the timing cover and toss it in your scrap bin. As I mentioned earlier about the rear main seal, don't even think of using the original rope-type seals. The Nailhead dealers have new neoprene seals available at a reasonable price. Some of the newer gasket sets may come with them.

2 Press your new seal into the timing cover and set it aside.

3 Prior to installing the timing cover, thoroughly soak the timing chain and gears in assembly lube. Using the drive hub, crank the motor over by hand, coat the chain and gears again with the assembly lube, and return it to top dead center.

4 Remove the drive hub and temporary timing indicator and set them aside.

5 Apply a thin coat of Ultra Black to the back side of the timing cover and the corresponding sealing area of the block and the exposed oil pan gasket.

6 Add an extra dab of sealant at the bottom corners of the timing cover by the oil pan. Be sure there is good coverage around each of the water inlets to the block.

7 Use a 2-inch set screw as a guide on the right side and set the timing cover gasket in place over the dowel and the guide screw. Then, install the timing cover.

8 Apply anti-seize to the bolt threads and start them all by hand to ensure the gasket is aligned correctly before tightening.

9 Use your 3/8-drive torque wrench to tighten these bolts to 18 ft-lbs.

10 Apply Ultra Black to the water pump flange and the timing cover. Use a stud along with the dowel to locate the gasket until the pump is put in place. Torque the 5/16 bolts to 18 ft-lbs. The 1/4-inch-fasteners only require 8 ft-lbs or 96 in-lbs. This is not much pressure and is a good opportunity to get out your 1/4-inch-drive torque wrench. With these small bolts and the small amount of torque required, it is easy to see why the water pump bolt holes get stripped out of the timing cover. As with the timing cover, these bolts were powder coated in an effort to minimize corrosion. Use a liberal amount of never-seize on these threads as well.

The aluminum thermostat housing is the third and final victim of the most serious coolant-related corrosion. The other aluminum components are less of a concern. Once again, the reproduction manufacturers have come to our rescue with new housings such as this one available from TA Performance. (Photo Courtesy TA Performance)

Intake Manifold

Installing the intake manifold is pretty straightforward. It has an exhaust crossover that was intended to enhance warm up from a cold start and warm the fuel for better vaporization and therefore better fuel economy. However, the exhaust gases can be very corrosive depending on how well tuned the motor is. Usually the crossover passages get plugged but hopefully are fixed before there is any damage from the corrosion.

The preferred method of isolating the exhaust flow is with stainless inserts at the intake manifold flange or using NPT pipe plugs threaded into the exhaust passages below the carburetor flange.

You can resume using stainless steel bolts to fasten the manifold, as it is remote from the coolant system. Remember to use nickel-based anti-seize with the SS fasteners. Include the kick-down switch bracket when bolting on the manifold and torque to 35 ft-lbs. Set the studs in the carb flange of the intake manifold with red Loctite to ensure that they are locked in permanently for locating the carb and gasket. Set the carburetor in place and torque the nuts to 18 ft-lbs.

For ease of installation, use studs to locate the intake gaskets and manifold. Once they are in place, remove the studs and insert the bolts. You could leave the studs in place and secure the manifold with nuts depending on what visual affect you want. Note that the exhaust crossover passages in this manifold have already been blocked off at the base of the carburetor flange with 1/8-inch NPT plugs at the carburetor flange.

Reproduction dampers, such as this one from TA Performance, are another welcome addition from the aftermarket parts suppliers. When you are working with 60-year-old parts, you have to scrutinize them carefully for your safety and to produce a quality rebuild. (Photo Courtesy TA Performance)

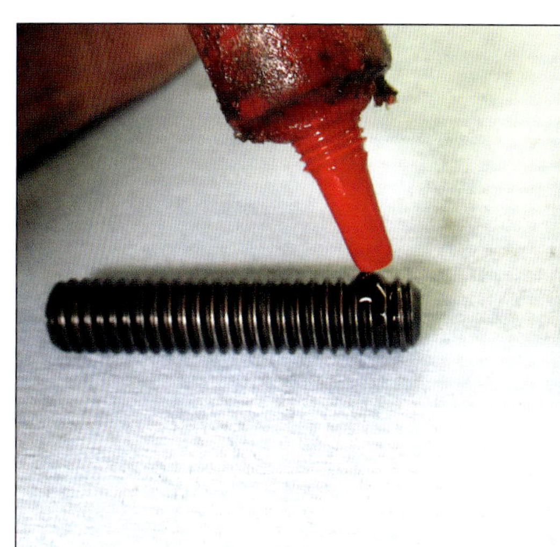

Install 5/16 NCx1½-inch socket set screws in the carb base. Thread 1/4-inch of the stud into the manifold with red Loctite and lock it in place with a jam nut. This will make it much easier for you to remove and replace the carb. The socket stud provides a clean method of removing the stud (should the need arise) without using Vise-Grips or a stud remover.

A locking compound is your best friend when fastening any components directly to the rotating assembly in the new motor, including the flexplate, crankshaft pulley, and especially the water pump pulley and fan. Use lock washers with these parts. You might not like it so much when you try to undo these fasteners, but it sure beats the alternative.

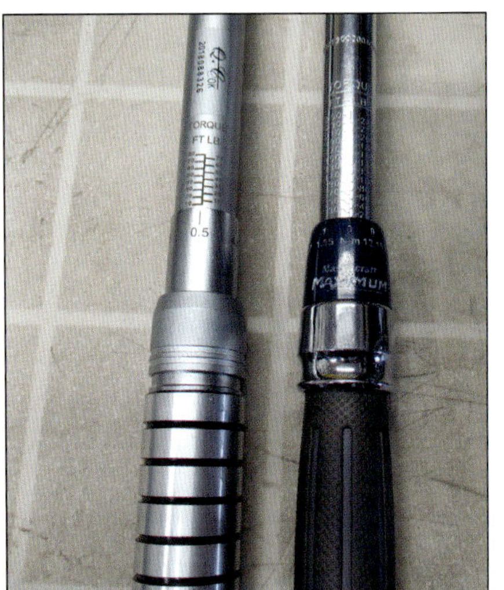

You may think that the torque specified for the damper is excessive, but bear in mind that torque requirements increase exponentially relative to the bolt size. It is important to apply the specified torque to retain the balancer. If you do not have a torque wrench in the range that you need, borrow or rent one.

In a perfect world, we would always use new bolts, but there are situations where we reuse some fasteners. Whether it is bolts, nuts, or even the engine block, only use thread chasers to prepare these parts. If you feel that it is necessary to use taps or dies to correct the thread, have a closer look. There may be more to that problem.

Harmonic Balancer and Flexplate

1 The flexplate is the next piece of the puzzle, but first slide the harmonic balancer onto the nose of the crankshaft and check that the timing marker on the balancer corresponds with the zero position on the timing cover. All Buick crankshafts have a faux dowel pinhole in the rear flange with an apparent receiver hole in the flexplate or flywheel. These are meant as a guide only to ensure correct orientation and should be aligned.

Now that you have the flexplate and the damper torqued to specifications, it should be the last time to use the locking device. Be sure to remove it.

When you want to verify TDC, the stock Buick balancer does not have gradients in degrees. Use one of these plastic tape measures from Ikea or a cloth tape if you have one. The millimeter increments shown here are much the same as a scale of degrees to reference the TDC.

As you can see here, it appears that the factory mark was right on the money. In spite of that, this is something that you need to check on any motor. You cannot take this for granted. There could be a factory error or the dampening rubber may have deteriorated and the balancer has slipped.

2 Install the flexplate and use blue Loctite. Torque the bolts to 40 ft-lbs, then install a crankshaft locking device and finish torqueing the bolts to 65 ft-lbs. Do not use the locking device with the bolts loose because it will put a side load on the bolts and distort the torque readings.

3 Turn the device around to prevent rotation in the opposite direction and tighten the balancer retaining bolt to 200 ft-lbs. Use blue Loctite here as well.

4 Attach the front crankshaft pulley, water pump pulley, and fan using blue Loctite and torque these fasteners to 18 ft-lbs.

5 Up to this point, you relied on the temporary marker and degree wheel to indicate TDC. Now you want to confirm the accuracy of the TDC mark on the harmonic balancer relative to the indicating marks on the timing cover. Use a cloth tape with metric measurements and tape it onto the balancer with the 10-cm point aligned with TDC. As much as you may not like the metric system, you will find it more user friendly in this situation. You can use either a dial indicator setup on the top of the piston or a stopper screwed into the spark plug hole and follow the same sequence that you used in chapter 6. All you need to do now is verify that the factory mark on your harmonic balancer is accurate and, in this instance, the mark was correct.

Before you install the distributor, check the relationship of the direction the rotor is pointing relative to the oil pump drive tang. Check the orientation of the oil pump drive slot in the top of oil pump shaft. You can reposition this with a long screwdriver to coordinate with the rotor pointing at the rear hold-down bolt for the right-bank valve cover. Lower the distributor into place and be sure you have the oil pump fully engaged.

Distributor

1 Before you install the distributor, remove the right-bank valve cover.

2 Turn the motor over by hand until the intake valve closes. Then, bring it up to TDC, and put the valve cover back on.

3 Stand at the rear of the motor and hold the distributor over the mounting hole with the rotor at the 1 o'clock position.

4 Put the distributor down in place. As it engages with the cam gear, the rotor should turn to 2 o'clock and be pointed at the rear hold-down stud of the right valve cover. As often as not, the distributor will not go all the way into position because the oil pump shaft did not engage.

5 If the oil pump did not engage, remove the distributor and use a long screwdriver to reposition the pump shaft.

6 Once it has a satisfactory fit, give the drive gear a good coating of assembly lube and put the distributor back in place with the clamp bolted down lightly. Mark the outside of the distributor cap with number tape to indicate where the rotor is pointing for the number-1 cylinder.

It is a good practice for you to establish a reference starting point when installing your spark plug wires and when you need to connect your timing light. Make a habit of aligning the distributor with the #1 plug terminal in line with the rear hold-down bolt for the right valve cover. By doing this and following it routinely, you will quickly establish a pattern and an intimate familiarity with your new Nailhead.

BREAK-IN

Our intention with this motor is to run it through a break-in cycle on the Dynojet 248 chassis dynamometer at Forrest & Forrest Racing. They fabricated an engine cart on which to mount the motor and made mounts to fit various engines, including our trusted Nailhead. Let's not get too far ahead of ourselves and get back to the garage and get our new motor ready to be shipped and ready to run. The assembly work was completed in chapter 7. In addition to equipment that you already used, you will need an oil pump driver, a 1/2-inch-drive drill, and engine break-in oil.

I use Amsoil break-in oil because it is synthetic and has the high levels of zinc and phosphorus additives that are essential during the break-in period for flat-tappet motors. It also eases the transition for fully synthetic oil beyond the initial break-in.

Engine Preparation for Break-In

1 Connect a mechanical oil pressure gauge to the oil passage port at the rear of the passenger-side head in the bell-housing flange. This will only be used to monitor oil pressure when priming the motor. Forrest & Forrest has its own fittings to connect the gauge.

2 Confirm that the motor was set up at top dead center (TDC) at the end of chapter 7 with the rotor pointed at the rear hold-down bolt for the passenger-side valve cover. Remove the distributor hold-down clamp and remove the distributor. Make note of the rotor position as the distributor gear disengages from the cam gear. Also make note of the oil pump shaft position.

3 Fill the engine with 30-weight Amsoil break-in oil and check for leaks. In response to environmental concerns, the zinc content has been deleted from both petro-leum- and synthetic-based motor oils; however, that zinc content

It feels good to start adding oil to a fresh new motor. It is a sign of getting to the end of a project.

is essential for the break-in period of any flat-tappet motor. Be sure to get a break-in oil with added zinc. After the break-in period, a regular 20- or 30-weight synthetic oil can be used. A multi-grade oil is only necessary if the vehicle will be used year-round in a colder climate.

4 Install the oil pump driver with the 1/2-inch drill attached. Run the drill clockwise for about a minute to fill the oil filter. Then, top up the oil level.

5 Remove both passenger- and driver-side rocker-arm covers.

6 This step will take several minutes, and you may need a helper at this point to

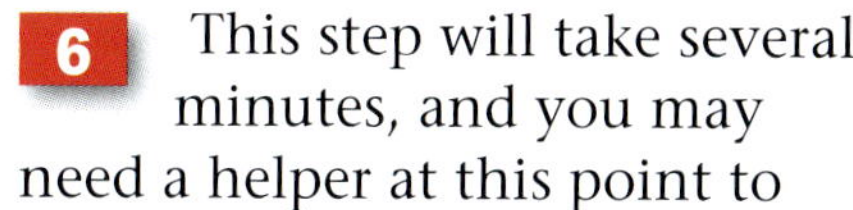

The oil pressure ran up to 45 psi when priming the pump to fill up the oil filter.

The oil supply is fed from the #1 cam bearing through the passages to each lifter bank, and a second passage runs from these up to the most forward rocker shaft stand on each head. You know you're done when oil begins to drip from the #7 and #8 exhaust rocker arms. They are the last ones in line to get oil.

The oil pump driveshaft is simply an old distributor shaft that has been shortened and cut off just below the cam for the points. The bushing is made from a leftover piece of stock used to make suspension bushings. It makes for much better control when running up the oil pressure.

watch for oil leaking from #7 and #8 exhaust rocker arms. Run the drill continually until the reading on the pressure gauge settles in at a maximum level. Continue until there is oil dripping from both of the monitored rocker arms. Once you have oil at these points, you can rest assured the motor is primed as they are at the end of the oil supply system.

7 Remove the oil pump driver. Then, replace both valve covers, and top up the oil level again if required.

8 Remove the oil pressure gauge and fittings, then temporarily plug the oil supply port with a 1/8-inch NPT plug to keep dirt out.

Mark both the distributor body and cap as a reference to where the rotor is pointed as a guide to estimate the initial timing and a start point for installing plug wires.

9 Reset the oil pump shaft to the position you noted when the distributor was removed.

Standing at the back of the motor and looking down the distributor hole, you can see the slot in the oil pump shaft is at the 11 o'clock position. You can easily reposition the shaft with a long screwdriver as needed to put the distributor back in place.

Looking from the rear of the motor, the rotor returned to the 12 o'clock position as the gear disengaged the cam gear when the distributor was removed.

10 Reset the rotor to the noted removal position. As you are ready to install the distributor, pour some assembly lube on the gear. When the distributor is installed, it should go into place and engage easily if the rotor and oil pump shaft were set up correctly. Install the distributor clamp, but only tighten the bolt so that it is snug enough to prevent easy movement but you

can turn it with some effort. You will have to adjust the timing once the motor is running.

The rotor returned to the initial 2 o'clock position when the distributor was replaced. Check how deep the distributor body settled into the block to determine if it is fully inserted before installing the distributor clamp.

11 Rotate the distributor so that the vacuum advance is pointed perpendicular to the front-to-rear axis of the motor and install the cap. Mark which terminal is closest to aligning with the rotor as #1 and extend the mark to the distributor housing. Move the distributor so it appears to be correctly aligned with the rotor and turn it counterclockwise about 1/4 inch. This should get you close enough to get the motor started.

12 The spark plugs of choice for this motor are NKG XR4 with the gaps set to 0.035 inch. Because this is a brand-new engine, put a small dab of Permatex Anti-Seize on the plug threads. Install the plugs with 20 ft-lbs torque. To index the spark plugs, mark each plug with a Sharpie to indicate which direc-

These are the new NKG plugs compared to an Autolite racing plug. Whenever getting new plugs, check that the terminal at the top of the plug is screwed tightly to the electrode. If this is loose, it can be the source of a miss. You will periodically get new plugs, but this terminal is loose.

This one of the racing plugs. Note that the stripe on the porcelain is in line with the ground strap. This plug has been indexed and numbered for a dedicated cylinder.

tion the ground electrode is pointing. Then, test fit each plug until you get one that points at the exhaust valve. Continue fitting the plugs until you have exhausted the supply of those that align with the exhaust. At this point, resort to using spacers to correct the positioning of the remaining plugs. Number each plug with a fine-tip Sharpie so that you don't have to repeat indexing. That being said, this is a good practice with a race engine, but it's not worthwhile with a street motor.

Silicon grease is a good way to seal the plug wire boots to the spark plug. At the other end, seal the boot to the cap terminal. This is a good practice to adopt, particularly if you live in an area with cold winters or high humidity.

13 Install the spark plug wires starting with #1 as marked on the distributor cap. Remember, Nailheads have their own firing order (1-2-7-8-4-5-6-3) and the cylinders are numbered front to rear with 1-3-5-7 on the passenger's side and the driver's side assigned 2-4-6-8. Start with the #1 marked on the distributor cap and work your way around clockwise according to the firing order.

14 Any accessories, including the alternator and fan, must be removed before the motor can be run on the dynamometer. Without a tensioning device left in the system, you will need a 33x3/8-inch V-belt to run the water pump directly from the crankshaft pulley.

Secure the cooling system by using a jumper hose from the coolant supply outlet at the water pump to the return fitting at the base of the thermostat.

A NAPA 3L330W belt is a tight fit to drive the water pump without the aid of tension adjustment. Keep this in a dedicated location so you don't end up wandering around your shop to look for it when another trip to an engine dynamometer comes up.

15 Before you transport your new engine to be broken in, put a hat on the carburetor and plug any orifices that you do not want debris to get into.

16 The exhaust ports have been plugged off with half-sheets of paper towels, which is adequate for transport; they will self-eject when the motor fires. Take a pair of exhaust manifolds with a short piece of exhaust pipe or headers to connect to the exhaust hoses at the dynamometer.

The same logic applies to the vacuum lines at the rear of the carburetor, except we need to maintain the PCV function.

The vacuum ports on the carburetor need to be sealed from dirt when transporting the motor and to prevent a vacuum leak during break-in. The fuel inlet needs to be plugged and kept clean until needed.

The motor is ready for transport with a lifting rig in place for loading and unloading. The stand is necessary to keep the motor stable during transport and provides decent tie-down connections.

Setting up the motor in the cart is routine for Paul and Glen. Although, in this case, new front mounts had to be fabricated because previous Nailheads were equipped with a front motor plate.

Now that the motor is up and running, it is easy to see how a fan or any accessories would be a safety issue unless a significant amount of time is spent fabricating guards. Those items would also present an obstacle course for Glen to make the water connections or access the timing marks.

It is a good thing that Paul and Glen have better hearing than I do when the motor is running without mufflers. This new rocker arm didn't last very long, which was frustrating, but this was a much better place for it to fail than when Dave is driving down the road. It was an easy fix, and we were back up running.

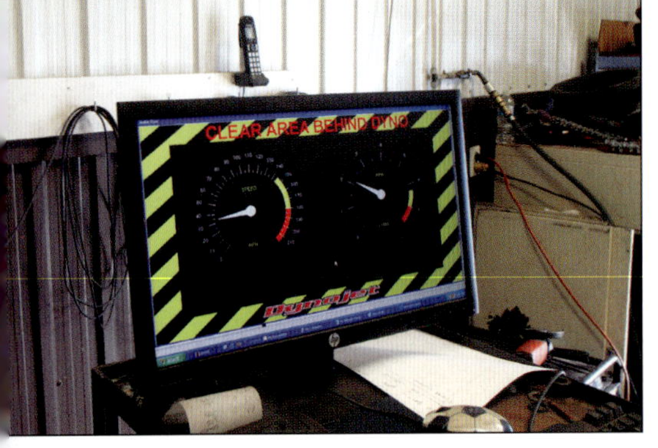

Paul held the RPM steady at 2,100 for the next 25 minutes. The temperature stayed at 160 to 170 degrees, and the oil pressure held at 45 psi throughout the break-in period.

Paul has a good practice of inserting a screen at the filter to pre-filter the oil supply from the pump. We only found a few pieces of fluff and no metallic particles, which is good news. You may feel a little embarrassed to see anything at all, and you may want to enhance your pre-cleaning and assembly practices, which is always a good approach. Most people will not show you this screen for the above reason, but this is actually good to compare yours to others.

17 The motor must be mounted on a secure stand so that it can be properly tied down for transport. Considering the weight of an engine, it should always be located as centrally as possible for transport to minimize any affects it may have on braking or steering. I have seen too many instances of a motor being set on an old tire in the very back of a pickup so that it will be easy to unload. That is waiting for a potential bad-braking situation that catapults the engine into the back of the cab. You also need a lifting device to hook onto the motor.

Once you arrive at the shop (in this case, Forrest & Forrest) technicians will unload the motor and set it up on a cart made to run an engine on a chassis dynamometer. They will hook up the shop's radiators and cooling system to the water pump inlet and thermostat outlet. Next, they will connect the electric fuel pump directly to the carburetor.

The shop will also have a drive connection with a self-contained starter motor that goes from the transmission and connects directly to the crankshaft flange. The technicians will install the headers we supplied and hook the extension

Dave is happy, and we are headed for home. Note that the motor is secured front and center in the truck. We were not quite ready to leave at this point because the weather was overcast, so the motor was protected with a plastic cover before we left.

hoses on to vent the exhaust gases outside. When the computer, distributor, and oil pressure sending unit are wired, they are ready to go. A pre-filter screen is inserted between the filter housing and the filter element. When this motor was tested, Paul sat in the cart, hit the starter, the motor fired up right away, and the oil pressure went right up to 47 psi. Glen was ready with his timing light to adjust the timing, and then they heard some noise from the motor and shut it down right away.

One of the new rocker arms had broken, but there was no other damage. It was replaced, and the motor restarted. The dis-

tributor had been set up with 1 degree of mechanical advance at 950 rpm and 12 degrees all in at 2,400 rpm. The initial timing was set at 8 degrees BTDC to achieve maximum power at 32 degrees of total advance. The vacuum advance was not used because it would be redundant when the turbocharger is added. Paul held the RPM at 2,100 for the next 25 minutes (which were uneventful), and the break-in was complete. The oil filter was removed to check the pre-filter screen. It was relatively clean, and there were no metallic particles.

The motor is now ready for the owner to take home and install.

BUILDING A NAILHEAD RACING ENGINE

The chapters leading up to this have been dedicated to building a performance street engine. The work practices required for that project all apply to assembling a race motor with some additional emphasis on part preparation and a different approach to tolerances. The number of Nailhead enthusiasts who are planning a future race engine project or who are currently racing one of these motors is a very small group.

The whole purpose of writing this book is to share some of my racing experiences and the things that I have learned from racing Nailheads for the past 18 years. I have no secrets. There is no "I am smarter or faster than you are" nonsense. I only hope that in some small way I might contribute to your success and enjoyment racing one of these motors.

The approach that Harold Watson and I took when we built the roadster was pretty basic. We were committed to using the latest in 1950s technology, to go as quick as we could, and to have as much fun as we could afford. We could not afford, nor did we have any desire, to delve into a high-tech, high-dollar electronic vehicle. Could we have made more horsepower with an electronic ignition versus a magneto? Yeah. Well, maybe. Could we have made more horsepower with electronic fuel injection? Obviously. But that was outside our mandate. Had we gone that route, could we have then been competitive with big-block Chevrolets, Rodecks, or Hemis? Absolutely not. So, we carried on throughout the whole project by following our intuition, trial and error, and fabricating anything and everything that we felt may give us a little more speed, and had a hoot doing it.

I have had the privilege of learning from two gentlemen. The most important influence with the race motor and racing etiquette came from Jack "The Motor Man" Greenhalgh.

I first met Jack on the Bonneville Salt Flats in 1988 where he

Tammy 10 *was a notorious super-modified that was raced throughout Michigan, Ontario, and Ohio from the 1950s to the 1970s. Most of the credit went to driver Harvey Lennox, but he could not have done this without support from the crew, especially Johnson's motors.*

was helping a mutual friend with his race car. I had spent the previous 10 years pitting with and learning from other racers that I had met during that period when I stumbled across this vehicle with Canadian license plates. I stopped and introduced myself to Gerry Davis and his crew, and he introduced me to this other Canadian, Jack Greenhalgh.

Oddly enough, I grew up less than 2 miles from Jack, but we had never crossed paths. His background was circle-track racing in the late 1940s as a car owner and builder. His forte was as an engine builder, and he produced motors for Canadian Association for Stock Car Auto Racing (CASCAR) racing as well as local competitors. I had grown up with drag racing and hot rods. We hit it off really well and have remained good friends to this day. He built the first Nailhead for the roadster and has mentored me with building my own engines ever since.

Harvey Lennox was the driver for the Kernahan Lumber sprint car and successfully campaigned *Tammy 10* with Nailhead power well into the 1960s. Harvey's success as a driver is well documented. However, credit for their motor was to a man named Johnson, and I unfortunately do not have any info about him. Harvey recalled that they purchased new short-blocks from General Motors, had the crankshaft polished to give them 0.003 main bearing and 0.002 rod bearing clearances, and reassembled it with Jahns pistons on the stock rods and stock oil pump. Unfortunately, I have thrown out most of that old stuff and don't have any of

If you are going to use a stroker crankshaft, you need to test fit the rotating assembly and check for clearance between the rods and the bottom of the cylinders. The main oil gallery will also interfere. Be sure to use a sonic tester to verify the material thickness as you grind clearance at this spot.

those old cast pistons left around. It would have been amusing for the younger generation to see an old piston with 0.200-inch-thick skirts that must have weighed about 1,000 grams each (close to one kilogram). This was the heart of a Hilborn-injected, alcohol-burning Nailhead that ran with an Isky roller cam and vertex mag. It routinely outran the Chevrolets and Chryslers until the late 1960s. The only engine problem that he could remember was piston breakage. They came up with a preventative maintenance plan and replaced them every 10 races.

That was almost 60 years ago. If only they could have seen some of the ultra-light pistons made today. Johnson did the motor work at home. Harvey recalled

that once when they were racing in Ohio in the mid-1960s, there was a man dressed in a suit wandering through the pits, which was odd enough to make anyone curious about who the person was. Anyway, he approached their pit and wanted to know who owned the race car and where they got those heads. Being somewhat suspicious of this person walking around the pits at a stock car dirt track in a suit, Harvey replied that he took them off a car in a scrap yard. The man didn't buy that, but Harvey stuck with his story saying that they came off of a Canadian Buick. He later heard that the person in the suit was the manager of Buick's experimental division in Flint, Michigan. When they returned home to London, Ontario, he found out that Johnson had a brother-in-law who worked in Buick's experimental division. Harvey told me this story in the early 1990s. That Nailhead was long gone and had been replaced with a big-block Chevrolet about 20 years earlier. He had no recollection of where the old motor went, and I have looked high and low with no luck finding the engine that came out of *Tammy 10*. You can try to connect the dots and guess which heads were on that motor.

I might as well start off this section from the bottom upward with the engine block. I saw friends and other members in our local car club painting the inside of their engine blocks with glyptol on the pretense of sealing the rough casting and improving the oil return flow. I was a little skeptical and thought that the paint could come loose and possibly plug the oil pump pickup.

Around the same time, I read an article about how grinding and polishing the surface of a casting would relieve stress. I was working on a job out of town for about six months with lots spare time on my hands and met another car guy, Steve Glibota. Thanks to Steve's hospitality, I had a place to work. Returning from my next trip home, I came back with a bare block, die grinder, and sanding drums.

I spent all of my spare time over the next several weeks grinding and polishing all of the rough casting inside the block. When I brought the block back at the end of the job, Jack took one look and said, "If you're going to stress relief the inside, then why don't you do the outside too?"

Thanks to Jack and Steve, preparing my own heads and blocks now includes grinding and polishing all of the castings inside and out.

That is the beginning of the learning process if you are going racing with a Nailhead. I don't care how much money you have available for this project. You cannot run down to Performance Improvements and purchase an extra 10 or 20 hp for your racing Nailhead. You can get your ARP fasteners and fuel lines and order a Hilborn setup and stuff there, but for the most part, you are going to have to learn how to improvise and fabricate. If you can do that, the world is at your fingertips.

At the beginning of this book, the discussion was about how you could rebuild a couple of small-block Chevrolets for what it is going to cost you to rebuild your performance Nailhead. The discussion will now move on to building a Nailhead race motor. Using what Nailhead race parts are available commercially will get you a respectable entry-level race engine in today's world. You will still to have fabricate or have parts made, such as scatter shields and headers. As with any kind of race motor, the further you want to go, the cost will increase exponentially. Follow your dreams.

Getting Started

1 Now that we are talking about race block preparation, some things are no different from any rebuild. Magnaflux the block to check for cracks or

Polishing the block can be a tedious and time-consuming job and is certainly more than just removing casting flashing and inclusions. It will improve oil return flow back to the oil pan and will also help improve the strength of the block by removing minor faults.

This crankshaft has been welded and ground for a 3.89 stroke and then nitrided by John at Canadian Chromeplating and Crankshaft. The rod journals were ground to 2.198 to accept big-block Chevrolet bearings and connecting rods.

flaws. Next, do a sonic test on each cylinder to determine if there has been any corrosion or core shifting that will eliminate this block as a good candidate. Be sure to check each cylinder at four quadrants and at the top, middle, and bottom of each.

2 The amount of grinding and polishing to do on your castings is up to you. I prefer to do all of the exterior and interior surfaces. At the very least, you must remove the vagrant flashing as we did in chapter 6. The final finish was with 120-grit sanding drums. If you are going to use a stroker crankshaft, you will also need to grind clearance in the center oil gallery and notch the bottom of the cylinders to clear the rod bolts. You must use a sonic tester to check the thickness of the main oil gallery.

3 Directions about how to tap the oil galleries for 3/8-inch NPT plugs were also partially covered in chapter 6. In addition to that information, you can tap the center frost plug in either side of the block for a 1½-inch NPT, which I will explain a little later. Do some port matching with the oil passages to and from the filter housing and clean up the oil flow route to the pushrod holes through the heads.

4 It is time to send the block and heads to the machine shop. They will send these parts out to be cleaned by baking and then shot-blasted.

5 Prior to boring and finish honing the cylinders, the water jackets in the block were filled up to an inch from the top with block fill to stabilize the cylinders. Before the material was added, a sock of sand was inserted to maintain a coolant passage from the center frost plug up toward the deck.

6 The machine shop will then proceed with the following machine work:

- bore and hone the cylinders to fit the pistons
- deck the block for zero deck clearance
- mill the heads
- cut the block and heads for O-rings if using copper head gaskets
- lighten the pistons
- machine the connecting rods for side clearance if using Chevrolet bearings
- resize connecting rods and install bronze bushings
- install cam bearings and fit the camshaft
- crankshaft ground for 0.003 main clearance and 0.002 rod bearing clearance
- balance the rotating assembly
- align bore only if required
The heads will then be sent to the head specialist to do the machine work and porting.
- install bronze guides
- port and polish ports
- port heads to match intake and exhaust flanges
- cut 3-angle seat in heads and seat valves to a standard depth
- flow heads

When the crankshaft connecting rod journals are offset ground, there is a radius to provide strength to the shaft. If the radius is too abrupt, it can become a fracture point. If the radius is too shallow, it will cause interference with the rod bearing insert. This was also done by Canadian Chromeplating and Crankshaft.

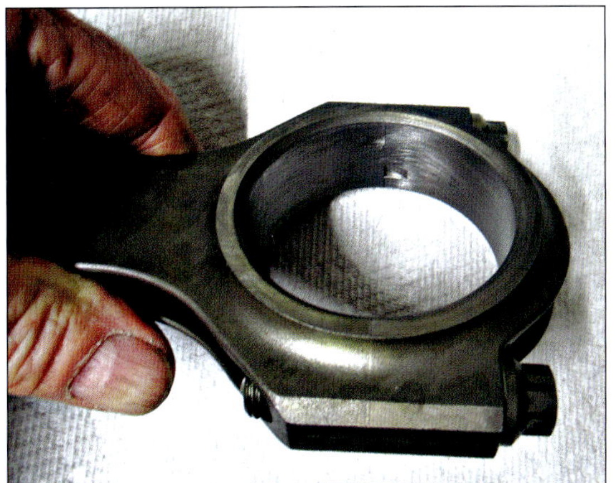

Note that the chamfer side on the rod boss is there to ensure clearance for the radius of the rod journal. When narrowing a rod, the clearance from that chamfer is important on the crankshaft side of the rod so the bearing insert clears the radius. When the rods are narrowed, the inboard side of the insert only needs to have a token amount of clearance.

Rotating Assembly

There are many options available when it comes to the rotating assembly. All Nailhead crankshafts are the same with some subtle differences. The important aspect is that they are all forged and there is no need to look for any special casting numbers. Similarly, Buick connecting rods are also forged and are more than adequate for a high-performance street engine, but it is much safer to avoid using 60-year-old rods in a race motor.

You cannot get aluminum or steel aftermarket rods for a Nailhead unless you want to step up to a high-dollar special order. However, you can get aftermarket small-block or big-block Chevrolet rods in a variety of different lengths up to 6.8 inches that can be adapted. To use either of these, the rod journals need to be turned down to 2.100 or 2.200, respectively. There are a variety rod bearings available in Chevrolet sizes that are more plentiful and usually cheaper.

While the crankshaft is being ground, use the opportunity to request an offset grind to gain up to 0.140 stroke. This is not expensive like a stroker crankshaft, which will have to be welded and ground. Both the small- and big-block Chevrolet rods are too wide and need to be machined to the Nailhead rod width of 0.965, which means about 0.009 inch of material needs to be removed from each side. The actual amount of material to remove from each side of the rod may vary with different aftermarket manufacturers.

The important factor is to keep more clearance from the outboard or crankshaft side of the rod to the bearing insert to provide clearance for the journal radius. Use an NH-series rod bearing, which is narrower than standard. You should have these on hand while machining the rods for side clearance so that you can monitor the clearance of the bearing insert from the rod journal radius. The clearance from the inboard side of the rod to the inboard side of the companion rod is not critical as long as you maintain a minimum of no less than 0.005 inch.

This all sounds kind of complicated, but it needs to be worked out as a package. The limiting factors that need to be determined

Fitting a piston as a sample mold for an order can be tedious. There was not enough aluminum in the edges of the dome of this sample piston, and the contour of the dome has been corrected with body filler. You might also note that the dome shape is not concentric to the head of the piston compared with the unaltered sample. You need to specify his and her valve recesses when placing your order.

Copper gaskets are essential if you are going to use power adders or extra-high compression. This particular set was ordered from Hussey Gaskets without water passages, so the coolant flow could be redirected. These are reusable only if kept in the original location. Properly sized holes for coolant flow have been drilled between each cylinder.

first are the finished deck height of the block and potential minimum compression height for your pistons. Consult a piston manufacturer to determine the minimum compression height with the ring package you want to use. From this information you can calculate the length of rod you need.

Some distinct advantages can be gained with the stronger aftermarket rods, such as the ability to alter your stroke-to-rod length ratio and obviously a bigger cubic-inch motor. Another benefit is when you target standard bore sizes, such as a 427 Chevrolet 4.250-inch bore. There is a whole world of ring packages available in that size depending on your intended end use. Rings for race applications may not be practical for street use, but you can gain up to an extra 20 hp by reducing parasitic drag in your race motor with the thinner rings. You cannot use those rings with off-the-shelf pistons; the ring grooves in custom pistons are cut to fit rings from a specific manufacturer.

I prefer to use zero deck clearance for race motors. Suppose you are starting with a 10.005-inch deck height (there is no correction required with zero deck clearance) and subtract half of the stroke length (3.64 / 2 = 1.820), which leaves you with 8.185 inches. A 6.8-inch rod would leave you with a 1.385 compression height for your custom piston. This leaves you a little more room to alter the deck height if needed as long as the pin does not encroach on the ring lands.

This combination provides a rod-to-stroke ratio of 1.87

compared to the stock ratio of 1.71. An increase in this ratio will enhance the torque output from the engine. As you reduce the compression height, it allows you to reduce piston weight with shorter skirts. Forged Nailhead pistons are notoriously heavy, (around 700 plus grams) because of the dome configuration, so every little bit of weight that you can eliminate helps. Don't expect to see any skimpy 500-gram pistons like you can get for small-block Fords or LS stuff.

7 Prep the block and heads and send them out for powder coating.

Pistons and Compression Ratio

You may wonder, "Why the zero deck height?" I have a lot of faith in controlling the squish or quench area to optimize combustion efficiency. The squish area also includes the sides of the dome as well as the piston deck area. This leaves a relatively small actual combustion chamber. The efficient squish area reduces the required flame travel, so you will get optimum power at a maximum 28 to 29 degrees advance. As the squish efficiency is reduced, the necessary spark advance to achieve maximum power can increase to as much as 32 or 33 degrees.

Originally, I made combustion chamber molds of Bondo, then tried fiberglass, and sent them in with piston orders but was never completely satisfied with the fit. More recently I have spent a significant amount of time hand-filing and fitting

piston domes to zero clearance using layout dye as a guide when fitting a head in place without a gasket. Continue this filing and fitting repeatedly until there is a near perfect fit. Send this sample piston to accompany your order. Through this process, I finally got exactly what was ordered from Racetec. This was the lightest out-of-the-box piston I had ever received, and the bonus was no additional file fitting required. Diamond Pistons has since been able to reproduce this piston.

Use 0.042-inch-thick copper head gaskets with the previously fitted domes to achieve the desired quench area; I believe 0.040 to 0.045 is an optimum for squish. The deck has been cut for

0.042 SS O-rings and the heads have a corresponding receiver groove. The copper gaskets and O-rings are necessary with the elevated compression and have worked perfectly. Initially there was an issue of sealing the oil and water passages. I tried several of the recommended gasket sealants and always had some oil or water seepage. I finally corrected that issue with The Right Stuff gasket maker. Problem solved.

So far, I have covered bore, compression height, and ring package for ordering your pistons. The missing factors are compression ratio, pin diameter, and valve pocket depth. You can discuss valve lift and duration with the manufacturer and they

The 1-inch-thick steel girdle helps stabilize the lower part of the engine block in high-stress situations. The fitment of the girdle to the main caps and pan rail is plus/minus 0.001 inch so that you do not induce stress to the block. It is critical to have zero clearance from the girdle to the main bolt head seat area for the ARP studs to work correctly. It is also a convenient mounting location for a crankshaft scraper.

An Oberg oil filter was originally installed as a space saver. It is a useful tool to monitor the engine and predict an upcoming issue within the motor. It is easy to check as often as you want without losing a half-liter of oil each time like you would with a cartridge filter.

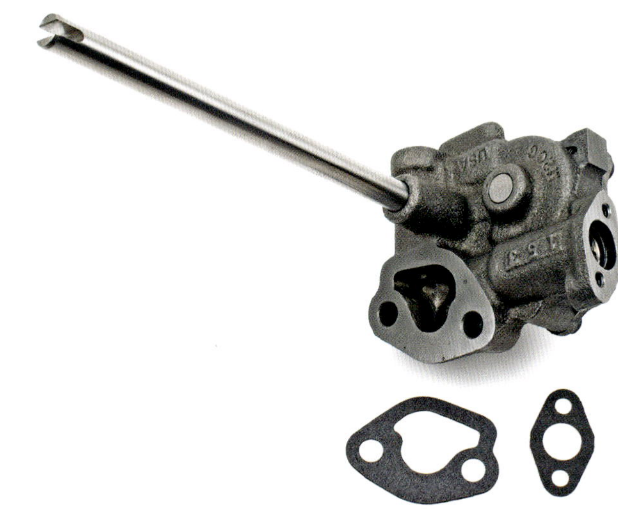

A high-performance motor requires a high-volume pump, such as this one supplied by TA Performance. The pump was not rebuilt but has been manufactured with a new housing and internal parts. (Photo Courtesy TA Performance)

The last piston-related item is compression ratio. I used 15.5:1 pistons in the motor for Bonneville. The actual compression is probably more like 14:1 when you consider the breathing limitation with Nailheads and then factor in the thin air with the corrected altitude on the salt flats.

As you increase the compression ratio beyond the stock 10.25, the returns diminish exponentially the higher you go. Depending on the efficiency of your air intake system, you will get some benefits at speed from the ram effect, but Nailheads did not have a competitive intake CFM airflow 50 odd years ago. Don't try to fool yourself with any expectation of coming close to the efficiency of airflow with the technology of current engines.

With a compression ratio of 15.5, I believe you have reached the end of the road for realizing any benefits by increasing compression any further. Without the ram assistance you could attain at speed and not having to contend with the thin air at the salt flats, you would probably be as well off with a maximum compression ratio no higher than 13:1 at any other venue. Even at that level, the actual compression may be as much as one full point lower. These comments about compression are related to a race-only motor. A performance street machine should not have more than the original Nailhead compression of 10.25 to 10.5, and your most aggressive street motor does not need any more than one point higher.

Crankshafts for the race motors are also ground smooth

will be reasonably close with an estimated valve pocket depth, but the ultimate test will be when you assemble the motor and check the piston-to-valve clearance. Piston manufacturers usually offer 0.990 pins for a bore over 4.125.

Bear in mind that as much as you might be able to, you are not going to make power like a big-block Chevrolet, nor are you going to do anything productive over 6,000 rpm. You may be able to save up to 25 to 30 grams with

0.927 pins; this can be another good discussion with your piston fabricator along with the grade of forging material.

I am not going to pretend to have any expertise about the metallurgy of the forgings required for race pistons. Some people can read a couple of paragraphs on this topic and instantly become an expert. Unless you have an extensive background in metallurgy, let's just leave this in the hands of the piston professionals.

The girdle is using up the pan rail bolts, so you will need a pan to fit a new bolt pattern, plus you may want to increase oil capacity. Making a new oil pan will give you an opportunity to add baffles to prevent the oil from sloshing around.

to reduce windage, and I use a 1-inch-thick girdle to support the bottom end. Is that a necessity for a 5,800-rpm Nailhead? Not likely. However, in my circumstance, when running the engine flat-out on a 5-mile straightaway with a 1/4-inch stroker, it is worthwhile for peace of mind. It is also a handy place to mount the crankshaft scraper.

No matter how well your rotating assembly has been balanced, there are a lot of harmonic vibes in the crank case. Mount your crank scraper with Loctite in the same manner as the oil pump body and pickup tube.

Oiling and Lubrication

A belt-driven Weaver single-stage oil pump is mounted on the front engine plate, and the purpose is twofold. First, I subscribe to the theory that you only need 10 pounds of oil pressure per thousand of RPM. The oil pressure is set and stays at 60 psi.

Second, it is easy to remove the belt and prime the engine with a drill. Given the infrequency of a motor like this running, pre-lube the engine for several minutes and turn it over periodically before starting it. This is a simi-lar process to pre-lubing before breaking in a fresh motor where the valve covers are removed and the oil pump is operated with a drill until oil drips from the exhaust valve rockers for the #7 and #8 cylinders.

The oil pan is a fabricated part with several baffles and a windage screen. In hindsight, we could have drained out the 20w50 oil at the end of a good run and made a follow-up run with straight 20-weight synthetic oil to see if there was a real difference. The oil filter is an Oberg unit that is checked after every run. I prefer using this as opposed to a cartridge-type filter in this particular application. You can pull out the screen and see exactly what material is being filtered out

Using four 180-degree thermostats to control the coolant flow from the front and rear of each head provides a more finite control of the cooling system and eliminates the potential for hot spots. Each of the four thermostats are mounted in inline aluminum housings and has a 1/8-inch hole drilled to maintain a minimal flow.

and is a good preview of a possible upcoming issue. It can help pinpoint the source of a potential problem. It is far more user friendly than cutting apart a used cartridge filter after the fact.

Redirected Coolant Flow

I mentioned earlier about running 1½-inch NPT threads in the center frost plug hole on each side of the block. The purpose is to use this as a central entry point for the coolant. The distribution of the water flow is metered with a 0.562-inch hole in the outboard side of the copper head gaskets between the center two cylinders and a 0.453-inch hole between the front and rear pairs of cylinders. There are also 1/2-inch holes in the front and rear of the inboard or upper side of the gaskets to relieve any potential steam pockets.

The coolant then exits front and rear of each head to inline 180-degree thermostats and down to dual aluminum radiators beneath the car. The airflow through the radiators is sucked from the underside of the car by four electric fans and ducted out through louvers in the trunk lid. The purpose of this is to cool the

We used Gotha adjustable rocker arms for several years without a single failure in spite of the high valve spring pressure with the roller cam. They are very reliable.

I believe these are Harmon & Collins roller lifters but have not been able to verify. I received these with the purchase of an old race motor and a backup set from the back shelf of a local machine shop that has been building race engines since the 1950s. The bare lifter weighs only 41 grams and I have yet to have a failure.

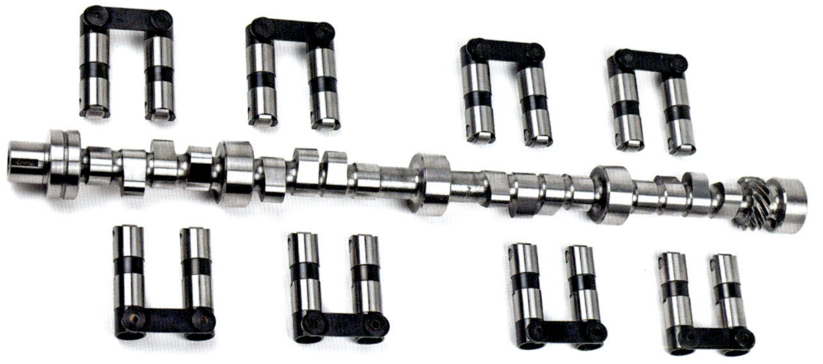

TA Performance now has roller cams and roller lifters for the 364, 401, and 425 Nailhead engines. Each camshaft is custom-ground to the customer's specifications or they will recommend a custom grind that will best suit your application. Its roller cams and lifters offer increased performance and reliability over comparable flat-tappet camshafts. It is also able to create the perfect camshaft for your engine, rather than use an off-the-shelf grind. (Photo Courtesy TA Performance)

radiators, but it also helps keep a negative pressure beneath the car and provides more stability. An electric 20-gallon-per-minute Meziere pump is used to circulate the coolant into the block via the center frost plug holes. Keep in mind that coolant for any race vehicle is water with water wetter added (not antifreeze).

Camshafts

Camshafts are another issue. I had a set of vintage solid-roller lifters that were made by Harmon & Collins in the late 1950s to early 1960s era. They were in excellent condition and have worked flawlessly. Finding old roller cams that can be reground with a suitable profile was always a concern. Cams that were made for the 364 motor did not have enough material left in the lobes to regrind with a decent amount of lift or duration. Some of the cams made for 401 motors had the same issue. Those that could be reground were only able to produce 268 degrees duration at best.

Around 2002, I found an unground solid-roller blank. I consulted with Harvey Crane, who suggested a grind with 284/289 duration at 0.050 lift with the idea that it can be easily reground for a less-aggressive profile if needed. I thought it was too much cam for the limited RPM from a Nailhead, but a friend ran the engine data through his computer program and it came up with the same numbers.

I had the blank ground with that specification and have used that cam with Tom Telesco's aluminum roller rockers for the last five years of racing the roadster. It pulled a lot harder but still can't push past the 197-mph wall.

8 At this point you are ready to assemble the motor. There's no need to repeat everything. Proceed here using the same instructions in chapter 7 with a few exceptions:

• Copper head gaskets require a sealing wire (in this case 0.042) to be tamped into the machined groove around each cylinder. Carefully trim the ends so they butt together with zero gap. Seal the coolant and oil passages with a thin layer of The Right Stuff. The head bolt torque is the same.

• If your camshaft uses solid lifters, either flat or roller, the valve lash should be set at 0.024 on the exhaust and 0.022 on the intake.

• This motor uses a magneto. The base timing is set at 5 degrees with 24 degrees centrifugal advance for a total of 29 degrees advance.

I don't believe there is a manifold made for a Nailhead to run a Holley carburetor. In the beginning we ran a Holley on this stock manifold that was heavily modified on the inside and with this adapter bolted on the top.

I am going to make a liar out of myself by having just said that there was not a manifold made for a Nailhead/Holley combination. I just came across this tunnel ram with the Holley-carburetor bolt pattern. There are no name or numbers cast into it, nor any sign of them being ground away. (Photo Courtesy Al Moffat)

Hilborn still makes the original mechanical fuel injection for the Nailhead and now offers an electronic version. Nothing makes a better traditional statement on a performance Nailhead than a set of stacks. (Photo Courtesy Hilborn Fuel Injection)

A drive stud was fabricated to run the fuel injection pump off of the front of the camshaft. My friend John Van Wyngaarden from Flamboro Machine Shop came to the rescue with this unit and incorporated a thrust bearing to limit camshaft movement.

A less-traditional statement is this in-progress, sheet metal, mechanical fuel-injection manifold. It provides better numbers on a flow bench but has not out-performed the original Hilborn unit as of yet.

An extension was required to space out the fuel pump out a little farther and reorient the mounting angle.

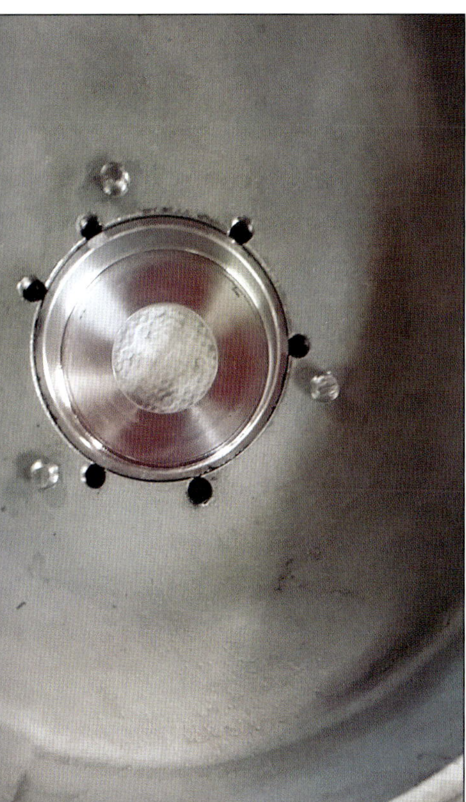

The inside of the fuel pump mounting extension became a receiver for the thrust bearing to complete the installation.

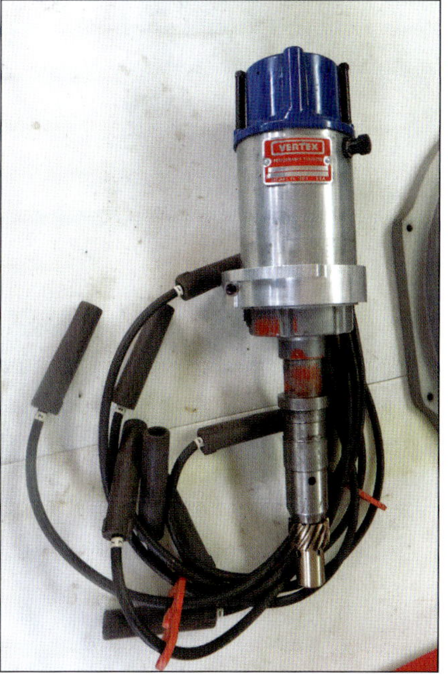

The Vertex magneto has been set up with 12 degrees advance. We normally use 4 to 5 degrees initial advance at the crankshaft. Total advance is from 28 to 29 degrees. Keep in mind that the gap for these Autolite Racing AR-73 plugs when used with a magneto is 0.020.

Hilborn Fuel Injection

We started running the car with a Holley carburetor, which was okay but was switched to Hilborn mechanical fuel injection shortly after. Being a novice with the mechanical injection, I spent a lot of time on the phone with the Hilborn technicians who were really helpful.

We started off with a 150A-1 pump using a primary bypass, and they set us up to start with a 0.150 bypass pill and 8A nozzles with additional pills plus or minus 0.005 and 0.010. We later moved to a smaller 150A-0 pump with a smaller 0.110 bypass and the smaller 7A nozzles. The whole purpose of this change was to increase the operating pressure to improve the atomization. This was a big improvement and produced the first 195-plus speeds.

The specific information provided here relates directly to this particular engine and how the injection system was set up and tailored to the environment where it would run. Do not try to apply this information to your own setup. There is a wealth of information within Hilborn's technical department that its personnel are willing to share to help you set up your own system.

A side benefit of fuel injection was to incorporate a thrust bearing into the fuel pump drive in the timing cover. That limited forward movement of the camshaft to 0.005 inch, and now the magneto timing is steady as a rock. Prior to installing the thrust bearing, the timing bounced around quite a bit, so the camshaft must have been dancing.

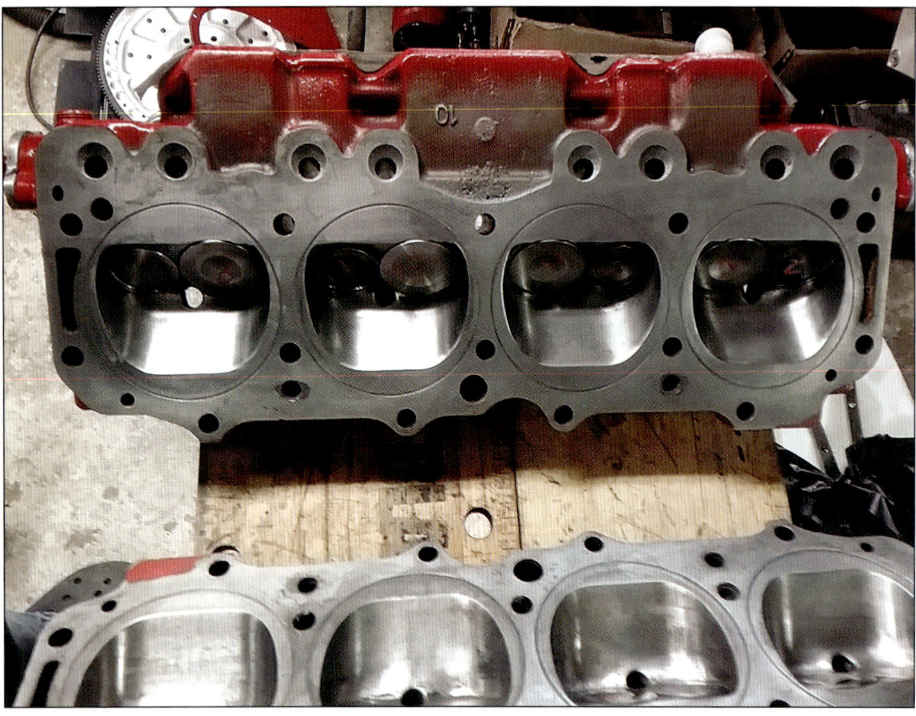

These heads were from the race car and ready to install. Note there is a receiver groove for the O-rings. The intake valves are 1.94 and the exhaust are 1.50 Chevrolet with 0.341 stems. Material was removed from the side of the combustion chamber to relieve the area adjacent to the intake.

Whenever you make any changes to the valvetrain, there will be at least one other area affected. In this case, Bill installed 0.100-inch taller valves that created an interference with the valve spring retainer and underside of the rocker arm. The remedy was to use offset keepers that lowered the retainer.

However, the fuel injection unit we had was still the small unit with the $1^{11}/_{16}$ butterflies. We tested it on the flow bench and lost 10 cfm when it was bolted to the head. That is a lot of lost air when you are talking about a starving Nailhead and not knowing they were still available. I had not been able to find one of the larger Hilborn manifolds. We did some research and fabricated a sheet metal manifold with primary butterflies at the front of the plenum. This restored lost airflow on the flow bench. We had success working this unit over the last couple of years, but it is still a work in progress to balance the airflow within the manifold.

The management of air flow with a race car and race engine is a science with so many variables that it warrants a book by itself. For example, take the numbers that need to be determined by calculations for optimum intake airflow to your throttle plates. You need cubic inches, volumetric efficiency of the motor, RPM, throttle plate size (determined by the intake manifold calculations), speed of the vehicle, radius of the opening of the air intake flange, and location of the intake opening relative to the vehicle. In some cases you also need to consider the temperature, corrected altitude for your race venue, etc.

This is only part of the four pages of formulas that are required to determine the square-inch area of just the intake opening. Numerous calculations like this are needed to properly build and operate a race motor. Most of us have to rely on the engineering and quality of workmanship in products from suppliers so we can reap some of the benefits of these sciences, or we revert back to our old trial-and-error methods.

Cylinder Heads

The heads and the approach to porting were covered in chapter 5 in the section about a performance porting for a street-driven vehicle. Porting and other modifications to the heads for the race engine are similar but with a more intense approach.

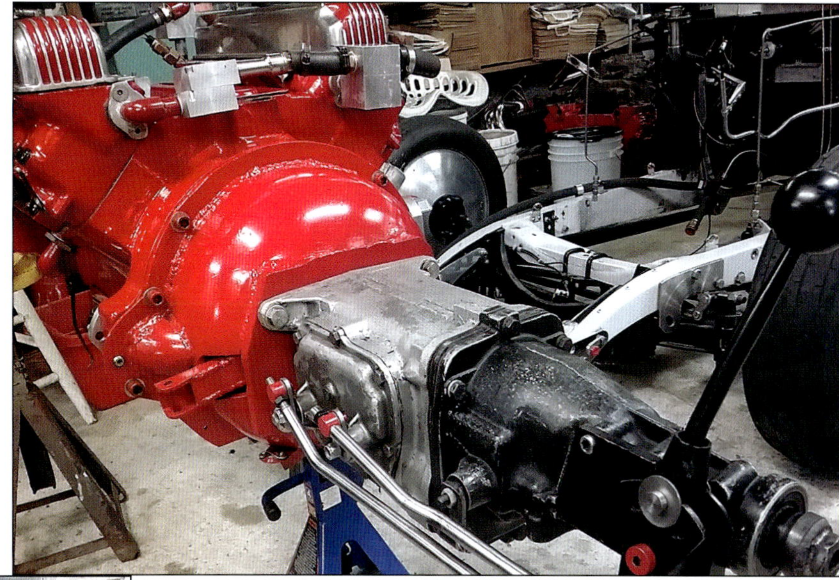

A 360-degree scatter shield is a standard requirement with any motorsports racing association with the intent to not only protect the driver but also anyone else who may be in the path of debris from a clutch or flywheel failure.

The old saying to never assume anything comes into play here. Whether your parts are fabricated or purchased, you must check for proper fitment. In this case, offset dowels are used to correct the alignment of the bellhousing to the crankshaft.

Due to the length of the Nailhead bellhousing flange, the clutch and flywheel assembly are inside the flange. A block protection plate was fabricated from an 0.125-inch plate to save the block in the event of clutch failure. Some material had to be removed from inside the block flange to fit this in. Do I plan to test this? No!

This clutch disc has ceramic pads to minimize any possible slippage. The ceramic friction material can withstand significantly more heat and still resist fading, which makes it more suitable to racing applications.

I am sure you understand by now that there is no individual magical trick to get good flow to or from a Nailhead. You need to scrounge every little bit from every corner you can find. Unshrouding both the intake and exhaust valves is one of the more productive areas. Be sure you have a sonic tester in hand while cleaning out this area.

Do not thin out the combustion chamber walls beyond 0.200 or even thicker like 0.220 if you are using any kind of power adder. You can replace the guides to accept 0.343 stemmed valves or even 0.312 if you can find a suitable valve. The return on your dollar is not very good here with the cost of guides and valves for a small increase in flow, but that's racing.

I used some vintage Gotha adjustable rocker arms for several years without any failures. More recently, I have used Telesco's aluminum roller rockers. There is additional lift but not any increase in speed. We made a couple of changes to the heads to maximize the benefit from these rockers. The guides were changed to accommodate Chevrolet 1.94 intake valves with 0.343 stems and 1.700 valve stem height. The extra stem height allowed us a better selection of valve springs and less deflection from the pushrod angle to the rocker-arm adjuster. With stock-height 1.6 valve stems and the valve wide open, the angle from the pushrod to the adjuster is 39 degrees. This lowers to 35 degrees with the 1.700 stem height. There was an increase on the flow bench but no increase in speed. I believe we are up against a wall pushing air and would need another 50 to 60 hp for that extra 3 mph.

Driveline

Another area that became an obstacle was the scatter shield. I believe Lakewood made one for Nailheads in the earlier years, but I could not find one. We ended up making one based around a weld standard carbon steel cap for schedule 40 12-inch steam pipe. The bellhousing flange was cut from 3/8-inch steel and the transmission flange was cut from 5/8-inch plate. A 60-inch length of 1-inch cold rolled bar was set up through the #1 and #5 main bearing saddles of an empty block, a machined ring was used to center the steam pipe cap, and a last spacer was machined to fit the transmission collar in the transmission flange. This acted as a setup jig for welding. The transmission flange was later milled parallel.

This is an oversimplification of the whole process, but the end result was an acceptable scatter shield to pass SCTA tech inspection. This is the same jig I have used to adapt/shorten the 700R4 transmission case to fit a Nailhead. The final test was to install a crankshaft with a dial indicator on the outlet flange to verify centering of the new bellhousing. A series of offset dowel pins were made to bring the runout to less than 0.002 inch.

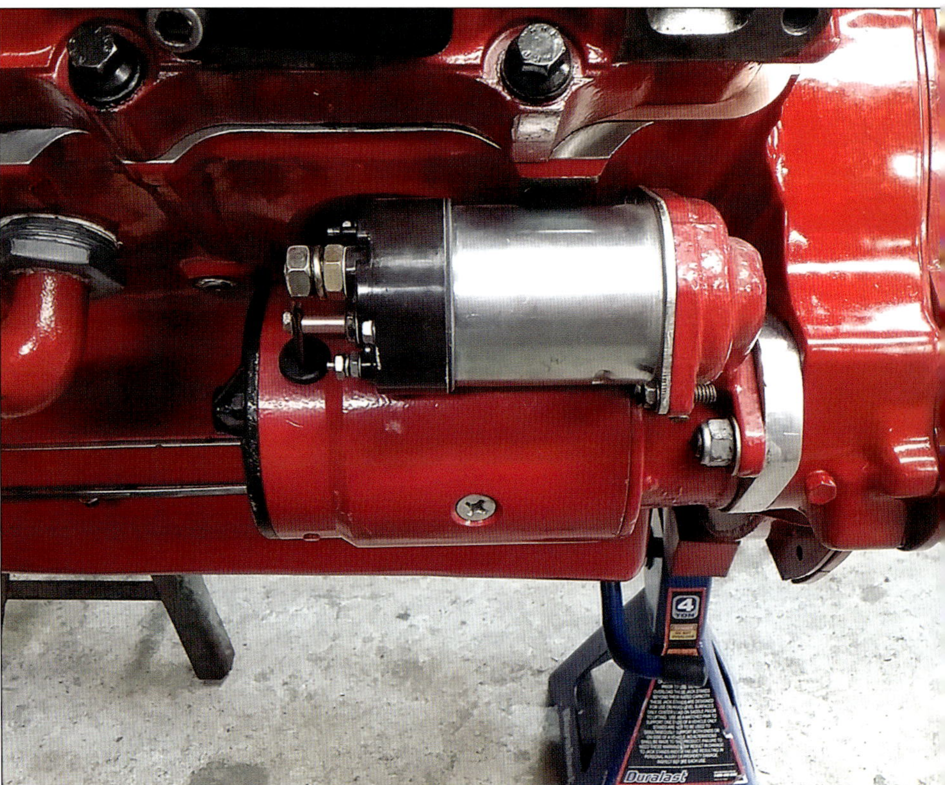

One of the issues with powder coating is that electrical current does not pass through it very well. In the case of the starter, you must scrape the coating from the mounting flange and apply dielectric grease or anti-seize to ensure a good ground. The spacer acts as an adapter.

Final Thoughts

I believe the following comments are relevant, but you may feel that I am just drifting off topic here for a little bit. We firmly believed that any motor-to-transmission misalignment would create a certain amount of parasitic drag. Remember the previous dialogue about airflow, how restrictive it is, and that every little bit helps. That same logic applies to our precious Nailhead where every little bit of drag becomes wasted horsepower, and we are all well aware at this stage that we cannot run down to the local speed shop and buy an extra 10 hp.

With that thought in mind, we used an empty engine block and transmission case with the same 60-inch piece of 1-inch cold rolled bar stock mounted in machined spacers at the #5 main bearing saddle and the transmission output shaft seal to set up the motor and transmission mounts.

The goal was to have zero deflection from the crankshaft through to the differential, including the driveshaft joints. I am sure that we have all heard about the importance of maintaining driveshaft angles for better universal joint life. Well, guess what? Your mandate here is to eliminate parasitic drag and not to maximize universal joint life.

Can you save a specific number of horsepower realigning your drivetrain? The answer is yes. A chassis dyno can measure wasted power as you decelerate after a pull. If you have a record from before and after pulls, the difference will give you the result.

This is the first time that I had come across Algon injectors. They may not have the straight-up appeal of other injections, but I was curious about how well they appear to align with the port angle and if this improved the airflow.

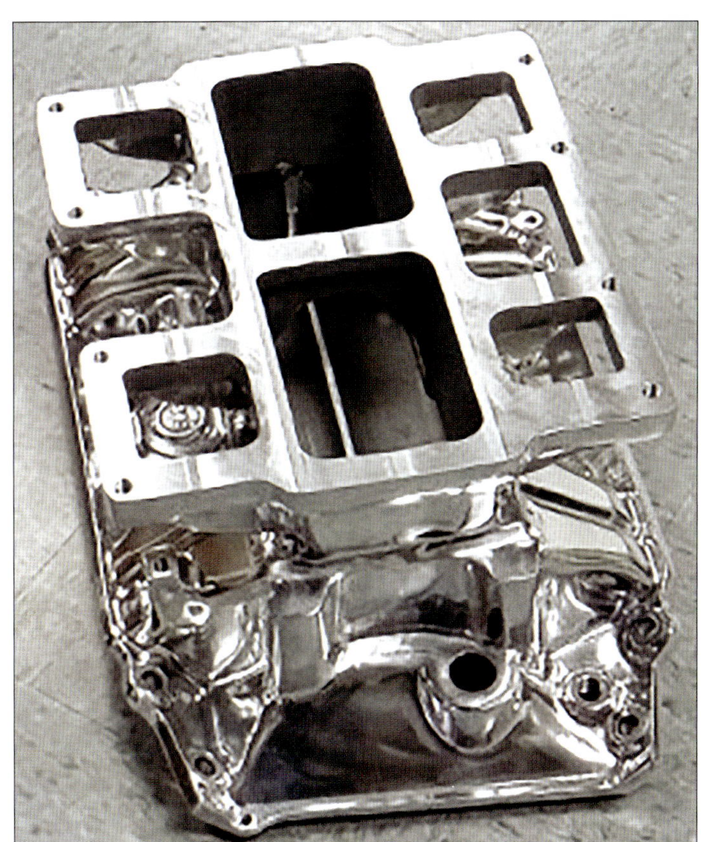

This blower manifold was fabricated to fit a 6-71 GMC onto a Nailhead. I believe Centerville Auto Repair and Ross Engines are remaking a manifold for 4-71 GMC blowers. (Photo Courtesy Carmen Faso)

While I am still running off-topic, there is another area that you may find interesting that came from experiences with land speed racing and is related to horsepower loss from parasitic drag. We started racing on the salt flats with a vintage quick-change rear end, as did most other racers out there. Some had a 9-inch Ford differential. From what I understand, it takes 25 to 30 hp to drive

a quick change. Both the 9-inch Ford and the General Motors 12-bolt rear ends require 18 to 20. Then there is the 10-bolt Chevrolet differential. It's ugly, a pain to work on, and spits out axles when it's unhappy. However, it only takes 10 to 11 hp to drive it.

This is a terrible photograph of a rare intake I believe came from Buick's Experiment Division. It had some pretty crude-looking carburetor spacers that I am certain did not originate from the same source as the manifold.

The Hilborn pump appears to be an early version of the PG150. The injector stacks are reminiscent of those that were on the motors that Balchowsky built in conjunction with a Buick dealership in California. Ten of those engines competed on road racing courses throughout the US for several years starting in 1956.

The harmonic balancers that I use on the race motors are Romac part number 0243SA. These are a quality part and were sourced through Tom Telesco. The belt drive and hub for the oil pump are shown.

The first time I saw one of these in land speed action was in the Holmes, Kugel, and McIness roadster. That differential could live through a 700-plus-hp, twin-turbocharged, alcohol- burning small-block that had just sheared off the input shaft from a Turbo Hydra-matic 400 transmission. I was sold.

You don't just roll this out from under a donor car and into your race car. You need to replace the skinny little axle tubes with 1/2-inch wall by 3-inch hydraulic tubing pressed in and welded to the center section. Then, 9-inch Ford outer bearing carriers and disc brake caliper brackets are welded on. The gears, posi-trac carrier, and/or locker blocks should be given a cryogenic treatment. Aftermarket race axles with the appropriate bolt pattern and spline will get you in business. A twin housing with all the internals will suffice for a gear change. Drag racing has significant more shock values than other motorsports, so use your own judgement.

There were multiple induction systems used for racing Nailheads through the late 1950s until these engines were no longer competitive in the last half of the 1960s. Experimental manifolds and some heads managed to escape Buick's Experimental Division and found their way onto some of the various racetracks, mostly in the northeastern states. Multi-carb manifolds found their way from the racetracks to hot rods on the street and into the hands of collectors along with the experimental stuff.

One of the more adventuresome setups I remember had a reverse flow with a front-mounted GMC supercharger blowing the intake charge, through the exhaust ports and header, and out of the intake flanges. Unfortunately, I have not been able to find a photo of that motor. The tried-and-true system that seems to have survived that era is the traditional Hilborn Fuel Injection.

Happy motoring with your Nailhead.

Torquing Sequence

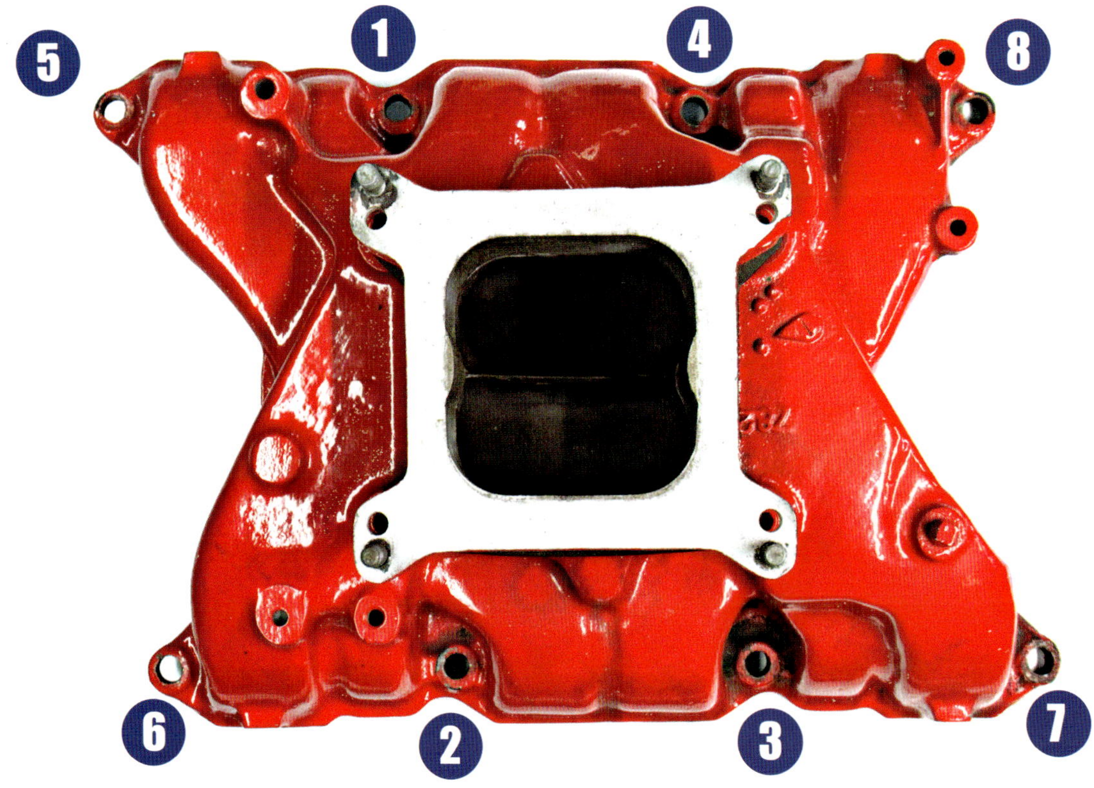

12
8
2
5
13
11
7
1
6
14
10
4
3
9

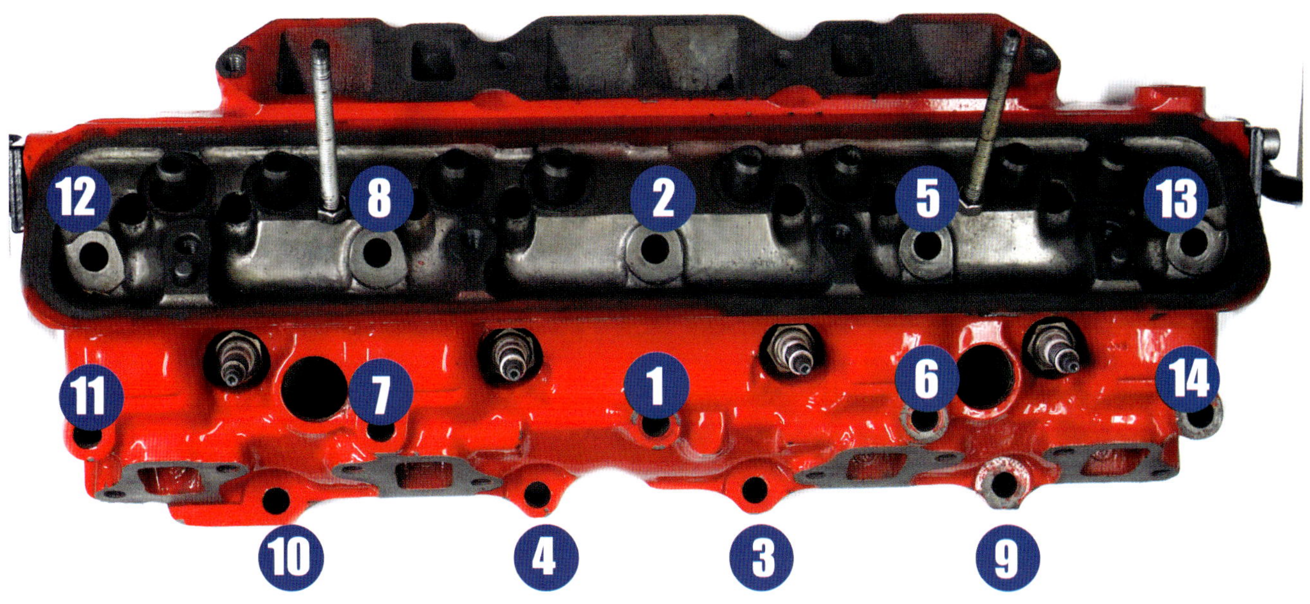

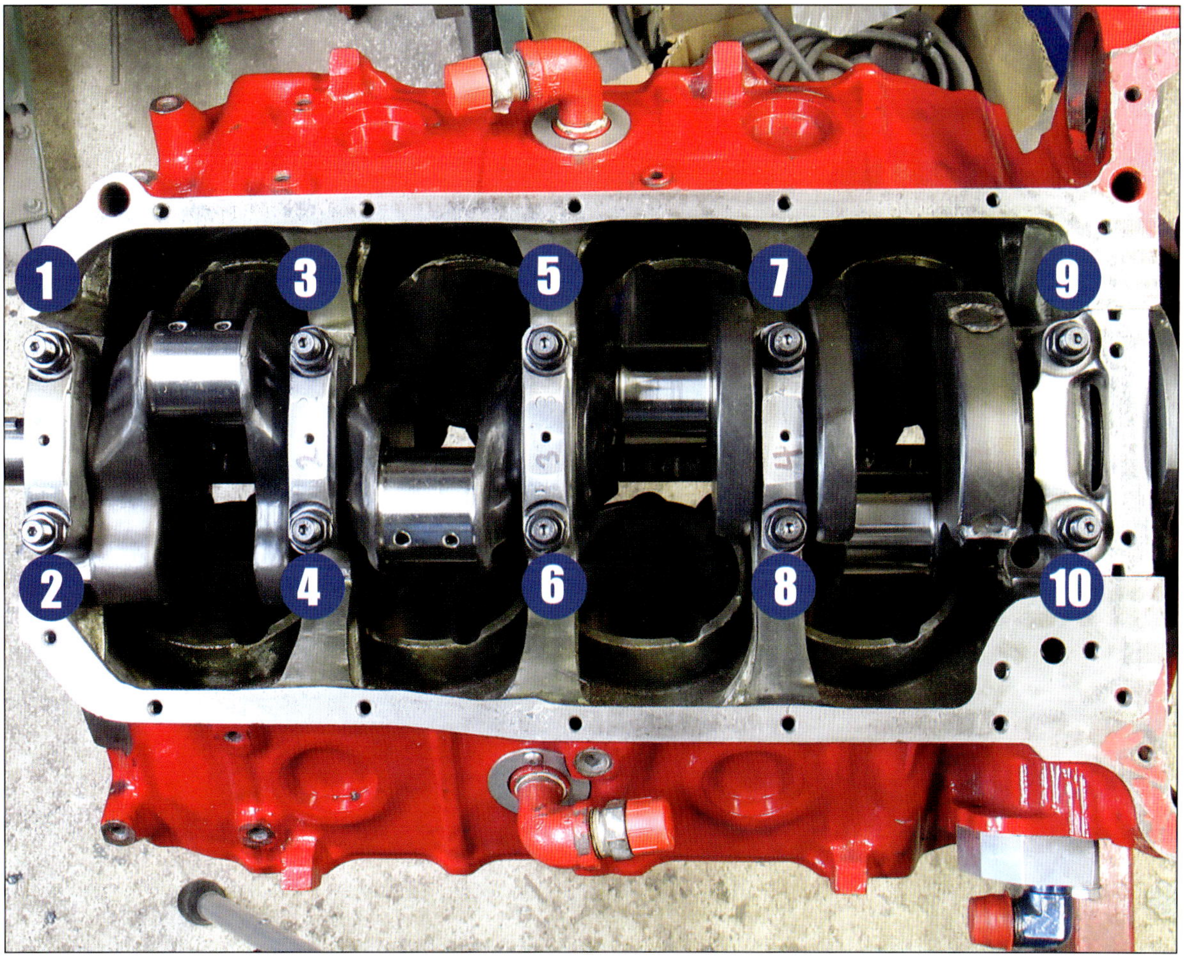
1
3
5
7
9
2
4
6
8
10

Torque Specifications

Part	Ft-lbs	Notes
Wheel studs	100	with anti-seize
Spark plugs	20	—
Oil drain plug	30	—
Oil pan	10	—
Valley cover	5	—
Valve covers	5	—
Timing gear to cam	60	—
Rocker shaft (ARP)	35	with moly
Rod bolts (Eagle Rods)	55–60	0.0064–0.0068 stretch
Rod bolts (Buick with ARP)	50	0.0055–0.006 with moly
Main cap bolts (ARP)	100	with moly
Girdle	20	—
Flywheel	80	with blue Loctite
Pressure plate	45	with blue Loctite
Head bolts (ARP)	75	with moly
Crankshaft damper	200	with blue Loctite
Crankshaft drive hub	20	with blue Loctite
Crankshaft center hub	60	with blue Loctite

Fastener Torque

Size	Grade 5	Grade 8
1/4 NC	8	12
1/4 NF	10	14
5/16 NC	17	24
5/16 NF	19	27
3/8 NC	30	45
3/8 NF	35	50
7/16 NC	50	70
7/16 NF	55	80
1/2 NC	75	100
1/2 NF	85	120

S-A Design Work-A-Long Sheet©

Project Statistics

Your Name____

Today's Date_____________________ Vehicle Engine Removed From ______________________

Engine Year _______________ CI ___________ Block Casting __________ ☐ 2 barrel ☐ 4 barrel ☐ Fuel Injection

Accessories Attached to Used Engine

☐ A/C Pump ☐ AIR Pump ☐ AIR Distributor Lines and Hoses ☐ Water Pump

☐ Flywheel ☐ Clutch ☐ Flexplate ☐ Transmission

☐ Starter ☐ Fuel Pump ☐ Exhaust Manifolds ☐ All Pulleys; Except____________

☐ Alternator ☐ Distributor ☐ Coil ☐ Carburetor

☐ Motor Mounts ☐ Motor Mount Attaching Brackets ☐ Spark Plug Heat Shields

☐ ECR Valve ☐ Dipstick Tube ☐ All Bolts; except ____________________________

Operational Notes

Oil consumption____________________________ Compression check pressure variation________________________________psi

Leak-down percent__________________________ Other observations________________________

Disassembly Notations

Crank uses centerbolt ☐ Yes ☐ No

Heat riser restricted on ☐ Left ☐ Right ☐ Both

Head gaskets ☐ Steel Shim ☐ Composition

Worn/damaged lifers ☐ No ☐ Yes; where___________

____

Vibration damper pulley screws ☐ 3/8-NC ☐ 3/8-NF

Location of timing-pointer attaching points:

Oil filter adapter type:

☐ Spin-on

☐ Long cartridge (late)

☐ Short cartridge (early)

Type of rear main seal:

☐ Rubber–two piece

☐ Rubber–one piece (late)

☐ Rope (early)

Initial Parts Inspection Observations

Block OK ☐ Yes ☐ No; describe problem ______________________________________

Heads OK ☐ Yes ☐ No; describe problem ______________________________________

Crank OK ☐ Yes ☐ No; describe problem ______________________________________

Bearings OK ☐ Yes ☐ No; describe problem ______________________________________

Pistons OK ☐ Yes ☐ No; describe problem ______________________________________

Cam/lifters OK ☐ Yes ☐ No; design problem ______________________________________

Damper OK ☐ Yes ☐ No; describe problem ______________________________________

Intake manifold OK ☐ Yes ☐ No; describe problem ______________________________________

Exhaust manifold OK ☐ Yes ☐ No; describe problem ______________________________________

Oil pump OK ☐ Yes ☐ No; describe problem ______________________________________

Oil pump/rear main cap mating surfaces damage/abnormalities ☐ No ☐ Yes

Identifying mark you placed on all part:

____

AT THE MACHINE SHOP

Parts Delivered to the Machine Shop

☐ Block   ☐ Main Caps   ☐ Crankshaft   ☐ Oil Pump   ☐ Oil Pump Pickup

☐ Connecting Rods   ☐ Pistons   ☐ Piston Rings   ☐ Camshaft   ☐ Lifters

☐ Vibration Damper   ☐ Main Bearings   ☐ Rod Bearings   ☐ Cam Bearings   ☐ Rod Bolts

☐ Gasket Set   ☐ Push Rods   ☐ Rockerarms   ☐ Head Bolts   ☐ Main Bolts/Studs

☐ Miscellaneous Nuts/Bolts/Brackets for Cleaning

☐ ______________________________________

☐ Water Pump   ☐ Timing Cover   ☐ Oil Pan   ☐ Flywheel/Flexplate

☐ Clutch   ☐ Exhaust Manifolds   ☐ Motor Mounts   ☐ Motor Mount Attaching Brackets

☐ Assembled Heads   ☐ Disassembled Heads with: ☐ Valves   ☐ Springs   ☐ Retainers   ☐ Keepers

☐ Rocker Balls and Nuts

☐ Intake Manifold   ☐ With Heat Riser Shield   ☐ Installed   ☐ Not Installed

☐ __________   ☐ __________   ☐ __________   ☐ __________   ☐ __________

☐ __________   ☐ __________   ☐ __________   ☐ __________   ☐ __________

☐ __________   ☐ __________   ☐ __________   ☐ __________

☐ Other Accessories_______________________________________

Special Instructions for Machine Shop

☐ Bore black   ☐ Use torque plates   ☐ Desired piston-to-wall clearance: 0. __________ -inch

☐ Grind crank   ☐ Rod bearing clearance: 0. __________ -inch   ☐ Main bearing clearance: 0. __________ -inch

☐ Deck to clean   ☐ Surface heads   ☐ Install cam bearings   ☐ _____________ ☐ _____________

☐ _______________________________________   ☐ _______________________________________

☐ _______________________________________   ☐ _______________________________________

Is pilot bushing to be installed in crankshaft (required for manual transmission)?   ☐ Yes   ☐ No

Are intake manifold heat shield holesto be tapped for 8-32 screwa?   ☐ Yes   ☐ No

After You Pick Up Your Parts

☐ Yes ☐ No   Threaded holes reconditioned/chased   ☐ Yes ☐ No   Drilled holes and edges chamfered

☐ Yes ☐ No   head/block dowels properly installed   ☐ Yes ☐ No   Are cam bearings properly installed

☐ Yes ☐ No   Galleries tapped for screw-in plugs   ☐ Yes ☐ No   Add 0.030-inch hole in gallery plug

☐ Yes ☐ No   Add 0.030 inch hole in thrust face   ☐ Yes ☐ No   Core plugs properly instaalled

☐ Yes ☐ No   Retaining straps on core plugs   ☐ Yes ☐ No   Crank keys properly installed

☐ Yes ☐ No   Manifold heat-shield holes tapped for 8-32 screws

PRE-ASSEMBLY FITTING

Measured and Recorded During Pre-Assembly Fitting

Yes   No   Do all valveguides have proper clearnce? If no, which are correct_______________________________________

Yes   No   Do all valveseats meet dimensional specs? If no, which are faulty_______________________________________

Yes   No   Do all valveseats hold solvent? If no, which leak_______________________________________

Yes   No   Have all valveguides been machined concentric for press-on seals?

Retainer to Valveguide clearance 0. ______ -inch; adequate on all vales?   Yes   No   If no, which valves have

insufficient clearance?_______________________________________

Recommened valvespring set pressure ___________ psi at___________ -inch installed height.

Measured valvespring installed height:

1____________   3____________   5____________   7____________

2____________   4____________   6____________   8____________

Spring shims used to obtain correct installed height:

1______________ 3______________ 5______________ 7______________
2______________ 4______________ 6______________ 8______________

Measured valvespring solid height ______________-inches

Calculated compressed spring clearance:

1______________ 3______________ 5______________ 7______________
2______________ 4______________ 6______________ 8______________

Connecting rod bore OK? ☐ Yes ☐ No; Which rods are defective______________________________________
Crank straightness OK? ☐ Yes ☐ No Runout on center main of O. ______________-inch
Main bearing clearance OK? ☐ Yes ☐ No Measured clearance O. ______________-inch
Crank thrust OK? ☐ Yes ☐ No Measured clearance O. ______________-inch
Main bearing clearance OK? ☐ Yes ☐ No Measured clearance O. ______________-inch
Camshaft bearing fit OK? ☐ Yes ☐ No; Describe problem ______________________________________
Block required clearance grinding for upper sprocket? ☐ ☐
Pin end clearance OK? ☐ Yes ☐ No Measured clearance O. ______________-inch
Piston-to-wall clearance OK? ☐ Yes ☐ No Measured clearance O. ______________-inch

Pistons with incorrect clearance ______________________________________

Measured ring end gap:

1 Top__________ 2nd __________ **3** Top________ 2nd ________ **5** Top__________ 2nd ____________ **7** Top__________ 2nd ____________
2 Top__________ 2nd __________ **4** Top________ 2nd ________ **6** Top__________ 2nd ____________ **8** Top__________ 2nd ____________

Rod bearing clearance OK? ☐ Yes ☐ No Measured clearance O. ______________-inch
Rod side clearance OK? ☐ Yes ☐ No Measured clearance O. ______________-inch
Piston-to-head clearance OK? ☐ Yes ☐ No Measured clearance O. ______________-inch

Cylinders with incorrect clearance______________________________________

Offset bushings/key used: ☐ + - 2°   ☐ + - 2°   ☐ + - 2°   ☐ + - 2°   ☐ + - 2°   ☐ + - 2°

Rotating assembly clearance OK? Yes No Cause of interference ______________________________________
Crank index OK? Yes No Maximum __________° out of index on journal no. ______________
Cylinder-to-cylinder deck height accurate? Yes No Maximum O. __________-inch variation.
Rocker geometry OK? Yes No; Describe problem ______________________________________
Rocker-to-stud clearance OK? Yes No Maximum O. __________-inch (Intake); O. ______________-inch (Exhaust);
Piston-to-valve clearance OK? Yes No Maximum O. __________-inch (Intake); O. ______________-inch (Exhaust);
Oil pump drive clearance OK? Yes No Maximum clearance O. ______________-inch
Intake manifold end-rail clearance OK? Yes No Maximum clearance O. ______________-inch
Mainfold surface parallel with head? Yes No Describe problem ______________________________________
Pulleys/accessories aligned? Yes No Describe problem______________________________________

____
____

SOURCE GUIDE

American Racing Products (ARP)
Contact: Trish Yunick
1863 Eastman Ave.
Ventura, CA 93003
800-826-3045
805-339-2200 (outside US and Canada)
arp-bolts.com

Mac's Motor City Garage
Contact: Bill McGuire
419-350-0687
macsmotorcitygarage.com
Email: mcg@macsmotorcitygarage.com

Bendtsen's Speed Gems
806H S. Division St.
Waunakee, WI 53597
763-767-4480
transmissionadapters.com
Email: sales@transmissionsadapters.com

Canadian Chromeplating and Crankshaft Inc
33 Peelar Rd., Unit 1A
Concord, Ontario, Canada
L4K 1A3
905-760-5561
www.canadianchrome.com
Email: info@canadianchrome.com

Carmen Faso
7127 Ward Rd.
North Tonawanda, NY 14120
716-693-4090

Centerville Auto Repair
12865 Pine Cone Cir.
Grass Valley, CA 95945
530-272-1564
centervilleautorepair.com
Email: nailhead_russ@yahoo.com

Forrest & Forrest Racing
60 Melair Dr.
Ayr, Ontario, Canada
N0B 1E0
519-632-1139

Gates Canada
222 Henry St. Unit #8
Brantford, Ontario, Canada
N3S 7R4
905-520-5582
Email: brad.dee@gates.com

Garry Thomson Metalworks
905-689-8757
Email: metalman@cogeco.ca

Hilborn Fuel Injection
22892 Glenwood Dr.
Aliso Viejo, CA
949-360-0909
www.hilborninjection.com
Email: info@hilborninjection.com

Performance Porting
Contact: Bill Bonnell
7 Adelaide St.
Brantford, Ontario, Canada
519-753-6318
Email: billb1998@hotmail.com

PML YourCovers
201 W. Beach Ave.
Inglewood, CA 90302
310-671-4345

Protech Racing
Contact: Mike Lewis
4531 E. San Gabriel Ave.
Fresno, CA 93726-1230
559-227-4773
protechracing.net
Email: mlewis6077@comcast.net

Sanderson Headers
Contact: Donna Smith
517 Railroad Ave.
South San Francisco, CA 94080
650-583-6617
www.sandersonheaders.com
Email: sheaders@aol.com

Schneider Racing Cams
1235 Cushman Ave.
San Diego, CA 92110
619-297-0227
schneidercams.com
Email: jerryc@schneidercams.com (sales/tech);
christianv@schneidercams.com (Spanish sales)

TA Performance Products Inc.
16167 N. 81st St.
Scottsdale, AZ 85260
480-922-6807
taperformance.com
Email: TAPerf@aol.com

Tom Telesco
465 Glanbrook Rd.
Stamford, CT 06906
203-324-6045
Email: telriv@yahoo.com